# IN HIS IMAGE

# In His Image

### THE JEWISH PHILOSOPHY OF MAN AS EXPRESSED

### IN RABBINIC TRADITION

### BY

### SAMUEL BELKIN

GREENWOOD PRESS, PUBLISHERS
WESTPORT, CONNECTICUT

Library of Congress Cataloging in Publication Data

Belkin, Samuel.
    In His image.

    Reprint of the ed. published by Abelard-Schuman,
London, New York, in series: Ram's horn books.
    Bibliography:  p.
    Includes indexes.
    1.  Man (Jewish theology)  2.  Talmud--Theology.
I.  Title.
[BM627.B44  1979]          296.3'8          78-10192
ISBN 0-313-21234-1

© 1960 by Samuel Belkin.

Reprinted with the permission of Harper & Row, Publishers,
as successor by merger to Thomas Y Crowell Company

Reprinted in 1979 by Greenwood Press, Inc.,
51 Riverside Avenue, Westport, CT 06880

Printed in the United States of America

10  9  8  7  6  5  4  3  2  1

# ACKNOWLEDGMENTS

I would like to express my gratitude to Professor Sidney B. Hoenig and Professor David Mirsky, both members of the faculty of Yeshiva University. The former took upon himself the difficult task of verifying the references quoted in the book and contributed greatly to the accuracy of the text. He also made numerous suggestions which I found most instructive. The latter was of great help to me in editing and revising the text and aided me with his suggestions in matters of style. I am particularly indebted to both of them, since the burdens of administrative work would have made it impossible for me personally to assume such onerous tasks. Neither of them is, however, to be held responsible for any inaccuracies in the volume. Likewise, with a deep sense of humility, I claim no perfection for myself.

I am also beholden to Mr. Jacob Dienstag, the librarian of the Gottesman Library of the Yeshiva, for assisting me with the necessary books, and to Mr. Joseph Ellenberg, the Secretary to the President of Yeshiva University, who relieved me of many technical phases associated with this publication.

It is my hope and prayer, with thanks to the Almighty, that this volume will serve as a guide to Jewry in its striving to understand and live up to the high ideals of Judaism and its way of life.

SAMUEL BELKIN

# CONTENTS

# IN HIS IMAGE

*"And thou shalt love thy neighbor as thyself"* — *Rabbi Akiba said this is the great principle in the Torah. Ben Azzai said, "These are the generations of man in the day that God created man; in the image of God did He make him"* — *this is even a greater principle.*

Sifra, Kedoshim, 19:18

# JUDAISM: A DEMOCRATIC THEOCRACY

Many attempts have been made to formulate a coherent and systematic approach to Jewish theology. All such attempts, however, have proved unsuccessful, for Judaism was never overly concerned with logical doctrines. It desired, rather, to evolve a corpus of practices, a code of religious acts, which would establish a mode of religious living. True, these acts and practices stem from basic theological and moral concepts, but most significantly, these theological theories of Judaism always remain invisible, apprehensible only through the religious practices to which they gave birth. Great rabbinic scholars and philosophers, therefore, found a greater measure of agreement among themselves in their *minyan ha-mitzvot*, the classification of the 613 religious duties which the Torah places upon the Jew, than in their attempts to present basic Jewish dogma in the form of articles of faith. Moses Maimonides lists thirteen basic dogmas but Joseph Albo lays down only three.[1] It is, therefore, futile to attempt to discover an articulate and organized body of doctrines which can be characterized as "Jewish Theology," in the full sense of the term. In Judaism, articles of faith and religious theories cannot be divorced from particular practices.

Probably the first Jew to endeavor to present a Jewish theology was the great Alexandrian philosopher Philo Judaeus; but even he was more concerned with a philosophy of Judaism, or better still, a philosophy of Jewish practice, than with mere theological dogma. Philo followed neither the Stoics, who considered theology a branch of physics, nor Aristotle, who considered theology a branch of philosophy. In his view, theology is part of the highest branch of philosophy, ethics, and is concerned with the worship of God and the regulation of human life in accordance with the divine laws of the Torah.[2] Thus, in a sense, Philo gave voice to the fundamental Jewish concept that theology and the rules of human conduct are almost indivisible.

Josephus, the great historian, defining Judaism to a non-Jewish world, was so aware of this fundamental concept that he felt it necessary to coin a new term to express the uniqueness of the Jewish religion. The word he chose was theocracy, and he wrote: "Some people have entrusted supreme political powers to monarchies, others to oligarchies, and still others to the masses. Our lawgiver, Moses, was attracted to none of these forms of polity, but gave to his constitution the form which—if a forced expression is permitted—may be termed a theocracy."[3] This, he explains, means "placing all sovereignty in the hands of God."[4]

Within the terms of his own definition, Josephus' characterization of Judaism as a theocracy is a true one. Judaism maintains that the sovereignty of man is dependent upon the sovereignty of God; that a man should view every act which he performs as the fulfillment of the wish of the Kingdom of Heaven. This is the meaning of the oft-repeated talmudic injunctions that man should act "for the sake of Heaven," and take upon himself "the yoke of the Kingdom of Heaven."[5]

Accepting this as a fundamental concept of Judaism, it becomes clear why it is wasteful for researchers in historic Judaism to seek to uncover or investigate abstract theological dogmas. Research ought rather seek to uncover the religious motives which underlie the body of Jewish practice and Judaism's concept of morality. The philosophy, or if you will, the theology, of Judaism is contained largely in the Halakah—in the Jewish judicial system—which concerns itself not with theory but primarily with practice. It is in the Halakah, therefore, that the philosophy of Judaism is to be sought.

Unfortunately, this is not the direction modern research in Judaism has taken. Instead of seeking to plumb the spiritual and religious motives which determine rabbinic thought, modern Jewish scholarship has tried to explain Judaism in terms which are alien and do not apply to it, and has attempted to force even those practices and rituals which define the relationship of man to God into the molds of current sociological and economic theories. One sage suddenly becomes a "New Dealer," and another a "conservative Republican"; one is credited with a "liberal" approach to life while another is stamped a "reactionary."

Of course the disagreements between the Pharisees and the Sadducees had a profound impact upon the sociological and economic life of the community, and the same is true of the halakic differences among the Tannaim, the mishnaic sages. For the most part, however, these disagreements did not spring from social or economic causes, nor were the disputants interested in championing one social class against another. The tannaitic sages were, above all, concerned with devising a code of living through which man, in his daily practices, could best serve God, and in such a system the duties of man to his fellow man are an organic part of his duties to his Maker.

Our Sages' chief concern was finding a system by which man, in his conduct, would apply the basic religious principles laid down in the Torah. Measured against practical western concepts of social justice, talmudic laws—recorded in the Mishnah, the Tosefta, the halakic midrashim, and the Gemara—appear quite impractical. Indeed approached from a secular and social point of view, many rabbinic laws are difficult to understand or appreciate. This is so, however, only because the underlying principles, and even the rules of procedure of rabbinic law spring from profound religious and theological concepts, and are not based at all on social theories. The laws pertaining to "crime" for example, often result from the religious concept of "sin," and the laws governing community life arise directly from the rabbinic concept of the sacredness of the individual personality. The laws of "the court of man" are seen as reflections of "the laws of Heaven" and the norms for the conduct of man in his relations with his fellow man are governed by man's relation to God. Human or social "practicality" was never accepted as a determining factor in Jewish law.

Our Sages did occasionally institute practical laws, but only when they felt that the ordinances would strengthen religious belief and practice, bring man closer to God, and help him reach the ultimate goal of penitence. Invoking rabbinic authority, they sometimes passed laws to help the poor or to insure fair conduct in the market place; at times they enacted rigorous laws for the protection of women. Such practical laws, however, they classified as *takkanot*, that is, innovations necessary to protect and aid the penitent, the poor and the weak. The classical example of a *takkana*, the *Prosbol*,[6] was enacted to aid the debtor in need of a loan and not to protect the creditor.

As one studies these rabbinic innovations or *takkanot*, it becomes quite apparent that the Sages were reluctant to enact them. They would have much preferred to preserve intact the practices set forth in the laws of the Torah, and enacted *takkanot* when compelled, primarily to bolster and strengthen the religious conduct of the community.

Given this understanding of the Jewish corpus of practice as divine law designed for the protection and defence of the individual, Judaism may well be characterized a "democratic theocracy," using the term "theocracy" as Josephus did, and not as understood by scholars today. It is a *theocracy* because the animating force of Jewish morality is not the protection of the state or community in the abstract, or of any mundane form of government. The entire system of Jewish morality derives from and is founded upon the concept of the sovereignty of God. It is a *democracy* because, unlike any other legal system, the rabbinic code places all emphasis upon the infinite worth and sacredness of the human being. In Judaism, the recognition of the *demos*, the individual and the infinite worth of his personality, are but a necessary outgrowth of the acceptance of God's *theos* (rulership), a relationship succinctly summed up in the phrase "democratic theocracy."

If the second element in this phrase is to be understood in the sense given it by Josephus, the first element is used as defined by Philo, who sought to explain the polity of the Torah to a non-Jewish world. According to Philo, democracy is "the most law-abiding and best of constitutions."[7] Understandably, Philo did not use the term "democracy" in the modern sense of a government elected by the whole populace, one in which every person is entitled to hold office.[8] To Philo, democracy, as an ideal form of government, "honors equality and has law and justice for its rulers."[9] It mattered little to Philo whether in the ancient polity of Judaism the functional government was vested in a monarchy, aristocracy or priesthood. Judaism to him meant the sovereignty of God as revealed in the Torah, the divine constitution which has as its goal the extension of justice to all. In this sense Philo characterized Judaism as a democracy and, as Professor Harry Wolfson has pointed out, he almost coined the term "theocracy" later used by Josephus to describe the Mosaic state.[10]

Upon these twin principles—the sovereignty of God and the sacredness of the individual—the religious philosophy of Judaism rests. Enunciated not merely as a theory, this philosophy is clearly reflected in the Halakah. In fact, only by properly understanding the Jewish concept of divine kingship and human worth can we fully understand many legal and spiritual institutions in Judaism. It is also true, however, that since Judaism is interested in practice rather than in theory, only a close examination of Jewish law can reveal its philosophic foundations.

This study is an attempt in that direction. By defining, in semi-popular terms, basic rabbinic concepts, and in studying the laws enacted by the Rabbis to govern various areas of human activity, it seeks to discover the religious doctrines which inspirit Judaism's legal definitions of man and society. Not a systematic study of rabbinic law, and far from complete, this work touches only upon a few fundamental concepts as they are revealed in talmudic literature, to demonstrate how the Jewish moral and religious principles manifest themselves in the rules of conduct and practice formulated by the Halakah.

# I. MAN AND THE WORLD

Underlying the spiritual structure of Judaism is the non-speculative but firm belief in monotheism—faith in God Who created the world and Who governs it with divine justice and righteousness. Man's religious responsibility is to worship the Creator and to refuse to worship that which is not the Creator. The Jew, therefore, must not worship the created things which came into being. He is forbidden to worship either a soulless material object or a human being, regardless of how great and saintly that particular human being may be. In fact, while the Jew reveres the Torah which, according to our Sages, was used by God as the architectural instrument for creation in general,[1] he is not permitted to worship it. Furthermore the Jew is forbidden to represent God by any material form or symbol, but not only because belief in the invisibility of God denies that He can be represented in visible likeness. The soul, too, though it is invisible, cannot be an object of worship, because it too is created.

This concept, incomprehensible even to a large segment of religious people throughout the world, is fundamental in Judaism. It represents, in a sense, the Jewish understanding of what the belief in pure monotheism is: the refusal to worship, as essence or as symbol, anything which represents that which is created. The religious Jew, therefore, is opposed to polytheism, which denies the existence of a sole Creator and Governor of the world. He is equally opposed to modern pantheism, which endows the physical world with the nature of God. For the Jew creation is not the Creator. The world is not, as the ancient Greek philosophers taught, merely the consequence of ultimate divine unity, nor are God and the world one.

The Jew rejects the idea that the world functions independently of God. At the same time, he refuses to identify the world with the nature of God, an act which would be tantamount to denying Him an independent and eternal existence. He does, however, hold firm to the belief, and accepts it as a major premise, that the world as the creation of the Uncreated is vested with holiness and that the human personality which was created in the image of God is infused with a divine spark of godliness. By necessity, the universe, which came into being through the free act of creation on the part of God, possesses sacredness. Moreover, since man was created in the divine image of God himself, the human personality is superior to all other forms of creation. Hence, according to the mishnaic sage Simeon ben Azzai, the fact that man was created in the divine image or likeness of God is the most comprehensive principle in the Torah and the fountainhead of Torah morality.[1a]

This premise also determines the attitude of the Jew toward the created world; accepting it, the Jew can never look upon the world and worldliness as evil. On the contrary, he always attempts to discover how to enjoy the things of creation without divorcing them from their Creator. Furthermore, since the world is the creation of God, it is, in a legal sense, His property. All created things belong to God. It is, therefore, the primary duty of man, who was created in the image of God, to strive continuously to develop, in deepest and profoundest measure, a sense of belonging to his Maker. Only when man realizes that he does not possess permanent and real ownership over either himself or created things in general, and that all created things belong to the Creator, can he begin to commune with God and establish an intimate relationship with Him.

Since the human personality is stamped with the divine likeness, it is man's duty to preserve that likeness and keep it physically as well as spiritually fit. Hillel the Elder perceived in the words of the Torah, "In the image of God He created man,"[2] an injunction to man to keep his body clean by bathing. The sage taught his disciples: "If there are men who are charged with the task of keeping clean the images of temporal monarchs set up in public places, and who are rewarded for such work, how much greater is my responsibility, who was created in the image of God."[3]

Moreover, since creation is the possession of the Creator, self-destruction is a sacrilege, and homicide is the greatest of all sacrileges. While one may use the objects of creation for the benefit of creation, one is forbidden to destroy purposelessly any object of creation, let alone that which stands highest in the scale of creation—man. It is the supreme duty of the human being, therefore, always to acknowledge and worship the Uncreated, and be ready to suffer death rather than worship any object of creation.

## THE PURPOSE OF MITZVOT

An understanding of this fundamental principle in Judaism gives us a true insight into the nature and purpose of the *mitzvot*, the commandments man must fulfill. When a Jew fulfills the positive and negative commandments of the Torah he is, in a sense, making the following pronouncement: "I am not the complete master of the world or of myself; I do not possess unlimited authority over the things of creation, and, therefore, whatever I do or fail to do with the things of creation depends on the will of the owner of creation—God Himself." This attitude, translated into action through the fulfillment of *mitzvot*, reaffirms a man's belief in the governorship of God and in the sanctity of creation. It indirectly brings him to a state of holiness.

This concept is not limited to material things only, as is indicated by the comment of our Sages on the verses, "But the soul that doeth aught with a high hand... the same blasphemes the Lord... because he hath despised the word of the Lord."[4] The Torah does not here specify the particular offense committed. One sage, Rabbi Ishmael, interprets the verse as applying to one who worships idols, but another, Rabbi Meir, says that the law is aimed at a person who is learned in the Torah but refuses to pass his knowledge on to others.[5] Such a man is arrogant, he despises God, rules Rabbi Meir. Rabbi Meir's intent is obvious. He teaches us that even one's knowledge must not be considered a personal acquisition and attainment. It, too, is but a gift of God; to refuse to share knowledge with others is, in effect, to despise God to Whom all things belong. Philo Judaeus, who often records in his writings ancient Jewish traditions, similarly recognized in this biblical verse prohibitions against arrogance—which leads to self-deification—and against selfishness—which leads man to regard all his endowments, intellectual and physical, as personal possessions, instead of as temporary gifts from God.[6]

This concept is the key to a true understanding of the laws which require man to pronounce a benediction before using the fruits of creation. The Talmud states:

Man is forbidden to enjoy anything without pronouncing a benediction, and whoever enjoys anything in this world without a benediction commits a trespass against sacred things [and].... is as guilty as if he would have derived enjoyment from the things dedicated to Heaven, for it is written, "The earth is the Lord's and the fulness thereof" (Ps. 24:1). Rabbi Levi raised the question: In one place it is written, "The earth is the Lord's and the fulness thereof," and in another place it is written, "The heavens are the heavens of the Lord but the earth He hath given to the children of man" (Ps. 115:16). The answer is that the former verse applies to the status prior to man's pronouncing the benediction; the latter verse applies after one pronounces the benediction.[7]

In other words, for our Sages all of creation is as sacred as are things dedicated to Heaven, for creation belongs to the Creator. A man must, therefore, before enjoying those things which are permitted him for his sustenance and pleasure, pronounce a *berakah* (blessing) over them to acknowledge that all things belong to God and are used only by His permission.

This concept is further developed by Philo Judaeus. He, more than any other Jewish philosopher, voiced the view that creation belongs to the Creator and that whatever dominion man enjoys over creation is limited and dependent upon the will of God. In fact, the greater part of his treatise *De Cherubim* is devoted to this concept. In it he writes:

No mortal can in solid reality be lord of anything.... God alone can rightly claim that all things are His possession.... To this sovereignty of the Absolutely Existent, the oracle is a true witness in these words: "And the land is not to be sold in perpetuity, for all land is Mine, because ye are strangers and sojourners before Me" (Lev. 25:23). A clear proof surely that in possession all things are God's, and only as a loan do they belong to created beings.... Yet he who has the use does not thereby become possessor, because there is one lord and master of all who will most rightly say, "All the land is Mine," (which is the same as "All creation is Mine"), "but ye are strangers and sojourners before me."[8]

Hence, the Torah regulates what we may enjoy and what we may not, and under what conditions enjoyment of the things of this world be-

comes permissible to us. Commenting on the same verse quoted by
Philo in the above passage, our Sages taught:

"*And the land shall not be sold in perpetuity*"—absolutely, irrevocably—
"*for unto Me is the land*"—look not sorely upon it, "*for you are strangers
and sojourners.*" Do not make yourself prime, for thus it is written, "For
we are strangers before you and sojourners like all our forefathers"
(I Chron. 29:15). And so does David declare, "For I am a stranger
with you, a sojourner like all my forefathers" (Ps. 39:13)—to teach us
that it is sufficient for a slave that he is like his master; "when it will
be mine, it is yours."[9]

Both sage and philosopher recognized man's temporal tenancy of God's
creation.

### SOCIAL JUSTICE: A RESULT, NOT A CAUSE

How pervasive this concept is in Judaism is indicated by the reasons giv-
en by our Sages for the law of the Sabbatical year. The Torah states:
"Six years shalt thou sow thy field, and six years shalt thou prune thy
vineyard, and gather in the produce thereof. But on the seventh year
shall be a Sabbath of solemn rest, a Sabbath unto the Lord, thou shalt
neither sow thy field, nor prune thy vineyard."[10]

Our Sages refuse to assign purely economic, agricultural or social
motives to this law. Rabbi Abahu, answers the question: What is the
reason for the law of the Sabbatical year? He states: "The Holy One
blessed be He said to the children of Israel: 'Sow for six years and leave
the land at rest for the seventh year, so that you may know that the land
is Mine!'"[11] Indeed, a careful reading of the twenty-fifth chapter of
Leviticus clearly reveals that underlying all the laws of the Sabbatical
year and the Jubilee year (during which property is returned to its
original owners and slaves are emancipated) is the concept that creation
belongs to the Creator, and that man cannot acquire permanent possession of either real property or of human beings.

Rooted in this religious concept, such laws must of themselves insure
justice for the poor, the slave, the vendor and the community in its
totality. But that is not their chief end. Animating these laws is the
religious belief that man does not acquire permanent possession of any-

thing in this world because the world is the property of God. Hence by observing such laws, the Jew, by means of his actions, reaffirms one of the root principles of the Torah.

Philo, too, understood this true significance of the laws pertaining to the Jubilee. He writes, "Do not pay the price of complete ownership, but only for a fixed number of years and a lower limit than fifty. For the sale should represent not real property, but fruits... [because] the whole country is called God's property and it is against piety to have anything that is God's property registered under other masters."[12]

The Mishnah likewise expresses the idea that all things of creation are the possession of God: "Rabbi Elazar of Bertotha said: Give unto Him from His own, for you and what you possess are His. This was also expressed by David: 'For all things come of Thee and of Thine own have we given Thee'" (1 Chron. 29:14).[13]

This concept is applied to human life too. Reflected in many midrashic passages, it finds particular and striking application in the story of Rabbi Meir's personal tragedy. Two of Rabbi Meir's sons died on the Sabbath while he was occupied in the Beth Midrash with his studies. When the Sage returned to his home Saturday night, his wife Beruria, who was famous for her scholarship and piety, did not inform him immediately of the great tragedy. Instead she asked a pointed question: "Yesterday, a man gave me a deposit: now he demands that I return the deposit. Should I do so?" Rabbi Meir answered: "My daughter, what an amazing question. Surely the depositary must return the deposit." But when Rabbi Meir saw his two sons lying dead before him, he became hysterical. Beruria then consoled him: "Did you not say that the depositary must return the deposit to its owner? Well, God gave and God took back. May the name of the Lord be blessed."[14]

Apparently it was standard practice to console mourners by reminding them that life is merely a divine deposit held by man and that God, the Depositor, can at any time demand the return of His deposit.[15] For Philo, the most consoling thought possible in cases of tragedy is that life is merely a loan given us by God.[16] In the same vein he records the Jewish tradition that one must not overindulge in grief. To mourn more than necessary for the dead is a sign of selfishness, an indirect declaration that human life, particularly that of close relatives, is one's own possession, and not the property of God.[17]

How fundamental this attitude toward divine ownership is in Judaism is further demonstrated by some features of the Temple service. Tradition records that every day a special chapter of the Psalms was recited in the Temple. The great sage, Rabbi Akiba, reported that on the first day of the week the Levites read, as we do today in our prayers, Psalm 24: "The earth is the Lord's and the fulness thereof." This psalm was chosen because it declares that "God acquired possession of the world and apportioned it to mankind, but He always remains the Master of His world."[18]

It is clear that the concept that creation belongs to the Creator is not an isolated principle in Judaism. Indeed, the entire structure of Judaism rests on it. The moral code of the Torah, its ritual pronouncements and man's obligation to observe the laws whether he knows the reason for them or not, all stem from this principle. God has instructed man, by means of Revelation, concerning what he is permitted to do or prohibited from doing with His creation. If man were to possess irrevocably the things of creation, were his life his own possession, then his own reason could dictate to him how to use it; he would even be permitted to abuse it. Since, however, creation belongs to God, He alone dictates the terms of man's tenancy in this world.

So important is a knowledge of God's law, that the study of Torah lays first claim to a man's time. This concept was given its extreme expression by Rabbi Ishmael, who believed it to be the will of God that man should dedicate his entire life to the study of the Torah and not occupy himself with secular learning. Asked whether a Jew is permitted to study the "wisdom of the Greeks," he answered, "Let him study during the time when it is neither day nor night."[19] By this answer he sought to emphasize that it is God's will that in His world the Jew should study only Torah.

MITZVOT AND REASON

Judaism lays particular stress on *mitzvot maasiot*, or religious action. Though we are forbidden to worship created things, the use of created things for the worship of the Uncreated One is regarded as the noblest form of worshipping God. This view lies behind Maimonides' declaration that man must fulfill those *mitzvot* for whose observance no rational explanation is apparent:

> For even wood, stone, dust and ashes become sanctified by mere word of mouth, as soon as the name of the Master of the universe is pronounced upon them, and if one treats them as things common, he commits a trespass against God; and even if it were done inadvertently, it requires expiation. How much more is it with the commandments inscribed for us by the Holy One blessed be He, that a man should not spurn them because he cannot divine the reason for their observance.[20]

Maimonides declares that when one dedicates a material object to the Temple it becomes holy and the property of the Most High, because we pronounce the name of its real Master over it, and since we proclaim that all things of creation belong to the Creator, no formal act of transaction is required to make an object Temple property. How much more sacred then, argues Maimonides, are the laws themselves over which the Master Himself pronounced His Name.

It would appear then that the purpose of sacrifices and monetary donations to the Temple was to actively proclaim, by the act of surrendering something to Him, that all things are God's. The sacrifice was merely a sign of gratitude to God Who permitted man to use all things of creation which, in themselves, as the property of God, are vested with a certain degree of sanctity. The same principle applies to the laws of tithes, first fruits, the tithe of the poor, and the many other ordinances concerning gifts to the priests, the Levites and the poor. Man was not permitted to enjoy any of his fruits until he had separated the necessary tithes. Every acquisition, even that which a man acquires by the labor of his own hands, is holy and must be redeemed; a share must be set aside for a godly purpose, to support the priest, the Levite and the poor man. By such acts man proclaims that the land and the produce thereof are not, in any sense of the word, his own. They belong primarily to God Who demands a share of them not because He has need of them but to ensure that the needy and those who are dedicated to His service may also benefit from His possessions.

Philo, speaking about the bringing of the *bikkurim*, the first fruits, follows a parallel line of thought:

It is no doubt just and a religious duty that those who have received freely a generous supply of substance so necessary and wholesome and also palatable in the highest degree should not enjoy or taste it at all until they have brought a sample offering to the Donor, not indeed as a gift, for all things and possessions and gifts are His, but as a token, however small, by which they show a disposition of thankfulness and loyalty to Him Who, while He needs no favors, sends the showers of His favors in never failing constancy.[21]

Similarly, the Midrash states that it is the custom of the world that when a man turns over his estate to be managed by a supervisor, he gives the supervisor a half, a third or a fourth of his produce, but God, Who supervises all of creation and causes the earth to produce, demands only one tenth of the produce.[22]

Commenting on the biblical verse, "Thou shalt surely tithe all the increase of thy seed, which is brought forth in the field every year,"[23] the Midrash declares:

The Holy One blessed be He said: I have commanded thee to honor Me, but not from thine own. Give Me what is already Mine, honor the Lord from the substance with which He graced you.... If thou shouldst say that I asked thee to give of thine own, see what I have written for thee: "When a bullock, or a sheep or a goat, is brought forth" (Lev. 22:27). When shalt thou offer a sacrifice? When I will first give thee.[24]

This midrash, enunciating the meaningfulness of the ancient sacrifices and tithes, repeats the basic principle in the religious philosophy of Judaism: Man must at all times recognize that the things of this world belong to God. When a man offers a sacrifice or gives his tithes in full awareness that he is returning to God that which belongs to Him, he performs a genuinely religious act. If, however, he believes that he gives of his own, his act is, in a sense, sacrilegious. The offering of an individual who regards creation as man's permanent possession and not as a mere deposit from the Almighty, is in effect a form of bribery and an act of superstition.

Similarly, commenting on the stress given to the pronoun "Me" in such phrases as "take Me a heifer,"[25] and "that they take for Me an offering,"[26] Philo remarks:

It says to us: You have no good thing of your own, but whatever you think you have, Another has provided. Hence, we infer that all things are the possession of Him Who gives, not of creation, the beggar, who ever holds out her hands to take.... Even if you take, take not for yourself, but count that which is given a loan or trust and render it back to Him Who entrusted and leased it to you, thus, as is fit and just, requiting good will with good will.... And so in the text He says, "Take ye *for me*." thus giving to Himself what is His due and bidding us not to adulterate the gifts but guard them in a way worthy of the Giver.... He "takes" in order to train us to piety and to implant a zeal of holiness, and to spur us to His service.[27]

Understanding this concept of God's ownership gives us an insight into the Jewish conception of man's obligations in this world.

To worship creation is a form of idolatry, but to worship God, the Creator, through the instrumentality of creation, is the essence of holiness. Thus, when man worships his fellow man he worships that which is not God, an act of idolatry. But when he renders service to his fellow man, he is, in the full sense of the term, worshiping God. By extending kindness to his fellow who, like himself, is made in the image of God, man imitates the ways of God who expresses Himself in the continuous extension of justice and mercy to mankind. Hence, Rabbi Hama ben Hanina said:

What is the meaning of that which is written "After the Lord your God ye shall walk" (Deut. 13:5). Is it then possible for man to walk after the *Shekinah* (the Holy Presence)? Is it not said: "For the Lord thy God is a devouring fire" (Deut. 4:24). Nay, [it means] walk after the attributes of the Holy One blessed be He. As He clothes the naked, do thou clothe the naked; as He visits the sick, do thou visit the sick; as He comforts the mourners, do thou also comfort the mourners; as He buries the dead, do thou also bury the dead.[28]

In many like passages do our Sages exhort man to imitate God by putting into practice His attributes of "being merciful, gracious, slow to anger, abundant in goodness and truth, extending loving-kindness, forgiving iniquity and transgression and sins." It is striking to note that nowhere do these teachers state that man should imitate God in His attribute of being a "zealous God." The reason is found in the *Mekilta*: "Rabbi says: A God above jealousy: I rule over jealousy, but jealousy has no power over Me; I rule over slumber but slumber has no power over Me."[29] Hence it is only God, who rules over jealousy, who is called a "zealous God." Man, who has no power to rule over jealousy, must rather imitate God in His attribute of kindness, and not in His attribute of jealousy.

### ELECTION AND BELONGING TO GOD

This concept of God's mastery also illumines for us the idea of Israel's "chosenness." Basic in Judaism, particularly in the relation of the Jew to God, is the concept of the election of the people of Israel, or "Israel as the Chosen People." Does this concept imply that Jews subscribe to the theory of racial superiority? Quite the contrary, such thoughts are foreign to the Jewish mind. The Jew, following the premise that all creation belongs to the Creator, believes that as a man, i.e., as the highest form of creation, he has entered into a covenant with God, his Creator. He promises to develop a greater measure of dedication and a greater sense of belonging to Him. The covenant is fulfilled only in the observance of the divine law. To that purpose is the Jew dedicated and chosen.

While it is true that all things of creation are the possessions of God, He designated particular parts of creation as His particular possessions in order to more vividly project the idea that creation in general belongs to Him. Our Sages set forth this concept as follows:

The Holy One blessed be He created days, and took to Himself the Sabbath; He created the months, and took to Himself the festivals; He created the years, and chose for Himself the Sabbatical year; He created the Sabbatical years, and chose for Himself the Jubilee year; He created the nations, and chose for Himself Israel; He created Israel, and chose for Himself the Levites; He created the Levites, and chose for Himself the priests; He created the lands, and took to Himself the Land of Israel as a heave-offering from all the other lands, as it is written. "The earth is the Lord's and the fulness thereof."[30]

The Sabbath dramatizes the idea that God is the Creator of the world. The festivals, which commemorate the historical experiences of the Jewish people, teach the continuous and particular providence of God. The Sabbatical and Jubilee years stand as a declaration that no human being has permanent possession of created things. Israel, by observing the Torah and through its willingness to assume greater moral responsibilities, becomes the "portion of the Lord," the "lot of His inheritance." All of the above elements, as well as the Land of Israel, a great part of whose produce must be dedicated to God, point to the central concept in Judaism: "The earth and the fulness thereof is the Lord's."

It is true that the universalism of God is the essence of Jewish monotheism, but accompanying this concept of pure monotheism is the idea contained in the midrash quoted above, that while the entire universe is the possession of God, He set aside certain created things as particularly His own. By their greater dedication to God and by their assumption of greater obligations in the service of God, these particularly elected portions continuously proclaim that "The earth is the Lord's and the fulness thereof." Hence, the election of Israel is based upon the covenant Israel made with God, in which Israel took upon itself to fulfill many duties not required of the rest of humanity.[30a] By these acts Israel constantly reaffirms that God alone governs the world and is the true possessor thereof.

Philo Judaeus expresses a similar notion in his comment on the verse, "Thou bringest them in and plantest them in the mountain of Thine inheritance,"[31] as well as in his interpretation of other verses which speak of Israel as the "portion of the Lord." He notes:

This expression would seem to apply to those who are on a special footing of more intimate relationship with Him as their Master. So kings are rulers of all their subjects but in an eminent degree of their household servants, of whose ministry they are accustomed to avail themselves for the care of their persons and their other requirements....[32]

In the mind of Philo the concept of Israel's election is thus easily explained. While the whole of creation belongs to God, the people of Israel are God's portion and inheritance because of their sacred ministration as servants of God, the Ruler of the entire universe.

Our Sages reach the same point in their own way. "Five possessions," they declare, "has the Holy One blessed be He made especially His own. These are: The Torah, heaven and earth, Abraham, Israel, and the Holy Sanctuary."[33] All creation is, of course, God's possession, but Abraham who proclaimed God in this world, Israel which practices His Torah and thus serves God, and the Temple which is dedicated to the service of God are the special possessions of God. Being the special possession of God demands unqualified recognition of Him as the Master of all things. The election of Israel, therefore, means, above all, the dedication of the Jewish people to the service of God. By acknowledging God as Master, the Jew feels that he becomes His servant. It is in this sense only that Jews, who strive to achieve a deeper sense of belonging to God through the observance of His Law, are known as a "Chosen People."

### BELIEF IN GOD AS THE OVERSEER

Thus, the belief in God as the Possessor of the world can be considered the keystone of Judaism. Many Jewish scholars, among them Maimonides, Judah Halevi and Nachmanides, accept the first of the Ten Commandments, "I am the Lord thy God," as a positive command which enjoins us to believe in the existence of God. While only one of the 613, this particular commandment is, in a sense, the very foundation of Judaism. In the words of Maimonides:

> The fundamental of all fundamentals and the pillar of all forms of knowledge is the realization that there is a First Being who brought all existing things into being... This Being is the God of the universe, the Lord of all the earth, and He is the Caretaker of the sphere with power that is without end or limit... And the knowledge of this truth is a positive command as it is said, "I am the Lord thy God."[34]

The duty of acknowledging the existence of God, however, is not met by saying "I believe that God exists." This *mitzvah* demands, above all, belief in God as the perpetual Possessor and Overseer of the world. Therefore does Maimonides incorporate into this fundamental belief not only the concept of God as the First Being, but also the concept of God as the *Manhig*, the Caretaker, of the world.

More striking, however, is the verse itself: "I am the Lord thy God

Who brought thee out of the land of Egypt, out of the house of bond-age."[35] To believe in God is not merely to believe in the existence of God; it requires that one have faith in God as a redeemer, a God on Whom our destiny depends. The *mitzvah* of believing in God is not fulfilled merely by pronouncing, "I believe in God who created heaven and earth." It requires an unwavering belief that God, of His own free will, acts favorably in behalf of man. Our belief in God rests not merely on our faith in a single historic act of creation. It is, above all, a belief in One Who ever, from moment to moment, continues to guide our lives: "Even from the time I brought thee out of the land of Egypt—I am the Lord thy God."[36]

But this, too, is not enough. Man must not only believe in God as the Caretaker of the world Who is directly and immediately concerned with the welfare of His creations; Man must also fashion for himself a way of life according to the pattern dictated by such a belief. All his actions and relationships must be directed by an awareness of God as the Possessor and Caretaker of the world and motivated by a desire to walk in His ways and care for all His handiwork.

In consonance with this understanding of man and his place in the world our Sages strove to develop laws affecting man's every act and relationship. Recognizing the difficulty men find in translating abstract principles into the simple actions of daily living, they moved to enact legislation which would so touch upon all aspects of human life that man's every act would demonstrate his acceptance of "the Yoke of Heaven." This is the essence and intent of the halakic life.

## 2. MAN AND SIN

In Judaism, monotheism is given universal application; all Jewish blessings, for example, contain the phrase, "Our God, King of the Universe." But God, the universal King, is at the same time the Jew's particular God. Abraham proclaimed a universal God, but the Jew feels no conflict in directing his prayers to "the God of Abraham, the God of Isaac and the God of Jacob." In the Jewish concept, God is not an absolute, remote, inaccessible Being; He is close to every man.

Our Sages assign greatness to Abraham, not so much in recognition of the fact that it was he who first acknowledged the existence of God, but because until Abraham did so, no one called God "Master."[1] In our Sages' view, what is important is that Abraham recognized God not only as the prime mover, the Creator of the world, but also as its continuous Master and Sovereign. In the homiletical midrash, *Sifre*, this point is most strikingly made:

> Before Abraham came into the world, the Holy One blessed be He, was Sovereign only in Heaven; our father Abraham made Him King of heaven and earth, as it is written, "I will make thee swear by the Lord, the God of heaven and the God of earth" (Gen. 24:3).[2]

In Judaism, therefore, monotheism is above all the belief in the sovereignty of God. Usually characterized by our Sages as the belief in the Kingdom of Heaven, it implies not only universal but also particular providence. God is the Father in Heaven, and by observing His law on earth, man creates a paternal-filial relationship between God and himself.

Hellenistic Jews also spoke of God as a father, but thinking in philosophical terms, they conceived of God as the Father of the universe, the Father of wisdom, the Father of all things intelligible and sensible, and the Father of mankind. For the Palestinian Jews, however, God was not merely the Father of the universe, He was the Father of Israel in general and of the individual Jew in particular. Therefore, they could address God in intimate terms—"Blessed art *Thou*,"—and speak of Him always in a personal way— "our Father in Heaven," "my Father in heaven," "his Father in heaven."[3] Commenting on the verse, "Ye are children of the Lord your God,"[4] Rabbi Judah said, "When you conduct yourselves like sons then you are sons, but when you do not conduct yourselves like sons then you are not sons." Rabbi Meir, however, declared that because of their election, the people of Israel remain His sons even when they are unworthy of God.[5]

In light of this intimate relation between God and man, and His accessibility to man, we can better understand why references to the need for intermediaries between man and God are hard to find in rabbinic literature. A man who transgressed one of the commandments had to bring a sin offering and confess his transgression, but the priest who sacrificed the sin offering on the altar was not considered an intermediary for the atonement of sin, nor was the confession of the sinner made to him.[6] The sinner confessed his sin silently, and directly to God; at the moment of repentance he stood in intimate relation with God, much like a sinful son making confession to his earthly father. For this reason confession was always offered silently.

But there was another reason, a result of the Jewish view of the human personality, why confession was always pronounced in silence. The Torah states that the sin offering and the whole-burnt offering are to be slaughtered in the same place.[7] This was done purposely, say our Sages, in order not to embarrass the sinner, since no one would be able to tell whether the sacrifice was being brought as a burnt offering or as a sin offering.[8] This attitude also shaped Philo's interpretation of the laws of the sin offering and the peace offering. It is God's wish, he writes, "that any sin which the penitent has previously committed should not be made notorious through the ill-judged judgments and unbridled tongue of malicious and acrimonious persons, and blazed abroad as a subject for contumelious and censurious talk but be confined within the sacred precincts which have also been the scene of the purification."[9]

The same reasoning accounts for one of the laws of prayer. The central prayer in the Jewish service, the *Shemoneh Esreh* (the Eighteen Benedictions), is recited silently. The reason for this, given in the Gemara, is to avoid embarrassing those who committed transgressions.[10] It was the desire of our Sages not to embarrass the sinner unnecessarily. They always endeavored to preserve human dignity, even the dignity of a sinner, wherever possible, and considered shaming a person in public to be morally equivalent to an act of murder.

Philo felt that there were two reasons why confession at the slaughtering of the sin offering was to be made in silence. First, since the confession was made directly to God, Who knows the thoughts of men, there was no need for an audible, and certainly not for a public confession. Second, silent confession would spare the sinner shame and ease the return of the penitent.

That confession is the expression of repentance is unquestionable. It was also the undisputed opinion of rabbinic scholars that there is a positive command requiring the sinner to confess. But there seems to have been a difference of opinion among talmudic scholars over the question of whether confession (other than the confession made at the sacrifice of a sin-offering) has to be made in public, or whether silent confession is sufficient.

Rabbi Judah, in the name of Rab, points to the apparent contradiction of two verses in the Bible. On one hand, the Psalmist said, "Happy is he whose transgression is forgiven, whose sin is *covered*,"[11] and on the other hand Solomon declared: "He that *covereth* his transgressions shall not prosper."[12] This apparent contradiction is resolved by two explanations in the Talmud. In one, the Talmud makes the following distinction concerning confession: if a man's sin is known, then it is his duty to confess in public; but if his sin is not known, then he may confess without acknowledging his sin publicly. The second answer follows a different approach. Sins committed against God need no public confession; it is sufficient if a man silently confesses to God the sins which he has committed. But sins committed against one's fellowman require a public confession.[13]

These distinctions point up the moral substructure of rabbinic law. The second statement teaches that man's relation to God is of such an intimate nature that no other human being need know of a man's sins against God. Maimonides held that audible confession was necessary and he begins his "Laws of Repentance" with the following statement:

With regard to all the commandments of the Torah, whether positive or negative, if a person transgresses any of them, whether intentionally or unintentionally, when he repents and turns away from his sins, he is duty bound to confess before God, blessed be He, as it is said: "When man or woman shall commit any sin that men commit, to commit a trespass against the Lord and that soul be guilty: Then shall they confess their sin which they have done" (Num. 5:6–7). This implies a verbal confession and such confession is a positive command. How does one confess? He says: "I beseech thee, O Lord, I have sinned, I have acted perversely, I have acted wickedly before Thee and I have done thus and thus, and lo, I regret and am ashamed of my deeds and I will never repeat them again." This is the essence of confession.[14]

But he, too, accepted the talmudic opinion that where sins committed against God are concerned, silent confession is sufficient. In confessing sins committed against God, he wrote, "The penitent does not have to pronounce them publicly... He should rather repent of them before the Almighty blessed be He, and enumerate the sins before Him."[15] This rabbinic concept is implied even in the ruling which requires public confession for sins committed against one's fellow man. That the purpose of public confession in such cases was not so much to ask the forgiveness of God as to secure the forgiveness of the person against whom the sin was committed, is indicated by the following midrash:

It is the custom of the world: If a man spurns his fellow man in public and later wants to appease him, the latter says, "You spurned me in public, and now you endeavor to appease me in the presence of only the two of us? Go forth and gather those people before whom you spurned me and appease me in their presence and then I will forgive thee." But the Holy One blessed be He is not so. Even when a man appears in the market place and shames and blasphemes His Name, the Holy One blessed be He says, "Repent between you and Me and I shall accept thee."[16]

Here, clearly stated, is the rabbinic view that even for sins committed against God before witnesses, one does not need to confess in public. God is accessible to every man and is particularly desirous that the sinner repent. Man can, therefore, in strictest privacy and without any intermediaries, confess his sin. It is different, however, when one sins against his fellow man. In such a case it is no longer confession which is the essence of repentance; it is the appeasement of the person injured or insulted that is important. Since it is assumed that, psychologically, a human being is more apt to forgive a wrong committed against him if the wrongdoer declares his culpability before all, public confession is required.[17]

CONFESSION AS A MEANS OF ATONEMENT

The attitude of Jewish law toward confession clearly reveals how Judaism's unique view of man and the world animates the halakah. In capital offenses, the Talmud required confession in public, or at least to a representative of the Sanhedrin, so that the execution should also serve as a means of atonement. This was, perhaps, an application in law of the rabbinic statement that if a man's sin is publicly known his confession must also be publicly known. Since, in the case of murder, there is no question of appeasing the victim of the crime, confession could be required only as a means of securing some measure of divine atonement.

That the Sanhedrin was particularly anxious to have the criminal confess is quite understandable. No modern judge, regardless of how deep his humanitarian principles may be, can ever be as disturbed as were our Sages when they had to pronounce the death penalty. Under our contemporary judicial system, it is the jury which makes the decision, and circumstantial evidence is accepted as proof of a capital offense. In ancient times, the decision of the Sanhedrin was based only on the faith and confidence which judges placed on the two witnesses who testified that the crime had been committed. We can understand, therefore, why the ancient Sanhedrin, composed of deeply religious men to whom the life of a single individual was as sacred as the life of the entire world, would welcome a confession. Yet, in their unfailing saintliness, they never forced the criminal to admit to the crime; they asked him, on religious grounds, only to declare, "May my death be an atonement for all my sins." Describing the procedure at the execution, the Mishnah states:

> When he was about ten cubits from the place of stoning they used to say to him, "Make thy confession"... for every one who makes his confession has a share in the world to come. And so did we find with Achan. Joshua said to him, "My son, give, I pray thee, glory to the

Lord, the God of Israel, and make confession unto Him, and tell me now what thou hast done; hide it not from me." And Achan answered Joshua and said: "Of a truth I have sinned against the Lord, the God of Israel, and thus and thus have I done" (Joshua 7:19–20). … It is written, "And Joshua said: Why hast thou troubled us? The Lord shall trouble thee this day" (Joshua 7:25)—this day shalt thou be troubled, but in the world to come thou shalt not be troubled. If he knows not how to confess, they say to him, "Say, may my death be an atonement for all my sins."[18]

One of the paradoxical legal concepts in the Talmud involves the legal validity of man's confession. On the one hand, the Rabbis rule that the confession or admission of the accused is equivalent to the testimony of a hundred witnesses.[19] Hence, if a man states that he owes another a hundred *zuz* he becomes legally bound to make payment. On the other hand, in criminal cases one's confession is of no legal worth, for the dictum in such cases is, "a man cannot incriminate himself."[20] Thus if a man confesses that he gave false testimony, or committed any other crime for which he is punishable either by a fine, stripes or death, his confession is void and is not accepted as legal evidence. He is not punished for the offense which he admittedly committed, nor does he forfeit, because of his confession, his trustworthiness as a witness. Confession, then, is binding only in civil matters but not in criminal matters. Maimonides offered the following rationalization for the rabbinic principle that a man cannot incriminate himself:

The Sanhedrin… inflicted neither capital punishment nor flagellation upon one who confessed to having committed a transgression, for it is possible that his mind became confused. Perhaps he is one of those troubled and bitter souls who look forward to death, those who thrust the sword into their bellies or throw themselves down from the roof. Perhaps it was for this reason that he confessed to a crime which he did not commit. The principle is a kingly [a divine] decree.[21]

Maimonides held the principle that a man cannot incriminate himself to be a "divine decree," a law which is difficult to explain. Nevertheless he saw psychological justification for it, reasoning that a man who incriminates himself is often not of clear mind and may be a victim of suicidal tendencies.

If self-incrimination is a result of an aberration, should it remove from a man his trustworthiness? Our Sages apparently held that self-condemnation cannot take from a man his legal status of trustworthiness. In fact, though in determining guilt self-incrimination had no legal significance, they often urged public confession upon a sinner as a means of repentance before God. To urge a sinner to repent and attain some measure of forgiveness before the Heavenly court, is natural if not inevitable in a society whose strongest cohering element is moral force.

## RESTITUTION AND REPENTANCE

The laws of repentance further reveal the religious and moral fundaments of Jewish law. When one reviews the 207 negative commandments, transgression of which makes one liable to punishment by flogging,[21a] one quickly realizes that most of them, with the exception of some fifteen, deal with sins against God.[22] Apparently, while physical punishment is not sufficient to absolve one of sins committed against one's fellow man, it is, in a sense, considered an atonement for sins committed against God, and returns the sinner to the same status he enjoyed in the community in his pre-sinful state. As regards the relation of the sinner to his Maker, however, physical punishment is not the most significant phase of man's restoration to his former worthiness. This can be achieved only by repentance.

One of the fundamental features of repentance in capital cases, as already mentioned, is confession before God.[23] The same principle applies when a man transgresses a negative command which involves some tangible action and for which the punishment is flogging. Though sufficient to restore a man to his former status among men, flogging is not sufficient as regards the laws of Heaven. In order to regain his former spiritual worthiness, a man must repent of his sinful actions before God. Maimonides states this explicitly: "So, too, those who incur the judicial penalty of death or the punishment of flagellation, do not receive their atonement by their suffering death or flagellation until they will repent and make confession in words."[24]

There is, however, one fundamental distinction between the transgressions which one commits against God and the transgressions which one commits against man. If one sins against God he sins against Him alone, but when one sins against his fellow man he sins against both God and man. Most striking is the statement, found in the name of Rabbi Jose ben Haninah, that if a man wrongs his fellow man and the latter dies, the offender must visit his grave in the company of a congregation of ten people and make the following statement: "I have sinned against the Lord of Israel and against so and so whom I have injured."[25] Though the declaration must be made before ten people, a religious congregation or community, one does not confess that he sinned against the congregation or community or state, but that in injuring his fellow man he sinned against God and man. This is, indeed, the philosophic concept of the Jewish democratic theocracy—by committing offenses against one's fellow man one automatically sins against God. Hence, the Mishnah states: "For transgressions that are between man and God the Day of Atonement effects atonement, but for transgressions that are between man and his fellow man, the Day of Atonement effects atonement only if he has appeased his fellow man."[26]

It appears to be the opinion of our Sages that if one commits an offense against his fellow man either by injuring him in body or by robbing his money, though the offender is legally responsible for money indemnity, his monetary payment does not restore him to his former worthiness. To atone for his sin and regain his *hezkat kashrut*, or former legal status of trustworthiness, the offender must perform three separate, yet interrelated actions: he must make restitution, he must appease the person whom he injured or robbed, he must repent his wrongdoing. The last means, above all, resolving never again to repeat his action.

### CORPORAL PUNISHMENT AND MONEY INDEMNITY

Recognizing the importance of repentance and restitution in Jewish law, it would be a serious mistake to assume that because the rabbis interpreted the law of "an eye for an eye" to mean money indemnity, as opposed to the *lex talionis*,[27] they considered an injury inflicted upon another's person to be equivalent to damage inflicted upon another's property. On the contrary, it was the rabbinic view that injuring a fellow being was a violation of a negative commandment punishable by flogging, a negative commandment derived from the verses: "It shall be if the wicked man deserves to be beaten then the judge shall cause him to lie down and to be beaten before his face, according to the measure of his wickedness, by number. Forty stripes he may give him, *he shall not exceed.*"[28] From this they deduced that if the messenger of the court applies more than the prescribed number of stripes, he himself violates a negative command for which he may be punished by stripes.[29] If such a rule applies to a person appointed by the court to punish an offender, how much more does this negative injunction apply to one who injures an innocent person. Obviously then, not only were the Sages of the opinion that money indemnity does not compensate for bodily injuries; they maintained that an offender should receive bodily punishment, though not on the literal scale of "an eye for an eye." Corporal punishment by the court, then, may have been a form of repentance dictated by the Sages.

In practice, however, such corporal punishment was not meted out. Following a great humanitarian principle, our Sages ruled that a man cannot be punished twice for the same criminal act. Guided by the rule of the Torah that a man should be punished "to the measure of his wickedness,"[30] they decreed: "You punish him according to the measure of one wickedness, but not as if he had committed two wicked deeds."[31] The legal question raised by this ruling—should one who injures another pay money indemnity to the injured person or should he be punished in body for his sinful act and be relieved of his monetary liability—was a matter of controversy in the Mishnah. Rabbi Meir ruled that witnesses who falsely testify that one man owes another money must be punished by flagellation and also pay, "for the name [the transgression of the negative command] which makes them liable to be flogged, does not make them liable for recompense." The Rabbis, however, held that "He that makes recompense does not suffer the penalty of flogging."[32] The opinion of the Sages was accepted as halakah, and the talmudic dictum is: "He pays money indemnity but does not receive bodily punishment."[33]

That this rabbinic ruling is directed by a high moral concept is self-evident. Were the offender to be freed from the responsibility of indemnifying his victim for the injury committed and be punished only in his body, the only satisfaction the injured person could derive would be the pleasure which comes with revenge—the satisfaction of seeing the offender suffer as he did—which is in fact the philosophy of the *lex talionis*. But when the offender is forced to indemnify his victim, two ends are served. First, the offender is punished for he sustains a loss, and second, the injured person is recompensed for the loss which he sustained.

The consistency of the Rabbis in their notion that money indemnity does not in itself absolve an offender is clearly indicated in the Talmud. It is the law that if the damage caused by the injury amounts to less than a *perutah* (the minimum sum for which a person may sue another), then the one who committed the injury is punished by stripes. The reason for this ruling is that since, under such circumstances, the principle of money indemnity cannot be applied, the offender must suffer the corporal punishment set for his transgression.[34] Money indemnity helps to set right a wrong but it does not bring automatic forgiveness. True, the one sinned against is urged to forgive the wrongdoer, but the latter is enjoined to sue for that forgiveness. In the words of the Mishnah:

> Even though he pays, forgiveness is not granted to him until he begs forgiveness, for it is said: "Now, therefore, restore the man's wife: for he is a prophet and he shall pray for thee" (Gen. 20:7). From what source do we learn that if [the victim] does not forgive he is considered merciless? It is written (Gen. 20:17): "And Abraham prayed unto God, and God healed Abimelech."[35]

This is the traditional moral concept of Judaism. Mercy and justice must supplement and complement each other. The sinner must act justly toward the one against whom he has sinned, and the offended man must be merciful and generous with the sinner who makes restitution and seeks forgiveness.

### RESTITUTION: A MORAL ACT

As stated, money indemnity or restitution does not restore to a person his former state of legal trustworthiness. For acts which are crimes against man and sins against God, perpetrators must seek forgiveness from both God and man. As a first step the offender must make property restitution and beg the forgiveness of the person he has wronged, and only then, following genuine repentance, will God grant His forgiveness.

But even the act of restitution in rabbinic law is shaped by profound moral and religious principles. Restitution is not merely a means of reimbursing a victim of theft or injury for his loss. It is rather an outgrowth of the legal theory that one cannot acquire or retain legal possession of those things which come to him through unlawful means. Hence, if one steals an article worth a hundred *zuz*, and returns to the owner a hundred *zuz*, the exact value of the stolen article, he is still considered a thief, because he brought the article into his possession in an illegal way.

As is evident, our Sages gave a literal reading to the words of the Torah: "He shall restore that which he took by robbery."[36] But this is more than a matter of interpreting a verse of the Torah literally. The rabbis drew from the Torah the profound moral lesson that things which are acquired by force cannot become one's legal possessions even if full payment of their value is made to the owner. If the stolen property is burned or destroyed, the robber is legally obligated to return to the owner the full value of the item, but as long as it is in existence the item itself must be returned. Furthermore, even after returning the stolen article, the robber must ask forgiveness of his victim because the violation of a negative command which affects one's fellow man constitutes a personal injury and requires personal forgiveness.

In this light we can understand the tannaitic statement: "The Sages of the School of Shammai said: 'If one steals a beam and builds it into a structure, he must pull down the entire structure and return the beam to its owner.'"[37] This attitude of the School of Shammai clearly accords with the law of the Torah that regardless of the expense involved, a robber must restore the original article, "that which he took by robbery," to the owner. Often, however, modifications in a law are permitted if it is felt that leniency will, in the long run, encourage moral conduct and lead to repentance. Hence the School of Hillel, disagreeing with the School of Shammai, said: "In such a case the owner can collect only the value of the beam, in order to assist the repentant sinner."[38] The

School of Hillel agreed with the School of Shammai that in accordance with the law of the Torah a robber cannot acquire possession of the stolen article and must restore it, but they instituted a rabbinic ordinance, called *takkanat hashabim*, a *takkanah* or ordinance which would ease the return of the penitent.[39]

The Mishnah records the testimony of Rabbi Johanan ben Gudgada, an early sage, that this was the purpose of the *takkanah* enacted by the school of Hillel.[40]

The second moral concept, that a robber sins against the individual whom he robs and, therefore, in addition to restoring the article must also appease his victim, is the source for a striking statement made in the Mishnah:

If a man robbed his fellow man of the value of a *perutah* [the minimum sum for which one is held legally liable] and swore [falsely] to him,[41] [if he wants to make restitution] he must restore it to him in person even if he has to travel as far as Media. He may not give it to his son or to his agent, but he may give it to the agent of the court.[42]

The moral philosophy behind this law is that robbery is a crime against the person robbed and therefore the robber is required to present himself, along with the restored article, to the person whom he has wronged. Unlike Roman law, in which the robber is considered an "enemy of the state," thus giving the state the right to institute penalties as punishment for his criminal acts, Jewish law maintains that a criminal act is a sin against the individual wronged and against God. The reinstatement of the criminal to his former worthiness, therefore, depends primarily on his personal contact with the individual whom he has wronged.

However, the mishnah quoted permits restitution to be made "to the agent of the court." This is but another example of a *takkanah* enacted by the Rabbis to ease the return of the penitent. A tannaitic statement in the name of Rabbi Elazar ben Zadok explains this:

[The Sages] instituted a great ordinance (*takkanah gedolah*) that if the expenses incurred in making restitution [to the owner in person] are greater than the value of the property [to be restored], he [the robber] may deposit the property plus a fifth of its value in the court of justice. He then may bring his guilt offering and thus make atonement.[43]

Hence, it is only in extraordinary circumstances that the Sages would grant atonement to a robber without his having restored the stolen property and begged forgiveness directly from the person he wronged.

## RESTITUTION AFTER ILLEGAL ACQUISTITION

The legal principle that one can never gain ownership over property acquired in a prohibited manner also manifests itself in the principle of *yeush* through which one may acquire ownership over *lost* property but not over *stolen* property. According to rabbinic law, the expression, by the owner of a lost article, of *yeush*, complete abandonment of hope of ever recovering his lost property, is equivalent to an express renunciation of ownership, making the property ownerless. Following such a declaration, anyone has the right to acquire possession over it. The source of this principle of *yeush* is of little concern here; what is important is its legal and moral application. The law is that any person who finds a lost article after *yeush*, that is, after its owner has publicly abandoned hope of its recovery, acquires legal possession thereof.

This principle, however, does not apply in the case of robbery. If one steals or robs, even if the owner abandons all hope of recovering his property, the principle of *yeush* is non-operative. A robber or thief can never assume title to the stolen article. The Talmud explains the difference between *yeush* in the case of *abedah*, loss of property, and *yeush* in the case of *gezelah*, robbery, thus: "In the latter case it came into his domain in a prohibited manner."[44] Hence, the original immoral act of depriving the owner of his property throws upon the robber the responsibility of returning the property to the owner even though the latter has abandoned all hope of its recovery. However, the *yeush* of the owner remains ineffective only for the robber, not for a third party. Thus, if the thief, after *yeush*, sold or gave the article as a gift to another person, that person does acquire ownership of the property. In rabbinic terminology this is called *yeush v'shinui reshut*, abandonment of hope and a transfer from the thief's domain to another's domain.

The logic of this principle is quite apparent. Since the owner has already abandoned hope of recovering his property, though originally stolen, the article is like a lost article after *yeush*. Just as a finder acquires ownership of a lost article, so too in this instance, the one who receives the article from the robber or thief acquires ownership over it, not through the power of the robber to sell the article, but through the *yeush* of the original owner.

The robber himself, however, cannot through *yeush* acquire ownership over the property. Even if he gives the property as a gift to another after *yeush*, and the latter acquires legal ownership of the property, the robber still must restore the value of the property to the original owner. Here again the religious principle involved is that the robber, through an act of restitution, must cleanse himself of his original immoral act.

## CRIME AGAINST MAN, SIN AGAINST GOD

The various legal principles discussed above may also be comprehended in an understanding of the division of the laws of the Torah into duties which man has toward God and duties which man has toward his fellow man. If one sins against God, it is against God alone that he sins, but if one sins against his fellow man, he also commits a sin against God, for by his act he transgresses a divine command.[']

This distinction is one of the cornerstones of the Jewish democratic theocracy. Indeed, our Sages went so far as to say that by transgressing a negative commandment which relates to his fellow man, man denies the very existence of God. By this they meant that such a transgression denies the authority of the law, for had the offender believed in its godly origin, he would not have intentionally flouted it. Expressed by Rabbi Meir in connection with lending money on interest,[45] this idea was stated most strongly by Rabbi Jose ben Halafta:

Come and see how blind are the men who lend money on usury... the usurer brings the scribe, the pen and ink, the writ and the witnesses and instructs them to write that he has no share in the One Who commanded against taking usury; and the usurer takes the writ to the office of a heathen court and thereby denies the One Who by His word created the world. Thus you may learn that they who lend money on usury deny the Root."[46]

In particular did our Sages regard the violation of the commandment against taking usury to be not only a sin against one's fellow man but also a sin against God. One's conduct in this was regarded by them as proof of whether one accepts upon himself the yoke of Heaven or casts it off.[47]

The severity of our Sages in judging crimes committed against one's fellow man was often dependent upon the offender's disregard for divine providence and the extent to which his acts revealed that he feared his fellow man more than he did God Himself.[48] In rabbinic thought, the seriousness of a crime is largely determined by the degree of its sinfulness before God. This concept is illustrated in the rabbinic interpretation of many laws in the Torah and manifests itself particularly in the rabbinic, as also in the Philonic, interpretation of the laws of theft, robbery, murder and the denying of a deposit.

According to the law of the Torah, if a case of theft is established on the strength of the testimony of two witnesses, the thief must pay double the amount stolen. The halakah applies this law only when one steals from a private individual. If, however, one steals Temple property, while legally he is bound to restore the stolen article, neither a bodily penalty nor the fine of paying double the amount stolen is imposed upon him. The Talmud derives this law from the verse, "And it be stolen out of the man's house."[49] Only when an article is stolen from a private house does the thief have to pay double the amount stolen, but not when it is stolen from the "sacred house," that is, from the Temple.[50]

It is extremely interesting to note that, in contrast, ancient Greek and Roman law considered the theft of temple property a most serious offense, punishable by death.[51] The Greeks and Romans looked upon their deities as something private, as the property of the state, province or city. Hence, to steal something private which is also vested with sacredness is a greater crime than to steal something from a private individual. The Jews, who believed in the universality of God, were of the opinion that one cannot steal from the domain of God, "for wherever the property may be, it is in the treasury of the Merciful, as it is written: 'The earth is the Lord's and the fulness therof'" (Psalms 24, 1).[52]

## THE SACRILEGE OF MURDER

The Greeks and Romans used the term *hierosulia*, a sacrilege, in relation
to the theft of temple property. Philo Judaeus, who often employed
Greek terminology in explaining Jewish law to a non-Jewish world,
made use of this term too, but applied it not in relation to stealing the
property of the pagan gods but in relation to the act of murder. He
writes:

> The term murder or manslaughter is used to signify the act of one
> who has killed a human being, but in real truth that act is a sacrilege
> (*hierosulia*) and the worst of sacrileges; [this is because] of all the
> treasures which the universe has in its store there is none more sacred
> and godlike than man, the glorious cast of a glorious image, shaped
> according to the pattern of the archetypal form of the word. It fol-
> lows necessarily that the murderer must be regarded as committing
> something ungodly and unholy: indeed, both the highest degree of
> ungodliness and unholiness.[53]

I have always felt that this passage underscores the Judaeus as against the
Philo in the thought of this great philosopher. Certainly, the Jewish
imprint is unmistakable in this fundamental declaration that the greatest
sacrilege is the destruction of human life and not the stealing of Temple
property. He who takes a human life commits the most sacrilegious act
possible, because man, created in the image of God, is more sacred than
Temple property or, for that matter, any other sacred object.

Since in ancient Greece, murder was considered a crime against the
individual, forgiveness rested with the victim. If a fatally wounded
man forgave his assailant before his death, all further persecution of the
murderer, either by relatives or the court, was barred.[54] In Judaism, on
the other hand, murder was considered the worst criminal act possible,
not only because it deprived a human being of his life, but because it
constituted the greatest sacrilege possible. Furthermore, since Judaism
did not consider the gift of life to be the personal property of the individual, forgiveness of a murderer is not man's, even the victim's, to grant
or withhold. Maimonides summarizes the Jewish philosophy of human
life, which is in direct opposition to the Greek concept of life in general,
thus:

They [the court] are warned against the acceptance of ransom from the murderer, even if he is ready to pay all the money in the world and even if the avenger of blood consents to let the murderer go free. For the life of the murdered person is not the possession of the avenger of blood, but the possession of the Holy One blessed be He.[55]

No human being, not even the avenger of blood or the person who suffered death, has the right to pardon the murderer for this most terrible and sacrilegious act.

This concept runs through tannaitic literature. On the sixth commandment, "Thou shalt not murder," our Sages say:

How were the Ten Commandments given? Five on one tablet and five on the other. On the first tablet it is written: "I am the Lord thy God." On its opposite [the second tablet] it is written, "Thou shalt not murder." Scripture instructs us that whosoever sheds human blood is regarded as if he had diminished the divine image...indeed... if one sheds blood it is imputed on him as if he had diminished His Likeness. For it is said, "Whosoever sheds man's blood... for in the image of God made He man" (Gen. 9:6).[56]

Similarly, Rabbi Akiba said, "Beloved is man for he was made in the image of God; still greater was the love in that it was made known to him that he was created in the image of God, as it is written, 'For in the image of God made He man.'"[57] And again, "Whosoever sheds human blood renounces the Likeness."[58]

It is no wonder that Rabbi Akiba's younger contemporary, Simeon ben Azzai, went so far as to say that the most comprehensive principle of the Torah is the statement that man is made in the image of God,[59] more fundamental even than the Torah's command, "Love thy neighbor as thyself." Love for one's neighbor may permit forgiveness for the greatest of crimes, murder. The concept that man was made in the image of God imparts not only the great universal and moral lesson of the common heritage of all mankind; it establishes as a fundamental principle that every human life is sacred and that an act of murder is the most serious offense against God. Even the forgiveness of the murdered person, if granted, cannot absolve the criminal of his great sacrilege.

### CRIME: A DENIAL OF THE DIVINE

In the Roman and Greek world the seriousness of a criminal act was judged in terms of the individual, his immediate family and the state as a whole. Among the Romans, the concept that a crime committed against an individual could constitute a crime against the state had greater currency than among the Greeks. Because of their view of the state, the authority vested in it and the great discipline it imposed on its members, the Romans found it easier to accept this concept than did the Greeks with their concept of government as a democracy.

The rabbis, too, judged man's actions in relation to the state, but only the divine state. To what degree do a man's actions constitute a rebellion against the sovereignty of God, and to what degree do his actions reveal him to be more concerned with the sovereignty of man than with the sovereignty of God? By this yardstick did the Rabbis determine the seriousness of a crime. This is illustrated by the technical distinction made by our Sages between robbery and theft.

In cases of secret theft, the thief paid, as a fine, double the amount of the stolen property, whereas in cases of open robbery, the robber had to make restitution, but no additional penalty was levied against him. Theft was considered a more heinous crime because by his secrecy the thief implies that whereas he fears the punishment of men, he does not fear the judgment of God. In contrast, Roman law considered robbery the more serious offense, often punishable by death.[60] Because the robber was considered to have committed a crime against the state by openly daring to defy its authority, he became a public enemy.

It is indeed striking that despite the fact that he drew so liberally on Greek and Roman thought, in this case, too, Philo Judaeus hewed faithfully to the Jewish line. Beginning like any Roman, he writes, with reference to the law of robbery:

Anyone who carries off any kind of property which belongs to another and to which he has no right must be written down as a public enemy, if he does so openly and with violence, because he combines shameless effrontery with defiance of the law. But if he does it secretly, and tries to avoid observation like a thief, since his shamedness serves to palliate his misdeeds, he must be punished in his private capacity, and as he is liable only for the damage which he has attempted to work, he must repay the stolen goods twofold and thus by the damage which he most justly suffers make full amends for the injustice of his gain.[61]

But writing further, he concludes like a Palestinian Sage, that the robber is to be treated more leniently than the thief. In his view, "The law has shown itself reasonable and exceedingly forgiving in its treatment of him... it has not punished him as a public enemy by sentencing him to death or banishment, or at the very least to forfeiture of his whole property, but merely called upon him to make good the damages to the owner."[62]

Similarly, Josephus,[63] who often played the role of an apologist, points out that a thief is treated more harshly than a robber[64] and declares that the punishments meted out to him "are not such as are met with in other nations, but more severe ones."[65]

Only one explanation is given in tannaitic literature to the query why the law is more lenient with the robber than with the thief:

The thief pays double the amount stolen, but the robber pays only the principal. For what cause is the Torah more severe with the thief than with the robber? Rabban Johanan ben Zakkai says: The robber [who commits his crime in the open] respects the servant equally with the Master [i.e., he respects neither]. The thief honors the servant more than the Master. The thief, as though such a thing were possible, regards the Eye above as if it cannot see and the Ear as if it cannot hear, similar to what is said, "Woe unto them that seek deep to hide their counsel from the Lord, and their work is in the dark, and they say: who seeth us and who knoweth us" (Isa. 29:15). And it says: "And they say: The Lord will not see" (Ps. 94:7). And it also says: "For they say, the Lord has forsaken the land, and the Lord seeth not" (Ezek. 9:9).[66]

Clearly, for our Sages, the person who demonstrates that he has more respect for the authority of man than he has for the invisible sovereignty of God commits the greater crime and is to be more severely punished.

This same principle is enunciated, in almost the same words, by Philo Judaeus and Rabbi Akiba. The law in Leviticus dealing with a bailee who falsely swears that he never received a deposit for which he is being sued,[67] characterizes his criminal action not as a transgression against man but as a transgression against God. Asking why this should be so, Rabbi Akiba gave the following answer:

A creditor and a debtor transact their business by written deed and witnesses, and when the debtor denies the debt, he denies the validity of the written deed and witnesses, but he who wishes to make a deposit does not desire that anyone should know about it but the invisible Third [God] and, therefore, when he denies the deposit he also denies the existence of the Third [i.e., God].[68]

Hence, for Rabbi Akiba the denial of a deposit is a sacrilegious act. Philo Judaeus voiced this theocratic concept in almost the same way:

The most sacred of all dealings between man and man is the deposit on trust, as it is founded on the good faith of the person who accepts it... a man gives something with his own hands secretly to another when both are alone.... The one wishes that nobody should observe his gift, the other that no one should know of his acceptance. And this unseen transaction has assuredly the unseen God as its intermediary, to Whom both naturally appeal as their witness, one that he will restore the property when demanded, the other that he will recover it at the proper time. So then, he who repudiates the deposit ... repudiates two trusts, one that of him who consigned his property, the other that of the most veracious of witnesses Who sees and hears all.[69]

Thus are crime and sin bound together in Jewish law. A man must respect his fellow man, for both are the children of God and both were created in the divine image. To infringe on a fellow being's rights is to deny him his God-given privileges and is, therefore, a rebellion against Him Who grants equal rights to all. Here, again, the unique character of Judaism as a democratic theocracy is clearly demonstrated. The acceptance of the sovereignty of God insures the equality of man.

### THE REPENTANCE OF THE SINNER
### AND THE REBELLION OF THE RIGHTEOUS

One of the fundamental concepts of our Sages is that while no man is completely free of sin, neither is he always in the state of sinfulness because of sins he once committed. Implicit in God's attribute of mercy is the idea that God forgives man his sins if he repents and asks for forgiveness—"that the wicked forsake his ways and the unrighteous man his thoughts, and let him return unto the Lord and He will have mercy upon him" (Isaiah 55:7). Similarly, says the prophet, God declares, "I do not desire the death of the wicked man, but that the wicked man turn from his evil way and live" (Ezek. 33:11).

Acts of sinfulness do not condemn a man permanently, for through the act of repentance man is able to remake himself and become a new creation.[70] Similarly, acts of righteousness do not guarantee man a permanent status. Man is always in a state of flux. In the words of the prophet: "The righteousness of the righteous shall not deliver him in the day of his transgression; and as for the wickedness of the wicked, he shall not stumble thereby in the day that he turneth from his wickedness; neither shall the righteous be able to live thereby in the day that he sinneth" (Ezek. 33:12). Hence, it is taught that if a man lives righteously throughout his life only to rebel at the end, he destroys all. If a man regrets the commandments which he fulfilled and says to himself, "What benefit have I of them, wouldst that I had not performed them," he forfeits all and his meritorious deeds are not remembered in his favor.[71] The classic case of the righteous man who forfeited all his merits by his final deeds cited in the Talmud is that of Johanan the high priest, "who ministered for eighty years and at the end became a Sadducee."[72]

Conversely, God is ready to accept a man who was wicked throughout his life if he repents at the end.[73] The sinner is received by God and his sin is forgiven when "he forsakes his sin, removes it completely from his thoughts and resolves in his heart never to repeat it again."[74]

### THE SINNER AND HIS PENITENCE

Another of the concepts in Philo's work which clearly bears the Jewish stamp, and is unquestionably based upon the same traditions as found in rabbinic literature, is the virtue of repentance. The Greek philosophers had nothing praiseworthy to say about repentance. To their way of thinking, good men do no wrong, and even a penitent is an evil person.[75] In Judaism, however, no man is so good that he can attain perfection,

nor is any sinner so bad that he cannot redeem himself through penitence. Philo's understanding of repentance differs in no way from the
teaching of our Sages. He formulates the essence of repentance in the
following words: "If shamed into wholehearted conversion, they reproach themselves for going thus astray and make full confession and
acknowledgment of their sins, first within themselves with a mind so
purged that their conscience is sincere and free from lurking taint,
secondly with their tongues to bring their heart to a better way, then
they will find favor with God the Saviour, the Merciful."[76]

The elements of repentance listed by Philo are standards of repentance
formulated by our Sages: genuine regret for the sinful action of the
past, a sincere resolve not to sin again, and confession by word of
mouth.[77] In the case of sins committed against a fellow man, Philo, like
our Sages, states that repentance avails not until the sinner rights the
wrong he committed. He must demonstrate "his repentance not only
by a mere promise but by his actions."[78]

Sin, if repented, is not a stain on man. In Philo's view no man can be
entirely free of sin, "for absolute sinlessness belongs to God alone or
possibly to a divine man." But this fact gives man an opportunity to
demonstrate his true worth, for "conversion from sin to a blameless life
shows a man of wisdom who has not been utterly ignorant of what is for
his good."[79] In fact, speaking of the penitence of the Day of Atonement
Philo states that "the gracious God has given to repentance the same
honor as to innocence from sin."[80]

Despite this, it would appear that Philo accepted the view that in the
scale of values the repentant holds second place to the one who is innocent from sin.[81] In the Talmud, too, there is a dispute over whether the
non-sinner or the penitent holds a higher rank in the eys of God.[82] It is
clear, however, that both Philo and our Sages were of the opinion that
if a man genuinely repents and does not repeat his sins, he is forgiven by
God and with good conscience may continue a normal life.

### SELF-EXILE OF THE PENITENT

There is a passage in Philo which indicates that much more is required
of the sinner than repentance and confession. In that particular passage

apparently, Philo does not refer to a man who sins occasionally in the normal course of life but to one who committed grievous or continuous sins and now, after a change of heart, is seeking complete reformation; not to a man who does *teshubah*, who repents particular sins he committed, but rather with the *baal teshubah*, one who goes through a complete conversion from a life of sinfulness to a life of blamelessness.

According to Philo, it was through Enoch that repentance came into existence, for Enoch was a sinner, and God, in His mercy, granted to him the gift of repentance. The verse in Genesis 5:24, "And Enoch walked with God, and he was not; for God took him," rendered by the Septuagint as "And Enoch pleased God and he was not found because God transferred him," Philo interpreted allegorically: Enoch who lived in vice was no longer found, because he repented his sins and thus became a new man.[83] The phrase "transferred him," explains Philo, means that Enoch imposed upon himself self-exile. Self-exile, for Philo, was of great importance in achieving true repentance, for he writes:

> If a man has really come to despise pleasures and desires and resolves in all sincerity to take his stand above the passions, he must prepare for a change of abode and flee from home and country and kinsfolk and friends without a backward glance. For great is the attraction of familiarity. We may fear that if he stays he may be cut off and captured by all the love charms which surround him and will call up visions to stir again the base practices which had lain dormant and create vivid memories of what it were well to have forgotten. Many persons in fact have come to a wiser mind by leaving their country and have been cured of their wild and frenzied cravings when sight can no longer minister to passion the images of pleasure.... And further, if he changes his abode he must shun great gatherings and welcome solitude. It cannot but be that even in the foreign soil there are many snares like those at home on which the shortsighted who delight in large assemblies are sure to be pinned.[84]

Unmistakably, the subject of this passage is not the occasional sinner who repents particular sins committed at one time or another. Philo here speaks of a man so completely under the influence of passion that even after penitence he must guard against the danger of reawakened unlawful desires. Part of the penitence required of such a sinner is self-exile and solitude to save him from the temptation of resuming his old life. A man undergoing conversion from a life of sin to a life of perfection must experience a complete change. To insure that his old life "is no longer found," he must leave his old surroundings, move to a foreign place and live in isolation.

The same penitence is prescribed by Maimonides for such a sinner. The true penitent, he writes, "keeps far away from that wherein he sinned; changes his name as much as to say I am another individual and not the one who committed those deeds... and exiles himself from his former place of residence."[85] Apparently Maimonides and Philo shared an ancient tradition requiring this type of penitence in such cases.

Moreover, both Philo and Maimonides, like Aristotle, stress another vital point. For both of them virtue consists of finding the mean and avoiding either extreme. In Philo's words, "deviations in either direction, whether of excess or of deficiency, whether they tend to strain or to laxity, are in fault."[86] Similarly, in discussing the dietary laws, which according to him teach man self-control, Philo states, "He approved neither of vigorous austerity like the Spartan legislator, nor of dainty living, like him who introduced the Ionians and Sybarites to luxurious and voluptuous practices. Instead he opened up a path midway between the two. He relaxed the overstrained and tightened the lax.[87]

Maimonides, too, taught that man should be neither volatile nor unfeeling; satisfy his physical needs, but avoid luxury; be neither miserly nor overly prodigal; neither frivolous nor melancholy. In short, "whoever observes the disposition of the mean is termed wise."[88] But he excepted two types of people from this rule, the saint and the sinner. The saint chooses an extreme not as a means of self-punishment, nor out of a disregard for his moral and lawful inclinations, but as a means of attaining a greater degree of self-control. The sinner, on the other hand, should strive for the extreme in self-denial as a part of his repentance to compensate for indulging in the extreme of unlawful desires and passions during his sinfulness.

Of the saint, Maimonides writes: "Whoever is particularly scrupulous and departs from the mean in behavior is called a saint. For example, if one refrains from haughtiness of heart to the utmost extreme

and is exceedingly humble, he is termed a saint; and this is the measure
of saintliness. But if one departs from the haughtiness of the heart and
is humble only as far as the mean, he is called a wise man; and this is the
measure of wisdom, and so with all other dispositions."[89] The sinner,
he writes, must seek the extreme in those pious virtues which are the
opposite to his sins. "If a man sinned in respect to property, he must
liberally spend his property in service of God; if he indulged in sinful
bodily enjoyment he must weary his body and trouble it by service of
privation and fasting and rising early before daybreak.... If his intellectual facilities have been concerned in sin... he must remedy his
fault by careful reflection on that which has to form the subject of his
belief."[90] In other words the sinner who repents must aspire to the
standard of the saint, and therefore exile, solitude and privation are inte-
gral parts of the sinner's penitence.

This concept of "measure for measure," expounded by Maimonides,
is also found in the *Testament of the Twelve Patriarchs*. Reuben, who
committed the great sin of lying with his father's concubine, denied
himself, as his penance, those things which would satisfy his desires.[91]
Similar stories are told about Simeon,[92] and Judah.[93]

Philo, too, favored the middle road and looked with disdain upon
anyone who thought to practice piety and self-control by being "careless about his clothing, or sleeping on the ground, and occupying wretched lodgings."[94] He also believed that while the average man could not
achieve piety by following extremes, such acts could "be considered a
great virtue in men who hold high offices of authority" and possess
"accumulated goods in vast numbers and abundant resources." He
therefore speaks with great admiration of people in high place who disdain luxury, and whose "cups are earthen, their loaves spitbaked... in
the summer they wear a girdle and a thin shirt, and in the winter a stout
rent-proof mantle. The floor will sometimes serve for their bedstead."[95]
In his view these extreme practices serve the great purpose of constantly
reminding the exalted among men "of their common humanity and
draws them away from lofty and overweening thought, reduces their
swollen dimensions and medicines their inequality with equality."[96]
This attitude helps explain Philo's admiration for the Essenes[97] who practiced a life of extreme frugality and in whom extremes were virtues

since they were saints, "wise and just and virtuous."[98] Philo saw in the practices of the Essenes what Maimonides saw in the conduct of the ancient saints, the *Hasidim Ha-rishonim*, an eschewing of the mean in favor of the extreme, justified in their case by their unceasing search for ultimate virtue.

# 3. THE EQUALITY OF MEN

It has already been shown that Josephus' term "theocracy" is a sound characterization of Judaism's view of the world in its relation to God. To avoid possible misunderstanding, it should be remembered that the term theocracy in no way implies a hierarchy headed by a high priest who is recognized as the sole representative of God among men. On the contrary, the term theocracy, as used here, posits that only God is infallible and that human beings, even those who occupy the most exalted positions, are never more than human. No human being is ever to be looked upon as the infallible vice-regent of God or the possessor of a particular approach to godliness, since all are subject to weakness and sin. That this evaluation is the true view of Judaism is clearly manifested by the laws of confession as applied to the high priest.

While the assumption of high priesthood marked the holder of the office as one who had chosen to dedicate his life to the worship and service of God, the high priest was never looked upon as semi-divine or as free of human weakness. In fact, the Torah prescribes the various sacrifices the high priest had to bring in the event he committed a transgression. The high priest was never considered a superhuman being nor did his ascension to the office set him apart from other men and dissolve all ties of family and of blood.

The Torah forbids a high priest to defile himself, even for his nearest of kin.[1] In tannaitic literature, however, this was not interpreted to mean that the office dissolved all ordinary family ties. It meant only that service to God takes precedence over all else, and therefore the high priest must guard against becoming Levitically impure and unable to continue his service in the Temple. These strictures were relaxed to permit him to mourn the death of his parents. Except for rending his garments and letting his hair grow wild, the high priest had to observe all the laws of mourning, and he also paid condolence calls on other mourners.[2]

That the high priest was human and not immune from sin was most plainly emphasized on the Day of Atonement by the high priest himself.

In the presence of a large congregation he openly announced that he was a human being, subject to sin and in need of repentance and forgiveness. Recorded in the Mishnah, the exact confession of the high priest, which he recited publicly at the slaughtering of the bullock of sin, differed hardly from that of an ordinary man:

O, Lord [pronouncing the Name], I have done wickedly, transgressed, sinned before Thee, I and my house. O, Lord forgive the iniquities and transgressions and sins which I have committed and transgressed and sinned before Thee, as it is written in the law of Thy servant Moses, "For on this day shall atonement be made" (Lev. 16: 30). And the priests behind him respond: "Blessed be His glorious Name whose Kingdom is for ever and ever."[3]

There was, as we have noted, some question as to whether a sinner had to confess his sins in public or whether silent confession was sufficient, but concerning the confession of the high priest on the Day of Atonement there was no such question. On this holiest day of the Jewish year the high priest publicly confessed and proclaimed before all that he too was a human being subject to transgression and sin. When he declared that he and his household had sinned, he was referring not to the priesthood in general but to his own immediate family, his wife and children.[4] Certainly this act, wrapped in sanctity and performed in the sight of all Israel, demonstrated for all the fundamental concept of Judaism that in the eyes of the law, and before God, all men are equal. No one, not even God's anointed, stands above the law nor is he to be judged in a manner different from all other men.

This, of course, is a root belief in Judaism. To deny that sacredness rests only on one human personality is to affirm the sacredness of every human personality. This principle inspirits Jewish law as it relates to man and his society, but if that law is to be properly understood, it must ever be remembered that it is built on a religious and not on a social foundation.

The disagreements between the Sadducees and the Pharisees,[4a] as recorded in the Mishnah and reported by Josephus, had almost no direct bearing on political, sociological or economic problems of the day. Through ingenious and fanciful interpretations it is possible to read sociological and economic motives into these controversies. But basically, the Pharisaic-Sadducean differences are concerned purely with ritual laws and beliefs, belief in angels, resurrection, immortality, free will, the authority of the Oral Law, and literalism. True, if one desires, one can credit such ritual matters as handwashing, defilement of sacred writings, and the religious calendar to differing political views. However, such speculative theories can never approach the true essence of historic Judaism nor can they explain the Pharisaic understanding of man's relation to his fellow man. Such conjectures cannot uncover the deep religious ideologies which are reflected in the thinking and decisions of the Pharisees.

An analysis of some of the controversies will reveal the basic ideological difference between the sects. The Mishnah states:

We cry out against you, O ye Pharisees, for you say: If my ox or my ass inflict damages I am liable for them, but if my male servant or my maidservant inflict damages, I am not liable for them. If I am held liable for damages inflicted by my ox and my ass, for whose observance of the commandments I am not responsible, should I not be held liable for damages inflicted by my male or female servants, for whose observance of the commandments I am responsible? To this the Pharisees replied: No! It is proper to hold an owner liable for damages inflicted by his ox and ass, for these animals do not have minds of their own. But can you hold an owner liable for damages inflicted by his manservant and maidservant who have minds of their own?[5]

Judged by practical standards, the logic of the Sadducean argument seems unanswerable. Given a community which tolerates slavery, it is only natural that the owner who looks upon the slave as his real property should be held responsible for whatever injury or damage the slave may inflict. Judged by these practical standards, the decision of the Pharisees seems most unfair, for it makes the slave owner the real beneficiary in any litigation involving damages caused by a slave.

Whatever may be said of the Pharisees, they certainly did not constitute the wealthier portion of the community, nor were their views and decisions shaped by a desire to protect "vested interests." Their refusal to hold a master responsible for his slaves' actions, therefore, was not directed by economic considerations. The opinion of the Pharisees can be understood only in the light of their concept of the sacredness of the human personality. A slave has a mind of his own, they maintained, and therefore has to shoulder his own responsibilities. No human being can so completely become the personal property of another as to lose all of his individuality. Complete and unequivocal ownership of a human being was alien to Pharisaic thought and contrary to its concept of the dignity of man. Therefore, according to the Pharisees, the owner was not liable, and the slave had to shoulder his own responsibility.

As for the observance of the commandments, the Sadducees, who regarded a slave as his master's personal property, no different in this respect from an ox or an ass, maintained that the slave's religious obligations were the personal responsibility of the owner. It was the duty of the master to see to it that the slave observed those commandments. The Pharisees, however, felt that in the observance of the commandments, the slave too had his own mind.

In this respect, it is interesting to note that in one of the Gaonic responses the following question was raised: "What is the law if a Canaanite maidservant violates the Sabbath? Is the owner held responsible for her acts since he is not permitted to have her work for him on the Sabbath?"[6] The answer given by the Gaonim was that a slave, who is considered a semi-proselyte, has his own religious responsibility. A master cannot be held responsible for his slave's violation of the Sabbath, whether it be done at his request or at the slave's own volition.[7] This Gaonic decision is an application of the Pharisaic attitude that the slave himself is responsible for his observance of the commandments, not his master.

Following this same line of reasoning, our Sages established the legal principle that anyone, be he the master of the slave or a stranger, who intentionally kills a Canaanite slave, must suffer the death penalty. It is as if he were to kill a freeman. The Tannaim derived this from the verse: "And if a man smites his bondsman or his bondswoman with a rod and he die under his hand, he shall surely be punished."[8] Though the Torah does not indicate whether the verse refers to a Hebrew or a Canaanite slave, nor does it define the nature of the punishment, the ruling of the Oral Law is that the verse refers to a Canaanite slave. A master who deliberately kills his slave is put to death;[9] ownership of a slave does not bring with it the power of life or death.

As much as the Rabbis speak of the master acquiring a *kinyan haguf*, property ownership, in a foreign slave, they never considered a slave chattel in the Roman sense of the word. In fact, Rabbi Ishmael, a Tanna of the first century, expressed the opinion that Canaanite slaves cannot be evaluated in terms of property ownership: "What the master possesses [in a slave] is only the right of service."[10] When slavery was still rampant in the ancient world, the Rabbis gave universal application to the concept of "the worthiness of the individual," translating it into laws which offered equal protection to all social levels. In their eyes all human beings are God's creatures.

### EQUALITY OF RESPONSIBILITY

The sacredness of the human personality is, in the rabbinic view, the cornerstone of all human relations, and our Sages were both consistent and consequent in giving this concept legal expression. Just as the Rabbis were of the opinion that the life of a foreign slave is as sacred as the life of a freeman, so did they maintain that insofar as legal rights and responsibilities are concerned, a king is to be treated like an ordinary man. Slave or king, all are alike in the eyes of the law when human life or rights are involved.

The Talmud records the incident which caused the final breach between the Pharisees and Alexander Jannaeus, 10a who served as king and high priest simultaneously. The Pharisees, in general, were opposed to placing "the crown of the priesthood and the crown of kingship" on one person. It happened, the Talmud relates, that a certain zealot among the Pharisees, by the name of Judah ben Gedidi(ah), rebuked King Jannai, saying, "It is sufficient for you to wear the crown of kingship; leave the crown of the priesthood to the children of Aaron." This same zealot, apparently, falsely reported that the mother of Alexander Jannaeus had been taken captive before his birth. Since, according to rabbinic law, the son of a captive woman is not permitted to officiate in the Temple, this implied that Alexander was ineligible to serve as an ordinary priest, let alone to occupy the office of high priest. Investigation proved the charge to be groundless. Seizing the opportunity, a Sadducee, eager to alienate the king from the Pharisees, said to him, "Should the same law that applies to an ordinary man apply to you, who are a king and a high priest?"[11]

The Talmud does not detail the penalty which the Pharisees proposed to impose on the one who had brought the false accusation. But, whatever it was, what really embittered the king was the fact that the Pharisees saw no greater offense in bringing a false accusation against a man who held the two highest offices in the land than in bringing a false accusation against an ordinary man.

A doublet of this narrative is found in Josephus,[12] who adds that the Pharisees ruled that one who circulates evil reports about another deserves the penalty of stripes since it is not right to punish reproaches with death.[13] Thus, in a manner, Josephus supplies us with the penalty the Pharisees imposed on the talebearer, lacking in the talmudic record.[14]

Closer examination of rabbinic sources reveals that Josephus' statement that the Pharisees considered stripes a sufficient penalty for circulating an evil and false report accords fully with rabbinic opinion. The Mishnah contains many laws which fall under the heading of *motzi shem rah*, one who maligns his fellow man. These are based on the passage in Deuteronomy[15] ordering that if a man "brings an evil name upon his wife" which is subsequently proven to be false, then the "elders of that city shall take the man and chastise him." The term "chastise him" means, according to tannaitic tradition, that the man is punished by stripes.[16] The Talmud finds the source for this rule in Leviticus:[17] "Thou shalt not go up and down as a talebearer among thy people."[18] A talebearer can be defined as one who peddles inconsequential gossip, or who brings false accusations against another.

On the basis of the traditional interpretation of the passages in Leviticus and Deuteronomy,[19] the Pharisees maintained that the man who circulated the false report concerning Alexander Jannaeus should be punished by stripes.[20] The Sadducees, however, argued that the law applies to an ordinary man and cannot be applied in equal measure to an extraordinary being who holds the position of king and high priest. They, therefore, demanded the death penalty for the man who had circulated the false report against Alexander Jannaeus.

In other words, the Sadducees maintained that the harshness of the penalty for an offense against a fellow man is determined by the position the latter holds in the community. The Pharisees, disregarding all social distinctions within the community, emphasized that Judaism is a democratic theocracy; that under the sovereignty of God all human beings are alike and must be treated alike. If the penalty for violating a negative command is stripes, it must be applied to all, regardless of rank or class.

This standard of equality the Pharisees applied in many other instances of law. Thus, a high priest who violated a negative commandment would be punished by stripes and then reinstated in his position. The fact that the high priest sinned did not disqualify him from the high priesthood.[21] This is summed up in the dictum of our Sages: "The high priest who... violates any of the positive or negative commandments, or any other commandment, is treated like an ordinary man" (hediot).[22] The Pharisees insisted that the high priest receive all the honors that go with his office, but they also insisted that as far as the law is concerned, he is not regarded or treated as a high priest. He is but a hediot, an ordinary human being.

The Sadducees accepted the logic of practicality. Inflicting harsher penalties for disrespect shown by an ordinary man toward one who holds high civil or religious offices, would certainly impose the fear and discipline needed to maintain the social structure. The decisions of the Pharisees, on the other hand, were not dictated by practical considerations. It was their religious conviction that in respect to the observance or violation of the law, all Israelites are alike and enjoy the same status. Since all authority originates in the sovereignty of God, in relation to God, all men are hediotim, ordinary men.

### KINGSHIP

Alexander Jannaeus was not only the high priest, he was also the king. What particularly incensed the Sadducees was the Pharisee position that the punishment for a crime committed against the king should not be more severe than the punishment for the same crime committed against an ordinary man. The Pharisees, however, had their own attitude toward kingship. Their over-all religious philosophy, and their firm, pious outlook on life, therefore, was bound to bring them into conflict with the Hasmonean kings of their day. This conflict, in essence a conflict between the Kingship of Heaven and the kingship of man, manifests itself constantly in rabbinic literature.

The wellspring of the theocracy of Judaism is the belief in monotheism, which implies not only the philosophic or theological belief in the existence of God but also the belief in the Fatherhood of God and His divine providence, general and particular—the belief that God is the absolute ruler of the world and that only He is infallible. A human being, regardless of how high a position he may hold, is still human, and therefore fallible.

True, the human king is considered the "anointed of God." When King Saul pursued David, and the latter's lieutenants had the opportunity to kill Saul, David cautioned them not to touch the king, saying, "The Lord forbid it to me that I should do this thing unto my lord, the Lord's anointed...."[23] Again, at a later date and under similar circumstances, David said to Abishai: "Destroy him not for who can put forth his hand against the Lord's anointed."[24]

To respect and honor a king was considered, in ancient Jewish life, a religious obligation of the highest order. But the king was not elected to his office by popular vote or by will of the people. Therefore, the obligation of bestowing honors upon him was not dependent upon his authority or upon their wishes. God revealed to the prophet the name of the person whom He had chosen to be king and according to the Tosefta, His designation was made official by the Sanhedrin.[25] Thus, in rabbinic tradition, the office of king is held by divine appointment confirmed by the prophet or the Sanhedrin of elders.

Compare this with Philo's notion of kingship. After criticizing the Greek system of appointing judges without regard to their qualifications for office, the philosopher makes the following statement:

Moses, wise here as ever... does not even mention appointment of rulers by lot, but determines to institute appointment by election. Thus he says, "Thou shalt establish a ruler over thyself, not a foreigner but from thy brethren" (Deut. 17:15), thereby indicating that there should be a free choice and an unimpeachable scrutiny of the ruler made by the whole people with the same mind. And the choice will receive the further vote and seal of notification from Him who confirms all things that promote the common weal....[26]

It is difficult to accept that Philo believed that in ancient times the king was elected by the people themselves. Most probably, his reference is to election by the Sanhedrin through whom the will of God and the will of the people was expressed. This was clearly the view of our Sages.

Interpreting the verse in Deuteronomy, "And there was a king in Jeshurun when the heads of the people gathered,"[27] the Rabbis concluded that the "king in Jeshurun" was Moses, and that the phrase "when the heads of the people gathered" meant that Moses was elevated to kingship with the approval of the Sanhedrin.[28] A similar comment is made on the verses, "and Moses and Aaron went and gathered together all the elders of the children of Israel... and the people believed."[29] It was only after the elders had accepted Moses as the leader that the people as a whole believed in him. Had not the elders accepted Moses as the leader appointed by God, the people themselves would not have recognized his rule.[30] Philo expressed similar views about the elevation of Moses.[31] It is a fair assumption then that when Philo said that the king was elected by the people, he meant that the high court (in a sense, the only body which represented the entire community) elected the king.[32] But in any case, the fact remains that in the entire field of rabbinic literature, we find no reference to elected offices. All relevant references speak only of appointments either by local courts or by the Sanhedrin in Jerusalem. Never is there mention of direct election to office by the populace.

Since the king was appointed to the highest office by God, he enjoyed the highest of honors.[33] In fact, the king did not have the right to forego the honors due him. The dictum of the Rabbis is, "In the case of a king who is willing to waive the honor due him, it is not waived."[34] The principle behind the halakah is that the office, not the individual, is being honored. A king, therefore, does not have the authority to waive the honors due his office. A scholar, on the other hand, who is honored not for his office, but for his learning, may waive all the honors due him.[35]

Because of his divine election, the king must be obeyed. Failure to obey him, even as a result of compliance with the direct commandment of the Torah, makes one a *mored bemalkut*, one who rebels against the king, and liable to punishment by death.[36] The rabbinic view of the prerogatives of the king, but also of their limits, is demonstrated in relation to David and Uriah. King David had the legal right to put Uriah the Hittite to death, according to the Talmud, because the latter had rebelled against him by failing to properly obey the royal command; David's sin in this matter was that he overstepped prerogative by punishing Uriah at his own discretion, instead of bringing him before the court for trial.[37] Thus, while rebellion against the king was a capital offense, the king did not have the right to take the law into his own hands, even in cases in which his personal authority was involved.

The description of life under a king, given by the prophet Samuel, would seem to imply that the king did enjoy unlimited and absolute authority. Apparently he could confiscate property at his own discretion and enslave whomever he wished.[38] However, some of our Sages maintained that not all of the acts described by Samuel were necessarily permissive. The prophet's intention was merely to make the people vividly aware of the danger inherent in kingship; he did not seek to establish kingly license.[39] The king could wage war, such as the war against the Seven Nations, but he needed the sanction of the court before he could declare war.[40] No doubt, even the Rabbis agreed that in matters pertaining to war and taxation, the king had great prerogatives. But it is also apparent that the Rabbis, particularly after the rise of Pharisaism, were wary of vesting supreme authority in the king. The Sages believed, basing themselves upon the dicta of the Torah, that even in matters which fell within the purview of the kingship, the sanction of the Sanhedrin was required before any action could be instituted.

A better appreciation of the rabbinic concept of the royal duties, responsibilities and privileges is acquired by comparing the attitude of the Rabbis with the understanding and practice of royal prerogatives common in the non-Jewish world. In Hellenistic literature, the political head of the state is often spoken of as the incarnation of the divine spirit of the law. He is pictured as a unique individual with a human body and a superhuman personality. His decisions become the law of the realm because he is looked upon as the "animated law" and, in a sense, as God revealed. His official pronouncements are divine truth; in his own personality he is the incarnation of the divine law.[41] When Gaius claimed that just as the herdsman does not share in the nature of the sheep, so the king, who is the herdsman of his human flock, does not share in their nature but is somehow divine,[42] he was merely echoing the Hellenistic philosophy of kingship. This concept permitted Gaius to regard himself as the Law.[43]

The superhuman attributes with which the non-Jewish world endowed the king resulted in his deification. The philosophers, of course, speaking of the ideal king as a divine or semi-divine being, had no intention of identifying him with the Supreme Being. But ultimately the masses came to regard the king as a divine and infallible authority, to whom they could pray and offer up sacrifices. The Jew, however, believed only in praying *for* the health of the king and regarded praying *to* and offering sacrifices *to* the king, as idolatry. Thus, even Philo Judaeus, who was greatly influenced by Hellenistic thinking and did not hesitate to speak of the Patriarchs as symbols of the "animated law" (because they observed the divine law even before the Revelation on Mount Sinai), would have given up his life before sacrificing to the king or worshiping the image of the king in the Alexandrian synagogue.

Many, including distinguished scholars, have failed to grasp the true significance of Philo's position or to recognize this basic concept of Jewish monotheism.[44] Central to the philosophy of Jewish monotheism is the concept that neither a material object nor any human being, be he dead or alive, may be invested with divinity. To imply such an investure through an act of worship or devotion, would be particularly abhorrent. The Jew may revere saints, who possess attributes of the highest order, but he still regards them as mere human beings, not divine beings. To do otherwise would be to fall into idolatry.

Philo's thoroughly Jewish attitude in this matter is manifest even as regards Abraham, whom he characterized as the "sage king." Commenting on the verse—"Then Abraham fell upon his face and laughed and said in his heart: Shall a child be born unto him that is a hundred years old?"[45]—Philo rebukes those who would see in this verse a "shadow or breath of unbelief."[46] For, he continues:

> It seems to me that this... amounts to a wish to make the created to be uncreated, the mortal immortal... and if it is not blasphemy to say it, man to be God... for the excellences of God must needs be unmixed, since God is not compounded, but a single nature, whereas man's excellences are mixed since we, too, are mixtures with human and divine blended in us and formed into a harmony in proportions of perfect music. Happy is he to whom it is granted to incline toward the better and more godlike part through most of his life. For it is impossible that it should be so with him throughout the whole length of life.[47]

This passage, more than any other, reveals Philo's philosophy that even the most saintly of men, such as the Patriarchs, have imperfections. Here Philo's words accord with those employed by the Palestinian teachers: "The great merit of the righteous man (*zaddik*) is that in the scale of life, his virtuous acts outweigh his evil acts; no human being can be perfect, just as no mortal can be immortal."[48] Hence, to regard any man as divine is blasphemous. Consequently, though a Jew may be versed in all of Greek philosophy and be fully cognizant of the symbolic significances relating to the divinity of kingship, nevertheless, as soon as he is asked to accept the royal prerogatives as a sign of divinity and to sacrifice to the king or worship him—even though that being is the "sage king"—the Jew must refuse. To do so would be to commit an act of idolatry. It was for this reason that the Alexandrian Jews refused to offer sacrifices to the Roman emperors or to admit images into their synagogue. To the Jew such an act would be the height of sacrilege, an act he must refuse to perform even though it costs him his life.

The view which regards the political head of the State, even philosophically speaking, as a superhuman authority and a vehicle through whom the divine law expresses itself, has therefore always been foreign to Judaism and contrary to its fundamental concept of monotheism. Furthermore, in historic Judaism, the formulation of law and the office of kingship are not in the same domain. Judaism is based upon the principle of the infallible sovereignty of God, not of man. Kingship is a matter for mortals; law is the revealed word of God.

Reviewing the polity of Judaism, Josephus, in his *Antiquities*, declares:
... let no craving possess you for another polity, but be content with
this, having the laws for your masters and governing all your actions
by them; for God sufficeth for your ruler. But should ye become
enamored of a king, let him be of your own race and let him have a
perpetual care for justice and virtue in every other form. Let him
concede to the laws and to God the possession of superior wisdom,
and let him do nothing without the high priest and counsel of his
elders.[49]

This statement is in agreement with the tannaitic concept of kingship,
emphasizing as it does that God is the true sovereign, that the king is not
the legislator, and that, even in the exercise of royal prerogatives, the
king cannot take the law into his own hands but must have his actions
sanctioned by the court. The king should, of course, stand as the public
symbol of justice, but he is not the lawmaker. Josephus also states that
Herod's greatest wrong was to assume the role of the legislator and
enact laws which were contrary to the traditions of Judaism. It was
this, writes Josephus, that made Herod a tyrant.[50]

### THE KING AS JUDGE

In the rabbinic view, the primary duty of the king was to be dedicated
"to the needs of the community."[51] Thus, for example, during the
Davidic dynasty, the king appointed judges and often acted as a judge
himself.[52] Philo similarly asserts that the king acted as judge, but he
adds:
... if the facts create a sense of uncertainty and great obscurity, and he
[the judge] feels that his apprehension of them is but dim, he should
decline to judge the cases and send them up to more discerning judges.
And who should these be but the priests, and the head and leader of
the priests? For the genuine ministers of God have taken all care to
sharpen their understanding and count the slightest error to be no
slight error, because the surpassing greatness of the king whom they
serve is seen in every matter.[53]

Here Philo[54] is undoubtedly referring to the verses in Deuteronomy:
"If there arise a matter too hard for thee in judgment, between blood

and blood, between plea and plea, and between stroke and stroke, even matters of controversy within thy gate; then shalt thou rise and get thee up unto the place which the Lord thy God shall choose. And thou shalt come up unto the priests, the Levites and unto the judge that shall be in those days; and thou shalt inquire and they shall declare unto thee the sentence of judgment."[55]

According to the Tannaim the passage pertains to decisions of the Great Sanhedrin which sat in the Hall of Hewn Stones. It was this court which had the final authority in certain legal matters of tradition to render decisions when judges of the lower courts were uncertain or doubtful of the law.[56] Coordinating the references of both Philo and the Tannaim, it is apparent that even according to the tradition which reached Philo, in cases in which the king sat as a judge, he had to apply to the highest court for a decision when he was uncertain of the law.[57]

On the same subject, Philo continues: "Another possible reason for sending such cases to the priests is that the priest is necessarily a prophet, advanced to the service of the truly Existent by virtue rather than by birth."[58] Apparently, Philo was of the opinion that the Sanhedrin was composed of the prophet, the high priest and other priests, a view shared by Josephus.[59] Both Philo and Josephus were probably describing the court as it was in the days of Moses, which consisted of Moses the prophet, Aaron the high priest, and the elders.

On the basis of these statements found in tannaitic literature and in Philo and Josephus, we can conclude that though in ancient times the king frequently acted as a judge, he was not even a member of the tribunal, let alone its head. In difficult matters he had to refer to, and be guided by, the decisions of the Great Court, which served as a court of appeals as well as the highest interpretive judicial body.

Though the Talmud makes no mention of a regal tribunal,[59a] we may assume that there existed a king's court which assisted the monarch whenever people appealed to him to redress the wrongs done them. This may be ascertained from Philo who, in addition to his reference to the court of "the priests and the head of and leader of the priests," also speaks of the king's lieutenants whose responsibility it was "to share with him the duties of governing, giving judgment and managing all the other matters which concern the public welfare."[60] These lieutenants were surely not the group which Philo described as having the greatest understanding of the law and to whom the king had to turn when he was in doubt. These lieutenants, who had to be men "of ability, of justice, of godliness" were primarily concerned with petty disputes and minor litigations.[61] The court to which the king appealed for guidance in obscure legal matters was the ultimate legal authority in the land—the Great Sanhedrin.

### THE KING AND THE LAW

In the rabbinic philosophy of kingship, one aspect stands out most strikingly. The king, despite the many royal prerogatives ceded him, was not looked upon as a superhuman being. He was not exempt from observing the law but was bound by it as was every other man. Nor was the standard of punishment applied to him different from that applied to all men. The biblical incidents of King David and Nathan the Prophet, or of Jeremiah and King Joash, are significant examples. The standard dictum of our Sages was: "If he [the king] transgresses any of the positive or negative prohibitions, or any other commandments, he is treated in all matters like a *hediot* (an ordinary man)."[62] The king did not represent a "higher law," nor was he considered "the animated law." To be paid honor and homage was the king's deserve; indeed, to serve him was a religious duty—but only when the monarch himself observed and bound himself by the divine law of the Torah. On the biblical verse, "a ruler of thy people thou shalt not curse,"[63] the Mekilta comments: "But a ruler might be one such as Ahab and his associates. Therefore the Torah says, 'Of thy people.' Only as long as they conduct themselves in the manner of thy people."[64] The Tannaim implied that if a king sets himself above the law he does not deserve to be treated as a king. In the eyes of the law, he remains in every respect an ordinary human being.

In their desire to emphasize that the kingship of man must always be subservient to the kingship of God, our Sages made a clear legal distinction. They declared a man who disobeys a direct order of the king to be a *mored bemalkut*, a royal rebel. For example, if a person is ordered by the king to go some place and he refuses, or if he is commanded to stay at home and he goes out, his act constitutes a "rebellion against the king" and is even considered a capital offense. However, if the failure of the person to obey the king is a result of his being engaged in the performance of a *mitzvah*, that person is not liable to any punishment. The reason for this, according to the Sages, is simple. When engaged in performing a *mitzvah*, a man is carrying out a command of the King in Heaven and obedience to His Kingship takes precedence over any obedience to the kingship of man.[65]

In this connection it must be recalled that the Rabbis included the rules of honor due a king as part of the Halakah. That honor far surpassed the honor due a high priest or scholar. With all this, there appear in rabbinic legislation rules which clearly reveal the view that the true king is the scholar, one who is well versed in divine law and who puts his knowledge into daily practice. Thus, it is stated, "Greater is [the learning of] the Torah than priesthood or kingship."[66] Similarly, Rabbi Nehunya ben Ha-kanoh said, "He who takes upon himself the yoke of the Torah, from him shall be taken away the yoke of kingly authority (*malkut*) and the yoke of worldly care."[67] There is also evidence that this view did not remain a pious wish, but was actually put into practice.[67a]

The balance between scholarship and kingship may also be perceived in such remote laws as those concerning the ransoming of captives. A tannaitic source notes:

> If one, together with his father, and his teacher were in captivity, his own ransom receives priority. The ransom of one's teacher takes priority over that of his father; but his mother's ransom obtains priority over all. The scholar has priority over the king because, when a scholar dies, we have none to equal him; however, when a king dies, all Israelites are qualified for kingship.[68]

Here again, our Sages emphasized that the "kingship of divine knowledge" is superior to temporal kingship. This conforms with Philo's oft-repeated statement that every sage is necessarily a king because genuine kingship is a matter of character and knowledge, and not of external position.[69] Interestingly, Hellenistic philosophers maintained that the ideal king must be a sage, while the rabbis constantly emphasized that the sage *is* a king.[70] This latter attitude was echoed by Philo in his assertion that kings in office "would be reckoned ordinary citizens when compared with great kings who received God as their portion."[71]

In review, we perceive that, according to our Sages, no human being can claim to be above the law, not even the king. Except for the royal prerogatives which went with the office, the king was given equal status with everyone else. He could not claim that the scepter gave him an exceptional position in regard to the law, or that the crown gave him immunity from punishment. Excepting the severe punishments meted out for rebellion against royal authority, any offense committed against or by the king was treated exactly like an offense committed by or against an ordinary man.

In light of the rabbinic notion of kingship, we can better understand the position of the Pharisees in the case of Alexander Jannaeus, alluded to above. The accusation against the king was that his mother had been taken captive before she was married, thus making Jannai ineligible for the office of high priest. Such accusation, even though false, could in no way be construed as an act of rebellion against the royal office. He who voiced the report had demanded only that Jannaeus be removed from the office of high priest. It is true that by this false assertion he may have insulted the king, but in no manner can his statement be interpreted as rebellion against the royal office. In consonance with their philosophy of kingship, the Pharisees maintained that since the accuser could not be regarded as a *mored bemalkut*, (a royal rebel) his punishment should be no different than that given for a false accusation leveled against any ordinary man.

Examining further the problem of kingship, we recall the mishnah in Sanhedrin which states that the "king can neither act as judge nor be judged."[72] This statement, on the surface, seems to be in direct contradiction to the rabbinic philosophy of kingship, as interpreted above. It seems to deny that the king is judged by the same standards which are applied to ordinary men. The answer is found in the talmudic explanation that the kings of the House of David "judge and are judged," but the kings of Israel neither "act as judges nor are judged." The Talmud adds further that this mishnaic statement was enunciated during the reign of Alexander Jannaeus and records the following incident which led to its pronouncement:

A slave of Alexander Jannaeus was charged with murder and the Sanhedrin summoned Alexander, as the master, to appear before it with his slave. We have already seen that in accordance with Pharisaic thought a slave was held legally responsible for his acts. Hence he could be brought to court. The master was also summoned because of his vested interest in the slave. The story continues: The king entered the court and seated himself. Thereupon Simeon ben Shetah, who was then the presiding officer of the Sanhedrin, said to the king: "King Jannai, stand on thy feet and let the witnesses testify. It is not before us that you stand, but rather before Him Who created the world by His word, as it is said, 'Then both men, between whom the controversy is, shall stand before the Lord.'"[73] The King replied that he would rise only if the other members of the Sanhedrin requested him to do so. The other members of the court, apparently afraid of antagonizing the king, did not utter a word. Angered by their timidity, Simeon ben Shetah publicly rebuked his colleagues and declared that He Who knows the thoughts of all men would punish them for their failure to act as judges should. Shortly thereafter, according to the talmudic narrative, all the members of the Sanhedrin, with the exception of Simeon ben Shetah, perished. It was then that the Sanhedrin decreed that a king of Israel "neither acts as judge nor is he judged."[74]

Josephus records a similar incident concerning Herod who killed an innocent man and, when summoned before the Sanhedrin, cowed the judges by his arrogant behavior.[75]

These two incidents, narrated in the Talmud and in Josephus, boldly illumine the fundamental issue about which revolved the controversy between the Pharisees and the kings of Israel, whether it was Alexander Jannaeus or the more evil-minded Herod. At issue was the question whether kings are subject to the same law as ordinary men, or whether, by virtue of their high office, they are regarded as superhuman beings who cannot be treated on the same basis as the average man. Stated somewhat more prosaically, the question was, can a king be hailed into a court of justice?

The Pharisees maintained that all men, regardless of their station or office in life, are equal in the eyes of God. When a man stands before a court of justice, he is not there to be tried by men; he stands in the presence of God before Whom kings and ordinary men are equals. The kings of the Second Commonwealth, on the other hand, yearned to emulate the Roman emperors who regarded themselves as constituting the law, free to judge and punish offenders as they pleased. These kings, ignoring the rabbinic decree that kings "neither act as judges nor are they judged," arrogated to themselves the role of legislators with tragic consequences. At their whim, they slew thousands of scholars without trial and regarded themselves as the "animated law."

Our study has thus revealed how deeply rooted were the differences between the Pharisees and Sadducees. The early Pharisees and later Tannaim, out of religious principle, refused to grant dictatorial powers to the king. Through their concept of a democratic theocracy, they set down the foundations of genuine democracy. Their desire was to emphasize the sovereignty of God; their unwavering dedication to this principle ultimately established the moral concept of equity and equality for all men.

# 4. MAN AND HIS TRUSTWORTHINESS

Rabbinic law, as we have indicated, rests on two fundamental principles: it constantly emphasizes the sacredness of the human personality and the sanctity of human life; it teaches that no human being, regardless of how pious or learned he may be, is immune from error. The latter principle determines many laws pertaining to the judiciary and much of the Jewish law of evidence.

The most powerful institution in Judaism during the Second Commonwealth was the judiciary. Jerusalem had the Great Sanhedrin, which sat in the Hall of Hewn Stones, and two smaller courts, composed of twenty-three members, while every town which had a minimum population of one hundred and twenty had a small Sanhedrin of twenty-three members.[1] In addition to these larger tribunals there were also smaller courts, made up of three judges, which ruled on civil suits, decided cases of money indemnity for injuries and had the judicial authority to inflict the punishment of flagellation for the violation of positive commands.[2] The various courts were always made up of an odd number of judges: three, twenty-three, and seventy-one. This was done purposely so that no tribunal should ever be deadlocked. The courts always rendered their decisions on the basis of a majority opinion and the odd number guaranteed against an evenly divided tribunal.

A single judge apparently had no authority to render decisions, even in the adjudication of civil cases. In fact, the Mishnah specifically warns against a single judge rendering a decision: "Judge not alone, for none may judge alone save One,"[3] driving home a great moral and religious lesson. God alone is capable of judging alone; a human being, never immune from error, should never undertake to render legal decisions alone.

There are indications that in Babylonia some of our Sages permitted the adjudication of civil cases by a single judge who was a *mumhe le'rabbim*, one who was recognized as an authority by the public, in addition to being *gamrina v'savrina*, qualified by his knowledge of the oral tradition and his personal resourcefulness.[4] Mar Samuel, on the

other hand, characterized a court of less than three as impudent.[5] Some
Rabbis were of the opinion that it is contrary to the law of the Torah
for a single judge to render a decision, whereas others maintained that a
single judge was disqualified by rabbinical authority. According to the
latter, this was true even of a court of two, particularly if they are not
mumhin (experts), and among those who ruled that in civil matters a
mumhe (an expert) could render legal decisions alone, some maintained
that such decisions did not carry the same authority as did those of a
regular court of three. Hence, an admission or a denial by one of the
litigants before a single judge did not have the same legal authority as
did the admission or denial of a claim before a court of three.[6] In any
case, the discussion in the Talmud concerning the validity of the decision
of a single judge applied only to civil cases. Insofar as the infliction of
penalties was concerned, it was the unanimous opinion that only a court
composed of the minimum number of three qualified judges could
render decisions.[7]

### MAJORITY OF ONE

This ruling is most significant. Although no reference is made in
rabbinic literature to election by majority vote, the entire judicial
system, which was, in fact, the chief instrument of government of the
Jewish theocracy, was bound by the rule of the majority.

Our Sages, however, were so strongly opposed to vesting final judicial power in a single individual that in some instances they even qualified the power of a majority. Thus, while in capital cases, as in civil
suits, the court was bound by majority decision, our Sages, in their great
care that an innocent man should not be condemned to death, ruled
that the death penalty could not be exacted by a mere majority of one.
In capital cases a majority of at least two was required.

The Mishnah states: "Thy verdict of condemnation shall not be like
thy verdict of acquittal; thy verdict of acquittal is reached by the decision of one, thy verdict of condemnation by a majority of two."[8] This
ruling is based on Exodus 23:2: "Thou shalt not follow after the many
to do evil," which the Rabbis accepted to mean that no death penalty is
to be inflicted on an accused by a majority of one.[9]

## MAJORITY OF HUMAN ACTIONS IN THE DIVINE SCALE

Interestingly, the rule prohibiting a court of men from issuing a death sentence by the slim majority of one, was also attributed to the Court of Heaven. According to rabbinic theology, in God's divine judgment of the human race, individuals are divided into three groups. Those whose merits on the divine scale outweigh their sins, are called righteous. Those whose sins outweigh their merits are called wicked and are condemned to death immediately. The third group consists of those whose merits and sins are balanced on the divine scale.[10] Not only individuals, but entire communities and humanity in general are judged by this standard. The fact that humanity still survives is evidence that, despite the abundance of wickedness, there still exists in the world a balance between good and evil. Were this not so, God would cause the world to be destroyed.[11] Our Sages further state that God does not condemn the sinner to death unless his sinful acts exceed his merits by three. If, however, his sins outnumber his merits by no more than two, God does not condemn the sinner to death.[12]

This in no way implies, of course, that in the divine scale every deed, for good or evil, is given equal weight, nor that God simply balances the number of sins and the number of good deeds one against the other. Rather, as Maimonides states:

[The divine scale] ... takes into account not the numbers but the magnitude of the merits and transgressions. There may be a single merit that outweighs many transgressions, as it is said, "Because in him was found some good thing."[13] And there may be one transgression that counterbalances many meritorious deeds, as it is said, "But one sinner [hait, i.e., one sin] destroyeth much good."[14] The scale of evaluation is in accordance with the knowledge of the Omniscient God. He alone knows how to evaluate the merits against the transgressions.[15]

It is most significant that in this theological concept, God does not condemn the sinner to death if his iniquities outweigh his merits by a slim margin. The sinner is condemned to death only if his iniquities outweigh his merits by a fair margin of three sins. The legal requirement of a recognizable majority in capital offenses, and the theological belief in the leniency with which the divine scale of merit was read, underscore the importance which, in our Sages' view, the life of the individual carries in the eyes of both God and man.

## THE INTELLECTUAL HONESTY OF THE INDIVIDUAL JUDGE

Another striking aspect of rabbinic court procedure is the insistence on the intellectual independence of judges. Although the final verdict rests with the majority, each judge is enjoined to retain his independent opinion, whether he joins with the majority or the minority. It is the duty of every judge to practice intellectual honesty regardless of whether he will or will not be overruled by the majority. In fact, he must not even permit himself to be influenced in his final decision by the opinion of another judge who is renowned for his scholarship. The Tosefta states: "Do not say at the time of decision: 'It is sufficient for the servant to be like his master'; state what is in your own mind."[16] Similarly, the Mekilta states: "Do not say: 'It is sufficient that I be like [i.e., vote like] the other judge; rather, express what is before you."[17] The rabbinic sources use as proof-text the verse in Exodus 23:2: "Neither shall you bear witness in a cause to incline after the many to change judgment," which is interpreted to mean that the individual judge should ever strive to arrive at an independent decision.[18]

A judge must never slip his responsibility by rationalizing that since the decision expressed by the majority is binding, he might as well support it. The judge, like any other man must be intellectually honest. He must clearly announce his conclusion, even when he knows that it will not be accepted. Once, however, the majority decision has been rendered, every judge, even one who held a minority opinion, is duty-bound by law to submit to the decision of the majority, and accept it as definitive.

## THE DISSENTING MINORITY

The rule of the majority applied not only in court, but also in disagreements over interpretations of the laws of the Torah. Disputes among our Sages over the true tradition or the exact interpretation of a law were resolved in accordance with the opinion of the majority. But it is of interest that the Mishnah, which is the tannaitic code, records the opinion of an individual or the minority along with the accepted majority opinion. For example, it records all the opinions of the school of Shammai though the halakah is in accordance with the school of Hillel, and it records the opinions of both Shammai and Hillel when neither opinion was accepted as final law.[19] Apparently, while the opinion of the majority prevailed, the opinion of individuals was not ignored even when not accepted. Moreover, the opinion of an individual, recorded as a part of oral tradition, is a part of Torah learning.[20] In fact, the practice of Maimonides, who was the first to codify Jewish law without recording the dissenting opinions, drew criticism.[20a]

The Mishnah itself explains why the opinion of an individual was recorded, even though not accepted:

Why do they record the opinion of the individual against that of the majority, if the halakah is accepted only in accordance with the opinion of the majority? So that [another or later] court, knowing the opinion of the individual, may rely upon him, since a court cannot revoke the decision of another court unless it exceeds it both in wisdom and in number: If it exceeds it in wisdom but not in number, or in number but not in wisdom, it cannot revoke its decision; only if it exceeds in both wisdom and in number.[21]

Clearly, the Mishnah here emphasizes that the opinion of the dissenting individual is never lost. It is possible that at a later time and in another court the majority may vote to accept the dissenting individual opinion even though it was not accepted previously. A court cannot revoke the unanimous decision of another court unless it exceeds it in wisdom and numbers. It may, however, under certain circumstances, decide in accordance with a minority opinion.[22]

Another mishnah sees in the practice of recording the unaccepted opinion of an individual a great moral lesson: while the individual has a right to record his opinion, in practice he must bow to the decision of the majority.[23] Our Sages respected the rights of the individual, and prized intellectual honesty and independence. They therefore recorded individual opinions, even when they went counter to the prevailing majority opinion and were rejected by halakic practice.

## AT THE MOUTH OF TWO WITNESSES

Just as no judge can render a binding decision by himself, so too did rabbinic law rule that no case, whether civil or criminal, could be decided on the testimony of a single witness. This rule is clearly stated in Deuteronomy 19:15: "One witness shall not rise against a man for any iniquity, or for any sin, in any sin that he sinneth; at the mouth of two witnesses or at the mouth of three witnesses shall the matter be established."

The *Sifre* enumerates the following matters in which the court cannot give legal decisions on the evidence of one witness: capital and civil cases, atonement, sacrifices, flagellations, promotion and demotion in priesthood.[24]

The *Sifre* apparently extended the rule that the evidence of a single witness is not binding to cover testimony concerning the status of another human being, for example, whether someone is a priest or an Israelite. The Mishnah, however, records diverse opinions about this question:

Rabbi Judah says: They may not advance any man to the standing of a priest on the evidence of a single witness. Rabbi Eleazar says: This applies only when there are some who protest; but when none protest they may advance him to the standing of a priest. Rabban Simeon ben Gamaliel in the name of Rabbi Simeon the son of the Prefect says: They advance any to the standing of a priest on the evidence of a single witness.[25]

The validity of the testimony of a single witness is questioned only when it involves the confirmation of the legal status of a man—whether a man is wicked or righteous, whether he owes money or not, whether he committed a capital offense or an offense punishable by stripes. But in cases involving merely the ritual status of a *thing* (i.e., is this object ritually clean or unclean? is this food permissible or not?), the testimony of a single witness is determinative.[26] The rabbinic attitude seems to be that the court cannot decide the status of a man upon the evidence given by a single witness. When, however, it is not the personality and obligations of a human being which are involved but rather the status of objects, then the evidence of a single witness is accepted.

Philo Judaeus thus explained the law prohibiting the court to render a decision on the evidence of one witness:

He added another excellent injunction when he forbade them to accept the evidence of a single person, first because the single person may see or hear imperfectly or misunderstand and be deceived, since false opinions are numberless, and numberless, too, the sources from which they spring to attack us. Secondly, because it is most unjust to accept a single witness against more than one or even against one, because their number makes them more worthy of credence than the one: against one, because the witness has not got preponderance of number, and equality is incompatible with predominance. For why should the statement of a witness made in accusation of another be accepted in preference to the words of the accused spoken in his own defense? Where there is neither deficiency nor excess it is clearly best to suspend judgment.[27]

Others offer different explanations of this rule. The *Sefer Ha-hinuk* writes:

The root of this commandment is that the inclination of man's heart is evil. At times there may arise in his heart a grudge against his fellow man, even if he may have remained firmly entrenched for a long time in the paths of uprightness, for it is still not impossible that he may change his mind and do wicked things. Our Sages of blessed memory said, indeed, that John Hyrcanus served in the office of high priest and at the end became a Sadducee; at the beginning he was a true prophet and at the end he became a false prophet. It is therefore fitting and worthy not to rely upon the heart of a single man to punish another by his word of mouth. And even if the accused be thoroughly wicked and the basest man and the witness a great scholar in Israel. But if two trustworthy men give evidence we have a presumption that two men will not consent to bear false testimony.[28]

Our Sages refused to assign to a single man the power to determine the worthiness and honesty of another human being. While this principle referred to judges, it was applied even more strongly to witnesses, upon whose trustworthiness and reliability judges had to lean in arriving at a final decision. Every man has a presumption of trustworthiness for himself, but not for the purpose of denying another's trustworthiness.

In the rabbinic concept there is, however, one fundamental difference between evidence and the judiciary. In the case of evidence, the court's primary concern is whether the witnesses are testifying honestly and truthfully. Since the presumption is that evidence given by two witnesses is truthful, the testimony of a hundred witnesses has no more weight than the testimony of two witnesses. "Two equal a hundred," rule our Sages.[29] If we cannot trust two men who have a presumption of worthiness we might as well not trust a hundred. Furthermore, commenting on the verse, "At the mouth of two witnesses or three witnesses, shall he that is to die be put to death,"[30] the Mishnah states: "If the evidence can be sustained by two witnesses, why does the Torah specify three? To make three analogous with two: as three witnesses may refute two witnesses, so may two witnesses refute three witnesses. Whence, do we learn that two witnesses may refute even a hundred? The Torah says 'witnesses.'"[31] Thus, the testimony of a hundred witnesses is of no greater weight than the testimony of two witnesses.

The judiciary, however, was always governed by the rule of the majority because it is presumed that judges will render honest decisions. The only question is whether their reasoning and conclusions are accurate, whether their opinions are in accordance with the law. The assumption is, therefore, that the concurrence of a majority of the judges is assurance of the correctness of the decision. In other words, as concerns evidence, our Sages felt that the truth is not made truer by the testimony of a hundred people than it is by the testimony of two. They therefore ruled that in establishing a truth whose source is human observation, "two equal a hundred." In matters of reasoning and judgment, erudition and knowledge, however, the aggregate thinking of equally competent men gains weight with number. Therefore, where a judicial decision is concerned, the majority opinion rules and becomes law.

The refusal to accept the testimony of one witness as sufficient is in no way an abridgment of man's inherent claim to trustworthiness. It is merely an affirmation of the principle that infallibility rests only with Him from Whom all justice flows.

## MAN'S LEGAL RIGHTS AND TRUSTWORTHINESS

Among the foundations of Torah morality are the principles that in the eyes of the law all men are equal, that every person can demand his rights, and that justice must be extended to all alike. The exhortation, "Thou shalt not show partiality to the poor man, nor pay respect to the person of might; but in righteousness shalt thou judge thy neighbor,"[32] was looked upon by our Sages not merely as a moral preachment, but as the very essence of legal justice.

It has become a sermonic cliche to point out that the Hebrew word for charity can also mean justice, but it would be dangerous to reverse the homily. While the word used by the Bible for charity may also imply righteousness, in deciding who is right and who is wrong the judge is forbidden to guide himself by charitable considerations. He must not say to himself: "This man is poor and inasmuch as this rich man and I are under obligation to support him, I shall decide in his favor and he will be able to make a clean living."[33] Just so is he forbidden to say, "This man is rich, he is a descendant of great men, how can I put him to shame and see him humiliated."[34]

Our Sages went yet a step further in defining the Torah concept of equality before the law. Not only are the poor and the rich, the strong and the weak, equal before the bar of justice, but also the just and the unjust, the righteous and the wicked, the scholar and the *am ha-aretz* (the unlearned). A judge must decide who is right and who is wrong not on the basis of the personalities of the litigants but on the legal aspects of the particular situation. On the verse, "Thou shalt not wrest the judgment of thy poor in his cause,"[35] the Mekilta states: "If a wicked man and a pious man stand before you for judgment, do not say, 'Since this man is wicked I will turn the judgment against him.' Therefore it is written, 'thou shalt not wrest the judgment of thy poor in his cause'— that is, one who is poor in the fulfilling of the *mitzvot*."[36] Similarly, though the *am ha-aretz* was generally looked down upon, his legal rights were always respected. Since it was the practice, out of respect for his knowledge, to seat a scholar who came to court for litigation, it was ruled that when an *am ha-aretz* and a scholar are litigants before the court, the former, even though he does not merit the respect, must not be left standing. He, too, must be given a seat, for no favoritism can be shown where right and wrong, guilt or innocence, are to be determined.[37]

In Jewish law the ignorant and the wicked share equal rights with the saint and the scholar. Our Sages often distinguished between the pious and the wicked, between the scholar and the ignorant, but never where it might affect a man's inalienable right to demand that justice be extended him. They held that this right was given to all men regardless of their station or their deeds. It is the duty of the judge to render an impartial decision uninfluenced by the litigants' piety or position in the community. It was only in assessing a man's trustworthiness as a witness and in determining his elegibility to testify in behalf of others, that our Sages did permit distinctions between the scholar and the unlearned, the wicked and the righteous. In other words, while all men have an equal right to demand justice in their own behalf, not all men are accorded equal trustworthiness in determining whether the claims of other litigants are just or unjust.

All rabbinic jurisprudence rests upon the acceptance of the trustworthiness of witnesses who testify in court. Circumstantial evidence, hearsay, personal admission of guilt, and other such forms of evidence, are not acceptable in court. The decision of the judge, particularly in capital offenses, is based on one and only one factor—the confidence that witnesses will testify only to what is true. The injunction, "At the mouth of two witnesses, or three witnesses, shall he that is to die be put to death; at the mouth of one witness he shall not be put to death,"[38] was taken by our Sages literally. They ruled that only on the testimony of two witnesses, in full conviction that they speak the truth, can the court condemn a person to death.

Concerning non-capital offenses, the Torah also teaches, "One witness shall not rise up against a man for any iniquity, or for any sin, in any sin that he sinneth; at the mouth of two witnesses, or at the mouth of three witnesses shall the matter be established."[39] Nowhere does the law suggest that because a man is of outstanding honesty his testimony should be accepted even if he is an only witness. The testimony of two witnesses is always required. The following personal experience was once related by Simeon ben Shetah:

May I not live to see the Consolation [of Israel] if I did not see a man run after another into a desolate place. I ran after him and I saw a sword in his hand dripping with another's blood and the murdered man struggling in the agony of death. I said to him, You wicked man! Who killed this man? Either I did or you did. But what can I do. Your blood [your life] is not delivered into my hand, for the Torah said, "Upon the mouth of two witnesses shall he that is to die be put to death." But He Who knows all thoughts will requite that man who murdered his fellow man.[40]

The trust bestowed upon witnesses and their probity was not only complete; it was irrevocable. Once two witnesses had testified in court and a final verdict had been rendered, the witnesses could not retract their testimony and claim that their testimony had been false or inaccurate. The standard legal dictum of the Rabbis is: "Since he once gave evidence he cannot give evidence to contradict his earlier testimony."[41]

It would be hard to find a parallel in any other system of jurisprudence to the legal philosophy of the Rabbis which placed complete confidence in the truth of the testimony of two witnesses and refused to accept circumstantial evidence, even of the most conclusive kind. Our Sages set up two principles in the admittance of witnesses. First the reliability and trustworthiness of the witnesses as persons must be established beyond any shadow of a doubt. Second, on the court rests the great responsibility of properly cross-examining the witnesses in order to affirm that they are not mistaken in their testimony. Hence Simeon ben Shetah, the leader of the Pharisees in the last century B.C.E., said, "Examine the witnesses diligently and be cautious in thy words lest from them they will learn to speak falsely."[42] Simeon ben Shetah could speak from bitter experience for he saw his own son executed upon the testimony of false witnesses.[43]

The Mishnah records in detail the cross-examination (bedikot) and queries (hakirot) to which witnesses had to submit before their testimony was accepted in court. The hakirot were designed to establish the exact time and place of the criminal act; the bedikot aimed to ascertain the exact nature of the criminal act.[44]

### WARRANT OF TRUSTWORTHINESS

Since the court based its verdict entirely on the word-of-mouth information it received from two witnesses, it was mandatory that the witnesses be beyond all reproach or suspicion. Thus a *rashah*, a man who transgressed a commandment for which he could be punished in court, was not considered trustworthy and was disqualified from giving testimony. Similarly, thieves and robbers were considered ineligible to give testimony in civil, criminal or capital cases.[45] It is, however, in borderline cases where, for example, a man is not a *rashah* in the strict sense of the term, and yet his testimony is not considered trustworthy, that the rabbinic philosophy of human trustworthiness best reveals itself.

According to our Sages, a trustworthy person is one who conducts his business in such a way that it benefits not only him but humanity in general. The Mishnah, for instance, states: "And these are ineligible [to be witnesses or judges]: a dice player, a usurer, and pigeon flyers.... Rabbi Judah said: This applies if they have no other trade; but if they have some other trade, they are eligible."[46] Discussing this law, the Talmud asks, "The dice player—what wrong has he done that he becomes ineligible to be a witness?" Since a professional gambler is not a thief or robber (for he acquires only that which was agreed upon beforehand and with the consent of the men with whom he gambled), why should he be ineligible to give testimony? He cannot, after all, be classified as a *rashah de homos*,[46a] a wicked man who benefits from another without the latter's consent.[47]

Rejecting one explanation,[48] the Talmud puts forth another which reveals a great philosophic principle.

"The professional gambler," says the Talmud, "is not engaged in a profession which furthers the welfare of the world [human society]."[49] The term employed by the Talmud in the above statement is "*yishubo shel olam.*" Translated into modern terms, this statement would read: "He is not trustworthy who is not engaged in the advancement of the civilization of the world." In other words, according to rabbinic doctrine, only that person who through his business or profession benefits society is trustworthy. Anyone who engages in a profession which does not advance the cause of human welfare is not considered a reliable person even if what he does is technically not illegal. Certainly there can be no clearer demonstration of how profoundly dedicated our Sages were to the principle that all human conduct must be rooted in an awareness that no man is an isolated, independent being, and that all men bear a responsibility for the welfare of their fellows.

This same yardstick is used in other cases. Another type of person who is not considered a member of the responsible community is the *am ha-aretz*, the ignorant man who through his lack of knowledge does not know how to observe the laws of the Torah. The Mishnah states:

> He who has knowledge of the Written Law (*mikra*), the Mishnah and proper conduct (*derek eretz*) will not soon fall into sin, for it is said, "A threefold cord is not quickly broken" (Eccles. 4:12). But he who has no knowledge of the Written Law, the Mishnah and proper conduct is not a part of the cultivated world.[50]

Rabbi Johanan, commenting on this mishnah, added, "And he is ineligible to be a witness."[51]

Maimonides, apparently, had a different understanding of this ruling. He believed that the Rabbis held the *am ha-aretz* to be untrustworthy not because his ignorance put him outside the pale of society, but because his ignorance leads him to violate the law and therefore lays him open to the suspicion that he may not tell the truth. Maimonides writes:

> One who does not possess knowledge of the Written Law, the Mishnah and right conduct has the presumptive status of a *rashah* and is ineligible to be a witness under rabbinical authority. The presumption is that a person who falls so low transgresses the majority of the commandments that may come to his hand... It therefore stands to reason that every scholar has the presumption (*hazakah*) of being eligible, unless he is found to be ineligible. And every *am ha-aretz* has the presumption of being ineligible unless he establishes for himself the reputation that he walks in the ways of uprightness.[52]

It is thus abundantly evident that, for our Sages, the presumption of a man's trustworthiness rested in great measure upon whether or not in his occupation, his personal conduct, his actions and his knowledge he served the community and advanced the welfare of society. But here again, the social outlook is a natural development of the underlying

principle that man is a child of his Maker, not of his environment. It is
the belief in the sacredness of man who was created in the divine image
which permits man to claim trustworthiness.

## THE PRESUMPTION OF ONE'S TRUSTWORTHINESS

The statement of Maimonides that, until proven otherwise, a scholar
has a *hezkat kashrut*, a presumption of trustworthiness,[53] applied not
only to a scholar but to every man. The term "scholar" in this instance
is used by Maimonides in contradistinction to *am ha-aretz*, one unlearned in the law. Just as it is accepted that a man is considered innocent
until proven guilty, so is it also a rabbinic doctrine that as long as there
is no definite evidence to prove that a man is morally wicked or unworthy, he is not required to produce evidence of his trustworthiness or
proper conduct. Every man is presumed to be a worthy person. Even
if a witness should come forward to testify that someone had committed
an offense, either criminal or religious, which would brand him as a
*rashah* and thus deprive him of his presumption of trustworthiness, the
testimony is not accepted. In a case such as this, the testimony of one
witness is not sufficient. To strip a man of his recognized status, of the
presumption of his worthiness, the testimony of two witnesses is
required. In its own way, this attitude reflects the rabbinic confidence
in the religious wholesomeness and moral fitness of the human personality.

This principle of "presumption" (*hezkat kashrut*) is applied scrupu-
lously and has halakic implications even in cases to which, on the
surface, it would seem to have little relevance. This is illustrated in a
mishnah which deals with marriage laws pertaining to priests. A priest
is not permitted to take for a wife a woman who has had intercourse
with a bastard, or any other man with whom she is not permitted to
have sexual relations. If she has had contact with such persons she falls
into the category of a *zonah* (harlot) and becomes prohibited to a priest.
The Mishnah states:

> If they saw her [an unmarried woman] speaking with some man in
> the street [under suggestive circumstances] and said to her, "What
> manner of man is this?" [and she answered], "He is one by such a

name and he is a priest, Rabban Gamaliel and Rabbi Eliezer say: She is believed [because she is presumed to be trustworthy]; but Rabbi Joshua says: We cannot rely on her word; rather, she must be presumed to have suffered intercourse with a *nathin*, or a bastard, until she brings proof for her words. If she was found with child and they said to her: "What manner of unborn child is this?" [and she answered], "It is of one by such a name and he is a priest," Rabban Gamaliel and Rabbi Eliezer say: She is believed; but Rabbi Joshua says: We cannot rely on her word; rather, she must be presumed to be with child by a *nathin*, or a bastard, until she brings proof for her words.[54]

The point made by this mishnah is indeed most striking. Even if viewed in the most lenient of lights, it is clear that the woman has not conducted herself properly. The point in question, however, is whether or not she has had intercourse with one who is forbidden to her in marriage. Upon the answer to this question depends her own legal status—whether she can marry a priest or not—as well as the legal status of her unborn child. Rabban Gamaliel was of the opinion that since there is no evidence to the contrary, we assume that her contact was with a man who is not forbidden to her in marriage. The legal presumption of trustworthiness operates in her own behalf and in behalf of the legitimacy of her child.[55] Rabbi Joshua, on the contrary, was of the opinion that since she had become pregnant through her relations with a stranger, we can presume that she lived with one of those men who are forbidden to her in marriage. Hence, she becomes ineligible to marry a priest and her child is considered illegitimate. The opinion of Rabban Gamaliel was accepted, and the halakah was formulated in accordance with his view that where there are no witnesses to contradict her, the presumption of her trustworthiness overrides all suspicions and her word is accepted.

That every person carries a *hezkat kashrut*, a presumption of moral and religious honesty and trustworthiness, is also illustrated in the law of contradicted evidence. The law states that if two witnesses testify in court that one person borrowed money from another, and then two witnesses appear who do not contradict the evidence itself but, instead, incriminate the first set of witnesses by stating, "On the very day and hour in which you testified that the money had been loaned, you were with us in an entirely different place," the testimony of the second pair of witnesses is accepted and the testimony of the first pair of witnesses is rejected. Such an act, in talmudic terms, is called *hazamah* and the first pair of witnesses suffers the same penalty that the testimony would have inflicted upon the man against whom evidence was given. If, however, two witnesses testify that one person borrowed money from another and two other witnesses contradict them, saying that the money was not borrowed, then the testimony of neither pair of witnesses is accepted. Moreover, neither pair of witnesses suffers a penalty, for the court can never determine which set of witnesses gave false evidence. In rabbinic law this is called *hakhashah*.[56]

Any witness who gives false testimony becomes a *rashah* and loses his trustworthiness as a witness in future cases. In fact, the entire principle that a *rashah* is ineligible to give testimony was derived by our Sages from the law of the Torah, "Put not thy hand with the wicked to be an unrighteous witness."[57] According to the oral tradition, this verse is a prohibition against accepting the wicked as witnesses.[58] Hence, when two sets of witnesses directly contradict each other, we are certain that two of the four witnesses involved have definitely committed the grave offense of giving false evidence. Since, however, we cannot ascertain which two have transgressed, and the trustworthiness of all four witnesses is brought under question, it would seem reasonable to deny all of them the right to give testimony in the future. Each of them, after all, is at least, a *safek rashah*, or, as it is called in the Talmud, a *safek deoraitha*, that is, a person whose trustworthiness is doubtful in accordance with biblical law. Therefore, each one of the witnesses should be disqualified from giving evidence in future cases.

The halakah, however, is that each pair of witnesses, as long as they do not unite into one set but give their evidence separately, is permitted to testify in other cases. The principle behind this halakah is the following: If two pairs of witnesses give contradictory evidence, and later one of each pair join together to give evidence in another case, their testimony is not accepted because we know definitely that one of the two has proven himself untrustworthy and has therefore disqualified himself from giving evidence. If, however, each pair, separately, should give evidence in another case, their testimony is accepted because, as long as it has not been proven definitely that they are untrustworthy, they are still covered by the legal presumption of trustworthiness which is attached to every man.[59] In other words, no human being can exist in a state of "doubtful trustworthiness" because, until he is definitely proven unworthy, every man has a *hazakah* of *kashrut*.[60]

In summation, two things are made manifestly clear by these halakic decisions. First, a man's right to be considered trustworthy is a God-given right, gifted to him as a creature made in the divine image, which only he, by improper action, can abnegate. Second, unless seen as evolving directly from the religious philosophy of the Jewish "democratic theocracy," these decisions might appear arbitrary and whimsical. It is the acceptance of the sovereignty of God as the governing principle in human relations which gains for man not only trustworthiness but also sacredness.

### WRONGDOING NOT A PERMANENT STAIN

This great privilege of a presumption of worthiness, bestowed upon every man from the day of his birth, is a clear expression of faith in the human personality. It is a manifestation of the firm belief of our Sages that man is not normally an "evildoer." Man was born in the image of God and he therefore retains his presumption of worthiness until it is undisputably proven that he is not worthy of this privilege. The concept of *hezkat kashrut* is not merely a legal concept; it is deeply rooted in the religious philosophy of Judaism which is based on the belief in the sacredness of the human personality. Our Sages very revealingly declared, "No man will go astray unless the spirit of insanity enters into him."[61]

Even when a person sins, the stain of his sinfulness does not constitute a permanent and ineradicable blemish on his person. If a person intentionally commits an offense, even a criminal offense, he is punished for his action. Once the punishment is executed, however, he again regains his status as a trustworthy individual. If a person transgressed a negative command which required human action, he was punished by stripes. If he committed a capital offense and his offense was proven by evidence given by two witnesses, he was liable to incur the death penalty. But once a person received his punishment he regained his former status of moral worthiness and legal trustworthiness. Man is the servant of God, and except under extraordinary circumstances, human beings cannot deprive a follow human being of his freedom, even if he has committed a crime. The Mishnah states:

> When a transgressor is already punished by flogging, then he is thy brother, for it is written: "Then thy brother should be dishonored (*veniklah*) before thine eyes" (Deut. 25:3). When he is punished by flogging (*ki'shilkah*), he is once more thy brother."[62]

The Mishnah apparently interprets the word *veniklah*, as if it stems from the root *lakah*, to flog, to mean that as soon as one is punished by stripes, he reassumes the normal status of "thy brother." Hence, even if a person forfeits his presumption of trustworthiness by becoming a *rashah*, he regains his *hezkat kashrut* and is treated like a fully worthy person as soon as he receives his punishment.[63]

# 5. THE SACREDNESS OF HUMAN LIFE

## THE SACRED WORTH OF THE INDIVIDUAL

The Mishnah declares that God created but a single man in order to teach mankind that whoever destroys a single individual God imputes it on him as if he had destroyed the entire world, and whoever saves the life of a single individual God imputes it on him as if he had saved the entire world.[1] This statement is not merely a noble preachment concerning the sacred worth of the individual; it is a principle animating rabbinic legislation. How careful our Sages were in putting this principle into practice can best be indicated by reviewing a few laws which deal with the loss or preservation of life.

The Mishnah states: "If heathens said to a group of women: 'Give us one from among you that we may defile her, and if not we will defile all of you,' they should all suffer defilement rather than surrender a single soul in Israel."[2] The principle, here applied in law, is that an individual may not be sacrificed for the sake of the group. The same principle is applied in the ruling which forbids the surrender of an individual to an unwarranted death in order to save the lives of an entire group:

> If heathens said to a group of men: "Surrender one of you to us so that we may put him to death, otherwise we will put you all to death," they should all suffer death and not surrender one soul from Israel. If, however, they [the heathens] specified one particular individual, in a case similar to that of Sheba, the son of Bichri, they should surrender him and not let all of them suffer death.[3]

It is forbidden for members of a group to save their lives by surrendering an individual to death, because the life of a single individual is as sacred as the lives of an entire group. It is different, however, if the heathens specify a particular individual whom they want to kill, for in such a case the group is not asked to select one from among them and surrender him to be killed. In the latter case the individual to be killed has already been clearly specified and all know that he will suffer death. If, therefore, by surrendering him they can save their lives, the group is permitted to surrender him. Yet, even in this case, it is stipulated that the position of the individual specified must be analogous to that of Sheba, son of Bichri, who had rebelled against King David and was, therefore, already legally sentenced to death. Should, however, the person specified be an innocent and guiltless individual, then all must suffer death rather than surrender him to an undeserved death.[4]

These laws give clear demonstration of the view of our Sages that the lives of a group or a community are not considered to be of greater worth than the life of an individual. If the survival of the group hinges upon the surrender of an individual to death, the entire group must suffer death rather than commit a murder, even if only indirectly. What makes this halakah even more striking is the fact that under Jewish law surrendering an innocent man to be killed does not constitute an act of murder punishable by death, since doing so is not in itself an act of murder. Morally, however, such an act can be considered an act of murder, and therefore an entire group must suffer death rather than surrender one innocent person.

### THY BROTHER SHALL LIVE WITH THEE

According to rabbinic law, a person has no right to save his own life by either directly or indirectly causing another's death. On the other hand, the halakah does not require of a man that he sacrifice his own life in order to save another's life, as long as he is not either the direct or indirect cause of his fellow man's death. The *Sifra* states: "And thy brother shall live with thee."[5] This verse was interpreted by Ben Paturi as follows: Two men travel in the desert and one has a jug of water; if the owner of the water should drink he will survive and reach habitation; but should they divide it, both will die; Ben Paturi said, "Let them both drink and let them both die, for it is said, 'And thy brother shall live *with thee*.'" Rabbi Akiba said to him, "And thy brother shall live with thee; your own life takes precedence over his."[6]

It appears that even Ben Paturi did not venture to suggest that the one who has the jug of water should give it to his companion and sacrifice his own life to permit at least one life to be saved. Such an act of supererogation neither Ben Paturi nor Rabbi Akiba required of a man. In the opinion of Ben Paturi, the verse "And thy brother shall live with thee" demands that both men share the same fate even if it brings death to both of them, while Rabbi Akiba recognized man's right to self-preservation if his act is neither the direct nor the indirect cause of another's death.[7]

## THE DUTY TO RISK ONE'S LIFE TO SAVE ANOTHER

While our Sages did not demand that one sacrifice his own life to save another, they did feel that one should *risk* his life in the hope of saving the life of another. On the verse in the Torah, "neither shalt thou stand idly by the blood of thy neighbor,"[8] the *Sifra* comments: "Whence do we know if you see your fellow drowning in the river or attacked by robbers or by a vicious animal that it is your duty to save his life? It says 'neither shalt thou stand idly by the blood of thy neighbor.'"[9] Similarly, if one sees one pursuing another with the intent to kill, or to ravish a male or a betrothed woman, he must risk his own life in order to prevent the commission of the criminal act.[10]

As a rule, our Sages refused to measure the merit of one life against another. The Mishnah states: "A one-day child can inherit property and bequeath it; he that kills him is culpable: and he is considered a full *hatan* to his father and mother and all his kinfolk [i.e., he is considered a full relative, and in case of death, the family must observe the laws of mourning]."[11] Hence, as soon as a child is born he is already, in the eyes of the law, a full-fledged individual and has the same rights to the preservation of his life as has any other mature human being. The Mishnah goes even further, stating that as soon as the greater part of the child is out of his mother's womb he is already a human being, and offers a most striking ruling: "If a pregnant woman has difficulty in giving birth, the child must be cut up while it is in the womb and brought out limb by limb, since the life of the mother has priority over the life of the unborn child; but if the greater part of the foetus is already born it may not be touched, for we may not set aside one human life in order to save another human life."[12]

Some religious denominations argue that it is forbidden to interfere with God's will and prohibit the destruction of a foetus in order to save the life of the mother. On the other hand, there are those who argue that the life of the mother always takes precedence over the foetus. Our Sages accepted neither of these two views. They asked but one question in arriving at their decision: "When can a person be considered a human being?" In their judgment, as soon as the greater part of the foetus emerges into "the lighted space of the world" it is considered a human being and may not be destroyed in order to save another human being. The Tannaim ruled in accordance with the religious and moral principle that no one has the right to set aside one human life for the sake of another. For them human life was sacred. They categorically opposed the destruction of human life, regardless of how immature and undeveloped it might be, in order to save another, even that of the greatest man in the world.[13]

It is interesting that Philo, quoting non-Jewish sources, maintains that one is considered a human being from the moment of birth, and that whoever kills a newly born child commits an act of murder. He writes:

No doubt, the view that the child, while still adhering to the womb below the belly, is part of its future mother is current both among natural philosophers whose life study is concerned with the theoretical side of knowledge and also among physicians of the highest repute.... But when the child has been brought to the birth it is separate from the organism with which it was identified and being isolated and self-contained becomes a living animal, lacking nothing of the complements needed to make a human being. And, therefore, infanticide undoubtedly is murder, since the displeasure of the law is not concerned with ages but with a breach to the human race.[14]

Among our Sages there is disagreement over whether the foetus "is a thigh [a part] of a mother" or not.[15] Philo, however, concluded that a child is considered a human being only from the moment of its birth. In effect, therefore, his view that killing an infant after its birth is an act of murder, accords fully with the halakah.[16]

There is, as we have already noted, a basic difference between destroying one life in order to save another, even one's own, and giving priority to the saving of one's own life over another's. Where the question is whether or not we are permitted to destroy a life in order to save a life, even one's own life, the answer is no. No one has the right to save himself or any other person by destroying someone else. In such cases the dictum of our Sages is: "What reason hast thou to assume that thy blood is redder? Perhaps thy neighbor's blood is redder."[17] If, however, two people are drowning in the ocean and it is possible to save only one, and in other such analogous cases, there are laws of priority. The Mishnah states:

> The saving of the life of a man takes priority over the life of a woman; the restoring of one's own lost article takes priority over another's. The covering of a woman's nakedness takes priority over a man's. The ransom of a woman out of captivity takes priority over that of a man. When both are in danger of being defiled [sodomy] the freeing of the man takes priority over the woman. The priest takes priority over the Levite, the Levite over the Israelite, the Israelite over the bastard, the bastard over a *nathin*, a *nathin* over a proselyte, a proselyte over a slave. This law applies only when, otherwise, they are all equal. If, however, a bastard is learned in the law and a high priest is ignorant of the law, the bastard learned in the law has priority over the high priest who is ignorant.[18]

Distinction of birth, particularly where birth brings one to dedicate his life to the service of God, bestows prerogatives. But, and this is most striking, it is those who have acquired knowledge of the divine law who are given the most prominent and preferential position in the theocracy of Judaism. The bastard who could not take for a wife even the lowliest, if legally born, maiden, takes preference, if he is a scholar, over one who occupies the highest position in Jewish life, if he is ignorant. It is not improbable that although our Sages set a scale of priority, they would not have considered it a criminal offense for one to save an ignorant bastard before saving a learned high priest. For them the overriding duty is to save human life, any human life, for in their eyes every life is sacred.

### THE SACREDNESS OF ONE'S OWN LIFE

Our Sages ruled that no man has unlimited rights over the life of his fellows. Their religious philosophy also posits that no human being is the "owner" and unlimited master of his own life. Life is not a personal possession which can be destroyed at will, and, therefore, regardless of the nobility of his purpose, man is forbidden to destroy himself. A man is not permitted to sacrifice his own life even to avoid violating biblical commands.

During the Hadrianic persecutions a special conference of Tannaim held at Lydda ruled that under duress a Jew could, in order to save his life, violate all the commandments except for the three cardinal prohibitions: idolatry (*abodah zarah*), adultery or incest (*gillui arayot*), and homicide (*shefikat damim*).[19] Transgression of one of these three cardinal sins was considered the highest form of *hillul ha-Shem*, profanation of the name of God, and a negation of the entire theocracy of Judaism. This ruling was based upon the often quoted biblical verse, "Ye shall therefore keep My statutes and Mine ordinance, which if a man shall do, *he shall live by them*, I am the Lord."[20] The rabbis interpreted this as follows: "He shall live by them—the law was given to live by, not to die by."[21]

Maimonides, summarizing the rabbinic law, states: "When one is enjoined to transgress rather than to be killed and he prefers to suffer death rather than transgress, he is considered guilty of depriving himself of life. When one is enjoined to die rather than to transgress and he suffers death, he sanctifies the name of God."[22] Thus, just as one must yield up his life in order not to transgress the three cardinal sins, so is one forbidden to sacrifice his life in order not to violate any other laws of the Torah. This is a clear illustration of the major tenet of Judaism that man does not exercise full authority over his own life, and that there is a sacredness in the human personality which transcends any form of "ownership."

Even in regard to the three cardinal sins, rabbinic commentators seem to differ over whether the law is *yaharog*—he should do away with his own life in order not to transgress the law—or *yehareg*—he should accept the penalty of death rather than violate the law. According to the latter view, under no circumstances may one do away with his own life; he can only submit himself to the death penalty. This principle, however, must not be misinterpreted to mean that one is permitted to do away with his life in order to avoid the temptation of yielding. "And surely the blood of your lives shall I acquire,"[23] is accepted by our Sages as a prohibition against doing away with one's life.[24]

The statement that he who commits suicide has no share in the world to come is not found in talmudic sources, but such a tradition is recorded by Josephus:

But as for those who lay hands upon themselves, the darker regions of the netherland receive their souls, and God their Father visits upon their posterity the outrageous acts of their parents. With us it is ordained that the body of the suicide should be exposed unburied until sunset.[25]

In another place Josephus, following tannaitic tradition, says that the penalty of exposure applied only to one who was executed on account of blaspheming God.[26] Apparently then, Josephus based himself on the tradition that the destruction of one's own individuality is primarily an offense against God in Whose image man was made.

Philo, too, voiced the idea that the human personality is not something which can be "owned" by man. In a beautiful passage he writes:

I am formed of soul and body, I seem to have mind, reason, sense, yet I find that none of them are really mine. Where was my body before birth and whither will it go when I have departed?... Where is the babe that I once was, the boy and the other graduations between boy and full-grown man? Whence came the soul, whither will it go, how long will it be our mate and comrade? Can we tell its essential nature?... Even now in this life, we are the ruled rather than the rulers, known rather than knowing. The soul knows us, though we know it not; it lays on us commands, which we must fain obey, as a servant obeys his masters, and when it will it will claim a divorce in court, and depart, leaving our home desolate of life.... All this surely makes it plain that what we use are the possessions of others, that neither glory, nor wealth, nor honor, nor offices, nor all that makes up body and soul are our own, not even life itself. And we recognize that we have but their use, we shall tend them with care as God's possession, remembering from the first, that it is the master's custom, when he will, to take back his own. The thought will lighten our sorrow when they are taken from us.[27]

With clear reason and in striking terminology, Philo here develops the idea that the human personality cannot be explained in rational terms. It is the possession of God, given to man as a trust which only He can recall, and it is man's duty to administer that trust in recognition of what it is—God's possession. This concept, of course, was not exclusive with Philo. In fact, the very words he uses, declaring our lives to be merely a loan given us by God to "lighten our sorrow when they are taken away from us," were the words with which the disciples of Rabban Johanan ben Zakkai comforted him upon the death of his son.[28] In a similar vein, as noted above, did Beruria comfort her husband on the loss of their two children.[29]

### BODY AND SOUL

In ancient Hellenistic sources, life was conceived of as a continuous struggle between the carnal impulses of the body and the lofty ideals of the mind. The body was regarded as the source of all evil and the material prison in which the immortal was penned. In this dualistic philosophy, body and soul were locked in continuous conflict within man. In Philo's terminology, the body with its irrational soul is an "actual hindrance" and "a plotter" against the rational soul.[30] For Philo the body is the symbol of passion and evil.

In rabbinic literature, on the other hand, the human body is neither a voluntary nor involuntary instrument, whether for good or evil. It is man, a composite of both body and soul, the creation and possession of God, man in his totality, who is responsible for his actions, whether good or bad. This, it may be said, explains why Hellenistic Jews spoke of the "immortality of soul" as the reward for man's good deeds in this world.[31] For them, steeped in Hellenistic thought, only the rational was the source of man's noble achievements, and they could not accept as a divine reward the resurrection of the body, the source of all evil. For the Palestinian Rabbis, however, "bodily resurrection" became the reward of the righteous because to them body and soul as a unity constitute man, and neither his good deeds nor his bad deeds are the results of a "half man."

With many parables do our Sages illustrate the fact that body and soul share equal responsibility for their deeds in this world.[32] In rabbinic theology, body and soul carry a joint responsibility and share a joint reward. It is for this reason that our Sages considered it a great offense to do away with oneself or inflict bodily injury upon one's self. For this same reason they opposed any form of asceticism. Only those who look upon life as a continuous struggle between body and soul can sanction asceticism, which is primarily a means of weakening the body to permit the soul to grow stronger. Therefore did our Sages forbid self-mortification by fasting except when participating in a public fast.[33] A Nazirite was considered a sinner because he abstained from wine,[34] and others condemned the practice entirely, saying, "Do not the prohibitions of the Torah suffice for thee that thou addest others for thyself?"[35] Maimonides sums up the talmudic approach to asceticism in the following words:

> Perhaps a man may say, "Since passion and glory and similar things are evil qualities to cultivate and lead to man's departure from this world, I will separate myself from them in greater measure," and seek their contrary extreme to such an extent that he will not eat meat, nor drink wine, nor marry, nor dwell in a decent home, nor wear comely apparel, but will clothe himself in sackcloth and coarse wool like the idolators' priests. This, too, is the wrong way, not to be followed. Whoever persists in such a course is termed a sinner. . . . And concerning this and similar excesses Solomon exhorts us, "Be not overrighteous, nor excessively wise. Wherefore shouldst thou be desolate?" (Eccles. 7:16.)[36]

Rabbinic tradition held that overindulgence results in rebellion against God,[37] but it also frowned on bodily mortification. Man must take proper care of his body and supply its needs because, created by God, it is vested with sacredness.

It is therefore interesting to note that even Philo, for whom the body is a perpetual "plotter" against the rational soul, speaks out against self-mortification in words almost identical with those used later by Maimonides. The verse (Deut. 16:20), "Justice, justice shalt thou follow," is translated by the LXX as "Justice, *justly*, shalt thou follow." Philo raises the question: Is it possible to do justice unjustly? His answer is:

> . . . we pursue justice and all virtue by doing deeds akin to it, but not those that are contrary to it. If then thou observest anyone not taking

food or drink when he should, or refusing to take bath and oil, or careless about his clothing, or sleeping on the ground and occupying wretched lodgings, and then on the strength of all this fancying that he is practicing self-control, take pity on his mistakes, and show him the true method of self-control; for all these practices of his are fruitless and wearisome labors prostrating soul and body by starving and in other ways maltreating them.[39]

Of course, Maimonides never read Philo's works. It is therefore, revealing to find these two Jewish philosophers, in different eras, using almost the same language in concurring on one idea, an idea so deeply rooted in traditional Jewish thinking.

## MAN'S RIGHT TO DIGNITY

The sacredness of the human personality, applied as a legal principle, bestows upon every man other rights besides the right to life. Most revealing and interesting is the rabbinic recognition of man's right to dignity. Inherent in the democratic theocracy of Judaism, this right receives legal delineation in the laws concerning compensation for injuries received.

The Rabbis interpreted "an eye for an eye" to mean money indemnity, and outlined how compensation is to be made:

If a man wounds his fellow man he becomes thereby culpable on five counts: for injury, for pain, for healing, for loss of time, and for indignity inflicted. How is one compensated for "injury"? If he blinded another's eye, cut off his hand or broke his foot, the injured party is evaluated as a slave who is to be sold in the market place, and they assess how much he was worth before the injury and how much he is worth now.... For "pain," thus: If he burnt his fellow with a spit or nail, even though it was on the fingernail where it leaves no wounds, they estimate how much a man would be willing to take to suffer so. For "healing," thus: If he struck him he is liable to pay the cost of his healing.... For "loss of time": He is looked upon as a watchman of a cucumberfield, since he has already been paid the value of his hand or foot. For "indignity inflicted": All according to the man who inflicts the indignity and the man who suffers the indignity.[40]

Most striking is the fact that even if the injured person is the greatest of dignitaries, his injury is assessed as if he were the humblest of men—a slave about to be sold in the market—and that the scale used to evaluate his loss of time is the wage paid to the watchman of a cucumber patch. It is apparent that in the rabbinic view, where human life or bodily injury are concerned, no individual is superior to or worth more than another.[41]

In cases of indignity, however, the Mishnah does consider the standing or place in the community of the humiliator and the one whom he humiliates. Where humiliation is concerned, the rabbis admitted a relation between the sensitivity of the individual, the place of his humiliation, and the station and intention of the one who brought the indignity upon him. The same mishnah, therefore, says that if a man slips off a roof and injures someone, he is liable for the injuries but not for the indignity inflicted because there was no intention to inflict injury. A distinction is also made between an indignity suffered by an ordinary person or a minor, and an indignity suffered by a dignitary or a mature person.[42] Consideration is also given to the fact that a man is more deeply hurt when he is humiliated in the street than when he is humiliated in a public bath.[43]

The great concern of our Sages with the exact definition of indignity and humiliation is not surprising, for they were deeply conscious of the dignity of man who was created in the image of God. For them, to inflict indignity on any man, be he a freeman or a Canaanite slave,[44] was one of the most serious offenses. Whoever humiliates his fellow man in public, the Talmud declares, is as if he had shed blood, for "the red disappears and the white comes," making the infliction of indignity akin to an act of murder.[45] Rabbi Eleazer of Modiim included those who humiliate a fellow man in public among those who have no share in the world to come.[46] We can, therefore, understand why the relative status of the injured and the humiliator plays a great part in determining the seriousness of the offense. A man must compensate his neighbor whom he humiliates primarily because by inflicting an indignity on his fellow, he commits a crime against the dignity of man.

Rabbi Akiba and some of his disciples were of the opinion that it is impossible to determine the relative worth of human personalities.

Rabbi Meir, therefore, said that for purposes of indemnity even the most insignificant persons are regarded as "freemen who lost their possessions, for they are all equally the children of Abraham, Isaac and Jacob."[47] Rabbi Akiba, too, strikingly expressed the respect which our Sages had for the dignity of man. The Mishnah states:

This is the general rule: All is in accordance with the person's honor. Rabbi Akiba said: Even the poorest in Israel are looked upon as freemen who have lost their possessions for they are the sons of Abraham, Isaac and Jacob. It once happened that a man unloosed a woman's hair in the street and she came before Rabbi Akiba and he made him liable for four hundred *zuz*. Said the culprit: Rabbi, extend for me the time, and Rabbi Akiba extended him the time [for payment]. He [the culprit] watched her standing at the entry of her courtyard and he broke before her a cruse that held an *issar* worth of oil. She then unloosed her hair and scooped up the oil in her hand and laid her hand on her head. He set up witnesses against her and came before Rabbi Akiba and said to him: Rabbi, should I give to such a one [who has no regard for her own dignity] four hundred *zuz*? Rabbi Akiba answered: Thou has said naught at all. For he who inflicts wounds upon himself, even though he is not permitted to do so, is not culpable; but if others wound him they are culpable.[48]

Rabbi Akiba here taught two profound lessons. First, that one cannot set relative standards for human dignity; that all upon whom indignity is inflicted are judged to be freemen, for human rights are not bestowed upon men in proportion to their worldy possessions. Second, that even if one does not stand upon his dignity, and even if he demeans his own dignity, it is forbidden to others to inflict indignity on him. Human dignity is not determined by one's personal attitude toward it or himself. Dignity graces man because he is made in the image of God and no man has the right to inflict indignity on his fellow being.

### THE RIGHT OF PERSONAL LIBERTY

Another of the rights granted man under the Jewish theocracy, perhaps a more basic right, is the right of personal liberty and freedom. For our Sages this right was a fundamental human right. Not only did they recognize it in their general social outlook, as might perhaps be expected, but their very penal code is so drawn as to preserve this right even for the lawbreaker.

In all rabbinic literature it is difficult to find reference to the punishment of imprisonment, which in essence punishes a man for offenses committed, whether criminal or religious, by denying him his freedom. Freedom was considered a most sacred and treasured gift of human life and our Sages rarely judged an offense so heinous as to justify depriving a man of this greatest of all human privileges.

In the Torah, imprisonment is mentioned twice, but not as punishment for the commission of unlawful acts; rather it implies temporary custody for those who commit grievous sins. In those two instances Moses did not know the exact penalty or mode of punishment to be inflicted upon the offenders and they were, therefore, held in detention. In one case, that of the son of an Israelite mother and an Egyptian father who blasphemed the Name, the Bible says, "And they put him in ward that it might be declared unto them at the mouth of the Lord."[49] Since the penalty for blaspheming the Name (*megadaif*) had not been revealed to Moses, he sought instruction from God. During the brief period between the commission of the crime and the final revelation to Moses that the punishment for the sin is stoning, the offender was kept in the ward. It is interesting to note that in the opinion of some of our Sages the *megadaif*, in accordance with a strict point of view of the *halakah*, should not have been placed in ward even temporarily, since it was not known at all what his penalty would be. The Israelites placed him in ward at their own discretion and only as a "temporary measure."[50]

The second reference in the Torah to imprisonment is in the case of the man who desecrated the Sabbath. Death is the penalty prescribed in the Torah for such an offense, but Moses did not know by what mode of capital punishment the offender was to meet his death. In both instances placing the offenders in ward was not a punishment for the offenses committed. It merely served as a safeguard against the offenders' escape before the proper penalties could be pronounced.

If a man smites another with a stone or with his fist and the latter does not die instantly but is confined to bed, the Torah states, "if he rises again, and walks abroad upon his staff, then shall he that smote be free."[51] Here the nature of the crime is in doubt; time alone will reveal whether the man committed homicide or not. What is to be done with the criminal until it is known whether he merely inflicted an injury or committed homicide? Should he be permitted to move freely and given the opportunity to escape and avoid the death sentence? On this the Mekilta comments: "'He that smote be free': Do I understand that he may assign bondsmen and walk freely in the market place? It tells us that they imprison him until the injured party is cured."[52]

It is unquestionable, therefore, that according to the strict law of the Torah, imprisonment was not to be used as a penalty for the commission of offenses. At most, offenders were placed in prison temporarily, particularly when it was uncertain as to what their ultimate penalty would be. It is equally certain that our Sages instituted imprisonment as a penalty for perpetual offenders or for murderers who could not, because of certain legal technicalities, be punished by death. The Mishnah states: "If a man was punished by flogging [and again committed the same transgression] and was flogged a second time, [if he transgresses a third time] the court puts him in a *kipa* and feeds him with barley until his belly bursts. If a man committed a murder and there were no witnesses, they put him in a *kipa* and feed him bread of adversity and water of affliction."[53]

The term *kipa* clearly refers to some form of imprisonment. According to the Talmud, a man who was flogged twice for the same transgression and again commits the same offenses is placed in prison only when the command he violates is punishable by *Karet*, premature death at the hand of Heaven.[54] Normally, however, a sinner who repeated an offense was not punished by imprisonment.

The penalty of imprisonment for a murderer who could not be convicted for his crime was also closely limited by the Talmud. The statement in the Mishnah, "And there were no witnesses," does not mean that there were no witnesses who saw the act of homicide. In such case there is no evidence that he is a murderer, and consequently he would not suffer even the penalty of imprisonment. The Mishnah refers rather to two witnesses who, "one after another," saw the act of murder from different vantage points, and whose testimony, therefore, is inadmissible in court. In these and similar circumstances, since the death sentence cannot be imposed, the offender suffers life imprisonment.[55] It is obvious, therefore, that the penalty of imprisonment was imposed by our Sages only in isolated cases.

In his *Mishneh Torah*, Maimonides expresses the view that life imprisonment was used only in cases of homicide, such as those mentioned above. However, a criminal who committed any of the other capital offenses enumerated in the Torah, under the same circumstances, was never punished by life imprisonment. In a moving preachment on the crime of murder, he writes:

> This [life imprisonment] is not given to any other person who commits crimes punishable by death at the hand of court. If one is condemned to death, he is put to death; and if he is not liable to be punished by death, he goes free, for though there are greater crimes than bloodshed, none cause such destruction to civilized society as bloodshed. Neither idolatry nor sexual immorality nor the desecration of the Sabbath is equal to bloodshed. For those are transgressions between man and God, while bloodshed is a crime between man and his fellow men. If one has committed this crime, he is deemed wholly wicked and all the good deeds he has performed during his life time cannot outweigh this crime or save him from judgment, as it is said, "A man that is laden with blood of any person shall hasten his steps unto the pit; none will support him."[56] We may also learn from Ahab who worshiped idols and of whom it is said: "And there was none like unto Ahab."[57] Yet when his transgressions and good deeds were set in array before the God of all spirits,[58] the one transgression that brought on him the doom of extermination, and the weightiest of all his crimes, was the blood of Nabot. For Scripture tells us, "And there came forth the spirit and stood before the Lord"[59]; this was the spirit of Nabot, who was told, Thou shalt entice him and prevail also.[60] Now the wicked Ahab did not commit murder himself. How much greater is the crime of one who commits murder with his own hand.[61]

The rabbinic opposition to imprisonment as a penalty is not a result of a "liberal" approach to punishment or a "modern" concept of penology. It is an outgrowth of the religious principle that man, created by God, is endowed with inviolable rights, among them the right to liberty, which can be abridged only by Him in Whom all rights originate.

Obviously, this is a far-reaching consequence of the belief in the sacredness of the human personality, one of the pillars upon which the Jewish democratic theocracy rests. This concept recognizes man's right to freedom and guarantees the preservation of each man's individuality. Needless to say, this guarantee is not limited to personal liberty. It insures all men against any form of slavery or subjugation.

### SERVITUDE OF PROPERTY AND PERSON

The religious concept of individualism in Jewish law means that the life of every individual is a sacred trust over which neither a group nor an individual can exercise unlimited authority. In the ancient Roman world, particularly during the epoch of the XII Tables,[62] it was common for one person to acquire complete possession of another as payment for an unfulfilled obligation. If, for instance, a debtor failed to pay his debt, ancient Roman custom permitted the creditor to do with the life of the debtor whatever he pleased. He could sell him into slavery, he could arrest him, he even had the legal right to put him to death—because, in the Roman concept, a debtor placed obligation upon his own personality when incurring a debt. The *obligatio* fell not only on the debtor's property; it implied that in the event of failure to pay, the creditor could assume ownership over the person of the debtor.

In rabbinic law, however, a creditor, in the event of default in payment, can secure ownership over the debtor's property, but he cannot acquire ownership over the debtor himself. The common term in the Talmud for *obligatio* is *shibud nekasim*, servitude of the property of the debtor, never servitude of the personality of the debtor.[63] Biblical law does permit the court to sell into slavery a person who cannot pay his debts,[64] but as interpreted by rabbinic sources, this law applied only to a thief who was unable to repay the principal he had stolen. But even in such a case, the person sold into slavery remained, in the full sense of the term, a free man, and his master never acquired real ownership of his personality. This device of "slavery" obligated merely the services of the thief through which he repaid the value of the theft.[65] The entire institution of Israelite slavery, furthermore, went out of existence during the Second Commonwealth.[66] Thus, the Jewish law of *shibud nekasim*, too, reflects the Jewish concept that one cannot acquire ownership of another person because only the Maker of all exercises true ownership over the things He has created.

## EMPLOYER AND EMPLOYEE

The rabbinic view that no one can acquire ownership in a human being, even in the most limited sense, also illumines for us the rabbinic concept of the relationship between employer and employee. The Mishnah, for instance, states: "If one hires artisans and they retract, they are at a disadvantage. If the employer retracts, he is at a disadvantage. Whoever changes [the condition of the agreement] is at a disadvantage. Whoever retracts is at a disadvantage."[67]

The mishnaic term for "disadvantage," literally translated, reads "his hand is lower." In practice, this means that if an employee undertakes to do something for twenty *zuz* per day and retracts after doing half a day's work, and for the other half a day the employer, because the work cannot suffer delay, has to engage laborers for twelve *zuz*, the employee who retracted is liable for the difference in cost to the employer; he thus receives only eight *zuz* for his half-day's work. On the other hand, if the employer retracts in the middle of the day and engages laborers for cheaper wages, he must pay his former employee at the rate originally stipulated.

It has been said that, in relation to labor, rabbinic law is so advanced that it approaches the modern view which recognizes the right of a laborer to strike. Do not the Rabbis, basing themselves on this mishnah, rule that an employee may retract even in the middle of the day?"[68] It is hardly necessary to point out the fallacy in this thinking, for the Mishnah extends the same privilege to the employer, thus protecting both employer and employee.

Biblical and rabbinic law, as a rule, are governed by the principle of equity: "Ye shall do no unrighteousness in judgment; thou shalt not respect the person of the poor, nor favor the person of the mighty; but in righteousness shalt thou judge they neighbor."[69] The Torah does not favor the protection of any particular group, rich or poor, employer or employee. It extends equal rights to and demands justice for all.

Giving both employer and employee the right to retract may not have been the most "practical" thing to do, but it did protect both groups against loss. Deeply rooted in this law is the Hebraic concept of human freedom. The Talmud states that an employee may retract in the middle of the day because the Torah says, "For unto Me, the children of Israel are servants,"[70] and not servants of servants.[71] Withholding from the laborer the right to retract would imply, even if only in a narrow sense, that an employer acquires a *shibud*, a certain kind of ownership, over the personality of his employee. To permit this would be to deny the guiding principle of the Jewish theocracy, that man is the possession of God and that one man cannot acquire rights of possession in the personality of another.

It is in this light that we can understand the legal difference between a *poel*, an employee who works by the day, and a *kablan*, a contractor who is paid for a particular piece of work done. The *poel* can retract in the middle of the day and is entitled to his wages for his half-day's work even if the employer should have to hire other workers at higher wages to complete the work. In the case of the *kablan*, however, if he completes only half of his job and then retracts, his employer has the legal right to charge to the *kablan* any extra costs involved in completing the work.[72] Rashi, with characteristic clarity, explains the difference between a *poel* and a *kablan* in the following few words: "In the case of an employee by the day, the reason 'they are Mine servants, not servants of servants' is operative, but a *kablan* works for himself."[73] In other words, the *kablan* is his own master and the employer has no possessive rights over his person. The day-worker, however, is in his *person* obligated to the employer, and therefore, not permitting him to retract would imply that there exists an *obligatio* of his personality.[74]

This principle was applied regularly and consistently, always with the aim of barring any relationship or contract which would even by implication suggest the assumption of possessive rights in a human being. Thus Maimonides ruled:

In things without material substance, no *kinyan* (act of agreement) is valid. For instance, if a written instrument sets forth that one person, by a *kinyan*, agrees to engage in business partnership with another, or that they should divide the field which they jointly possess, or that they should become partners in a trade and other such like things, this is a *kinyan debarim* (an oral agreement), and is of no validity at all. For he has not transferred to his friend a known and determined thing, neither a definite principle, nor definite fruit thereof.[75]

In another place, Maimonides states:

If artisans establish a joint partnership in the future earnings of their artisanship, even though the agreement was confirmed by a *kinyan suddar* (a symbolic exchange), the partnership is not valid. For instance, if two tailors or two weavers stipulate to share equally whatever each one of them will earn by his work, the partnership is legally void, because one cannot transfer to another that which has not yet come into the world. But if the two purchase cloth with money which they hold in joint partnership and manufacture garments and sell the garments, or if they buy yarn with money which they hold in joint partnership and weave cloth and sell the manufactured goods, then they are legal partners and whatever profit will result from their joint earnings or business transactions they share equally.[76]

Behind this law, as defined by Maimonides, lies the principle that a contractual obligation can be incurred only on property. Thus, if two people who do not possess equal ownership in a determined and known object wish to obligate themselves legally to share their future earnings or their future business transactions, they wish, in effect, to bind their personalities. This, in accordance with Maimonides' legal opinion, is a *kinyan debarim*, an oral agreement which has no validity. To legally bind one person to another, without their being bound by property, is a form of slavery.

The equation of such an agreement with slavery is clearly set forth by the Rabbis. The reason given by the Talmud for the right of an employee to retract even in the middle of the day was used by the Tannaim in rebuking slaves who refused to accept their freedom. Rabban Johanan ben Zakkai, commenting on the biblical law that if a Hebrew slave, after completing six years of service, refuses to go free, "his master shall bore his ear through with an awl and he shall serve him forever,"[77] said: "Why has the ear been distinguished from all other organs of the body to be bored. The Holy One blessed be He said,

'The ear heard My voice on Mount Sinai saying, "For unto Me are the children of Israel servants," but not servants to other servants, and yet he went and acquired a master for himself, therefore, shall it be bored through.'"[78]

In brief, the rabbinic view that man is a servant of God precludes his becoming the personal property of another man. Hence, the Halakah formulated rules outlawing and voiding any action which could imply, even in the slightest degree, that one man can establish ownership or legal obligation in the personality of another.

The sacredness of the human personality, which expresses itself in the acceptance of servitude before God, prohibits even the suggested enslavement of one human being by another.

# 6. THE COMMUNITY

## THE INDIVIDUAL AND THE COMMUNITY

The belief in the sacredness of the human personality not only governs the relations of one individual to another; it defines man's relation to society as a whole. In the theocracy of Judaism each individual must share in the responsibilities of the social order, but is guaranteed that just as no individual can acquire ownership in him, so the group will never be given unlimited authority over his person.

In the Roman and Greek order, the "city," "state," or "society" had a value in themselves. The state, as a state, had metaphysical value, and the "state," "city," and "social order" are often spoken of as abstract institutions which take priority over the individuals who compose and constitute them. Thus we often hear of "crimes against the State" or "enemies of Society." This view ceded to the state unlimited authority over the individual.

In Jewish tradition, however, all such terms are unknown. The only reference found in the Bible to a standard of law which differs when applied to a community than when applied to an individual is that of an apostate city. If the majority of the residents of a city were seduced to worship idols, their sacrilegious act was considered a more serious defection than that of an individual. The verse, "Thou shalt smite the inhabitants of the city... destroying it utterly and all that is therein" (Deut. 13:16) comes to teach, the Mishnah tells us, "that the property of the righteous in the city is destroyed, but the property of the righteous which is outside the city is saved; but the property of the transgressors, whether inside of the city or outside it, is destroyed."[1] In this case, then, the property of the righteous is destroyed with that of the transgressors, but this is the only instance in which an innocent individual is made to suffer because of the group. In any other cardinal offense, even if a majority of the inhabitants of a city transgressed, all were judged as individuals.[2]

Rabbi Simon explained the destruction of the property of the righteous who lived in an apostate city by declaring, "What caused them to dwell in this city? Their property! Therefore, their property suffers destruction."[3]  A deeper moral significance is attached to Rabbi Simon's words by the Tosefta which adds the following to his statement: "Is it not a syllogism: If property is to be destroyed by fire, though it possesses no power of hearing, of listening, of speech, but only because it caused the righteous to dwell among the wicked, how much more should a man who leads his fellow man from the path of life to the path of death be punished by destruction through fire."[4]

In general the Rabbis held that a righteous inhabitant of a city extends his merit to the entire city, and one righteous member of a family lends merit to an entire family,[5] but they also considered it a moral wrong for a person to continue to live in a morally corrupt environment. Indeed the Mishnah records the counsel given by Nittai the Arbelite, "Keep thee far from an evil neighbor and consort not with the wicked and lose not belief in retribution."[6] In much stronger words does Maimonides offer the same advice in the *Mishneh Torah*:

> It is the natural instinct of man to be drawn in his attitudes and deeds after his friends and associates and conduct himself after the customs of his fellow citizens. Hence, a person should constantly associate himself with the righteous... and shun the wicked who walk in the darkness so that he may not learn from their conduct.... So too, if one lives in a province where the customs are evil and whose inhabitants do not walk in the right path, he should leave for a place where the people are righteous and follow the ways of the good. If all the provinces of which he has personal knowledge, or concerning which he received reports, follow a course which is not right...he should then live by himself in seclusion, as it is said "Let him sit alone and keep silent" (Lamentations 3:28). And if the inhabitants are evilminded and wicked and do not permit one to stay in the province unless he mixes with them and conducts himself in accordance with their customs, let him withdraw into caves, thickets or deserts and not habituate himself to the path of the sinners.[7]

Hence, according to Maimonides, complete seclusion from community life may be, under certain circumstances, the only path to follow.

## COMMUNITY RIGHTS

Despite the fact that Judaism has no concepts analogous to the Greek and Roman concepts of "state" or "society," it would be wrong to assume that the word "community" had no significance in the ancient Hebraic theocracy. There is no doubt that central authority did exist in the Jewish communities. Thus, it was the duty of the Great Sanhedrin to appoint qualified courts in every city.[8] There also seems to have existed a governing board of seven in most cities during the talmudic period.[9] The existence of such authority is further indicated by a statement in the Talmud which took on great importance during the Middle Ages, when the lay authority of individual communities had to take over control as the central authority of the judiciary and the rabbinate declined. The Talmud states that the residents of a city have the right to establish, by mutual consent, standards of measurement, market prices, and wages for employees, and can apply sanctions against those who violate such rules.[10] In other words, every community, by the mutual consent of its inhabitants, has the legal rights to develop its own city ordinances. This talmudic passage was the source for the development, in the Middle Ages, of the concept of a *kahal*, a congregation, and its right to introduce innovations and apply sanctions in community affairs.

It is important to note that when the Rabbis speak about communities, they never speak about the cities *per se* or about the authority of the cities. The reference is always to the inhabitants of the city or, to use the literal mishnaic term, "the children of the City." Furthermore, the Rabbis ignore the concept of "city property," and speak rather of the property which belongs to all the inhabitants of the city. Each citizen of the town is looked upon as a joint owner of all the things which belong to the people of the city. The following mishnah underscores this attitude:

If a man said to his fellow man: May I be to thee as *herem* [a thing that is banned], the latter is forbidden by his neighbor's vow to have any benefit from him. If he says: Be thou to me as *herem*, he that makes the vow is forbidden to have any benefit from the other. If he says: May I be to thee as *herem* and thou to me as *herem*, then each is forbidden to have any benefit from the other; both are permitted to benefit from the things that belonged to them who came up from

Babylonia, but are forbidden to benefit from the things that belong
to the [people of that] town. What are the things that belonged to
them who came up from Babylonia? Such as the Temple Mount,
the courts of the Temple, and the well that is midway on the road.
And which are the things which belong to the [people of that] town?
The public places, the bathhouse, the synagogue, the Ark [of the
Law] and the Books [of the Bible].[11]

The Temple Mount, the courts of the Temple, and the wells of the
road obviously were not considered the property of particular individuals or groups of individuals. Public places in the city, on the other
hand, were considered neither ownerless nor "city property." Every
individual who lived in the city had an equal share in its public places:
the synagogue, the Ark, the Books, and so on. Underlying the ruling
of this mishnah is the principle that there is no such thing as a state or
city in the abstract and metaphysical sense, but that every individual is a
joint owner and equal partner in all the things that the members of the
community share in common. Hence, if two people forbid each other
from having benefit from one another, they are forbidden to use those
things which may be called the belongings of the city, because in
reality each individual has an equal share in them.

Nowhere in tannaitic sources do we find acceptance of the concept
that the group, by virtue of its numbers, can create an abstract "society"
which has authority over the individual. The only source of authority
recognized by the rabbis was the court which interpreted the Torah and
rendered decisions applicable to the life of the individual as well as to the
life of the group. No group or society, simply by virtue of its numbers,
could exercise any authority independent of the individuals who composed it, nor is any authority ever granted to the group over the
individual.[12]

The only state the Rabbis were conscious of was the divine state of
God as revealed in the Torah and interpreted and transmitted by the
oral traditions. Any crime committed by an individual was never
thought of as an offense against the community or state. It was looked
upon as an offense against the individual who suffered by the act and as
a serious sin against the theocracy of Judaism which united all Israelites
in the "religious nationality" of Judaism.

### THE LAWS OF FINES

Many rabbinic laws emphasize that a man's actions are judged primarily by how they affect his relations with his fellow man and what we may call the divine state. It is certainly significant that such terms as "public enemy" or "enemy of society" are completely unknown in our sacred literature. This concept is also clearly revealed in the rabbinic understanding of the law of fines.

Rabbinic law concerning monetary matters is divided into two categories: monetary statutes in civil law are designated as *dinei mammonot;* fines, which are monetary penalties, are designated as *dinei kenasot.* While any court can render decisions in litigations of civil law, the authority to levy fines as penalties for forbidden actions was given only to those courts whose members had been ordained in Palestine by qualified judges who, in turn, were ordained by their teachers. Hence, the Exilarch in Babylonia could appoint judges to carry out the normal judicial functions, but such judges had no legal right to adjudicate cases involving *kenas* [fines].[13] The authority to levy fines, even such fines which are explicitly set forth in the Torah, rested only in a qualified court. This the rabbis adduced from the verse "He whom God shall condemn shall pay double unto his neighbor."[14] By "God," the rabbis declared, is meant the judiciary, and fines can be levied only by a qualified court upon the evidence of two witnesses.[15]

The most striking aspect of the Jewish law of fines, those that are specifically mentioned in the Torah as well as those which were instituted by the Rabbis, is that there was never a fine that had to be paid either to the court, the community, the society, or the state. True, the Torah never specifies to whom the fine should be paid,[16] but it is certainly significant that our Sages never even entertained the thought that monetary penalties be paid to the state or community. Their very silence on the subject is the strongest proof of their full acceptance of the principle that a fine is always to be paid to the one against whom the transgression was committed.

As stated, this principle applied not only to fines prescribed in the Torah, but also to fines instituted by rabbinic authority. This is illustrated by the tannaitic definition of a man's legal liability for damages caused by him.

Our Sages ruled that the law of the Torah which makes one legally responsible for damages caused to another's property[17] applies only to physical, that is, visible damages. If, however, one renders another's property valueless in that it can no longer be used *religiously*, then, according to the law of Moses (*deoraitha*) he has not caused damage for which he may be legally sued and no court of man can make him responsible for restitution. An example of this kind of damage is mixing a neighbor's produce, from which the *terumah*, the priestly offering, has already been separated, and which can, therefore, be eaten by everyone, with a *terumah*, which only a priest may eat. This act depreciates the value of the produce, for the owner can now sell it only to a priest, but does no physical, or visible, damage to it. Another example would be pouring libation wine used in pagan temples into another's wine, which prevents the owner from deriving any benefit from his wine. The Torah forbids the use of such products, but the person who commits such acts cannot be held legally responsible for the damages because he has not committed a visible act of damages. The dictum of our sages is, "An invisible act of damages does not constitute damages."[18]

The principle of *nezek she'eino nikar*, damage which is not visible, it can be seen, does not mean only "invisible damage." It refers to a type of damage which results from the acceptance of the principle of *din*, adherence to law. It is a loss suffered by the owner only because he is willing to abide by the religious law. Should he choose to disobey the law, such "damage" would cause him no loss at all. Perhaps another illustration will make this distinction clearer. If one pushes another's coin so that it rolls down into the sea, though the coin is still visible and no physical damage has been done to the coin, nevertheless, since the owner can no longer recover his property, the act constitutes a legal act of damage and is so considered by law.[19] In such cases, the Mishnah does not invoke the principle of "invisible damages." Rather, it states that anyone who commits such acts intentionally is responsible for damages caused.[20] The Tosefta explains this ruling by noting that it is a *kenas*, a fine, instituted by the authority of the court in order to prevent mischievous persons from committing such acts.[21] This is another of those ordinances enacted by our Sages for *tikun ha'olam*, "the betterment of the world," or more directly put, for the welfare of the group. Yet, and this is the important feature, the fine levied against such an individual is paid directly to the person who suffered the "invisible damage" and not to the court or state, as would normally be done in non-Jewish jurisprudence.

In this connection it is worth noting another point which emphasizes the uniqueness of the rabbinic understanding of the purpose of fines. Josephus, speaking of the penalties for causing a miscarriage to a pregnant woman, says: "He that kicketh a woman with child, if the woman miscarry, shall be fined by the judges for having by the destruction of the fruit of the womb diminished the population, and a further sum shall be presented by him to the woman's husband."[22] Philo also speaks of a double penalty, one for the outrage and the other for obstructing nature "in her creative work of bringing into life the fairest of living creatures, man."[23] It would appear, particularly from Josephus, that fines for having "diminished the population" ought to be paid to the state,[24] but such penalties are unkown in rabbinic literature. Tannaitic sources also state that a double fine must be paid in such cases, one for the injurious act to the woman and one for depriving the husband of a child. These indemnities, however, in accordance with the rabbinic tradition, are paid directly to the party who suffered the loss, and not to the state or community.[25]

## COMMUNITY LAWS AND TAXES

The Mishnah and the Talmud contain many laws touching on public worship, sacrifices and the procedures of congregational services. Such laws regulate and outline the structure and order of service to be followed in community worship. These laws pertain to what may be called "the religious community." It is therefore even more striking that there are almost no laws which relate to the community as a community or define the community as a legal entity.[26]

Most of the scattered laws in the Talmud pertaining to the authority of communities revolve around their right to levy taxes or to protect themselves. The Mishnah lays upon every resident of a city the responsibility of sharing in the expense of raising a wall around the city and setting into it gates and bolts.[27] Similarly, all residents of a city are

compelled to share in the expense of building a synagogue and purchas-
ing scrolls of the Laws and Prophets for it.[28] The Talmud tells us that
one of the ordinances enacted by Ezra the scribe was that spice merch-
ants who travel from town to town cannot be prohibited by the
dwellers of the town from plying their trade, to ensure "that cosmetics
may be easily available for the daughters of Israel," but that they cannot,
without the consent of its residents, settle permanently in a city.[29] In all
laws affecting the rights of municipalities, however, the scholar is
accorded an honored and favored position, for his presence in a city is
considered to be beneficial to that city. If, therefore, a spice merchant is
a scholar, he does not need the permission of the residents of a city to
settle there.[30] Another dictum of the Rabbis is: "All, including orphans,
pay taxes for the protection of the city, with the exception of scholars,
because their learning is their protection."[31]

The most unique aspect of the Jewish community, unparalleled in
the ancient world, was the attitude toward philanthropy. Viewed not
merely as a religious obligation, philanthropy was a legal responsibility
which could be enforced by the courts. Much has been written about
the Hebrew term *zedakah*, which denotes both charity and righteousness. But the most revealing feature in the concept of *zedakah* is that
while private philanthropy, that is the giving of charity by an individual
to an individual, was left to one's own discretion, contributing to the
common charity fund was enforceable by law. In one instance, as
related in the Talmud, Rabba, a fourth generation Amora, forced his
contemporary, Rab Nathan, who was a wealthy man, to give four
hundred *zuz* to the charity chest.[32] Maimonides outlines rabbinic
judicial procedure in such cases in the following words: "Whoever does
not wish to give charity or one who gives not as much as he can afford,
the court forces him to give and he receives the "punishment of rebellion" until he gives as much as they estimate he can afford to give."[33]
Communities everywhere generally have the right to levy taxes on
their residents "for all things from which all derive benefits."[34] But the
concept that the court can force a man to give to charity was unique to
the Jewish community, a concept unparalleled in ancient or modern
history.[35]

## RIGHTS OF NEIGHBORS

As against the scattered references in the Talmud to the authority of the
community, there is a vast literature in the Mishnah, Tosefta, and Talmud pertaining to *hilkhot shekhainim*, laws outlining the mutual responsibilities of immediate neighbors in a community. The principle of
individualism is so deeply ingrained in the philosophy of Judaism that
the Rabbis preferred to set laws governing man's relation to his fellow
man instead of detailing man's responsibility to the community and the
responsibility of the community for the individual. These laws clearly
illustrate the great consideration the Rabbis required every man to
extend to his neighbor.

Notable is the law which states that first call on the moral and legal
responsibilities a man owes his neighbors belongs to those closest to him,
whether by blood or proximity. This principle applies not only in
charity but also in financial transactions. On the verse in Exodus, "If
thou lend money to any of My people, even to the poor with thee, thou
shalt not be to him as a creditor,"[36] the Mekilta makes the following
statement:

> If a poor man and a rich man stand before you to borrow, [the poor
> man should be given preference. If it be your own poor relative]
> and the poor of your city, your own poor should be given preference
> over the poor of your city. If it be the poor of your city and the
> poor of another city, the poor of your city should be given preference,
> for it says, "Even to the poor with thee."[37]

Even stricter is the law governing the sale of property. If a man sells his
property, the neighbor whose property adjoins his has a legal right to
purchase the property, for he is a neighbor in the literal sense of the
word. Furthermore, according to rabbinic law, if one sells property,
his adjacent neighbor has the legal right of preemption. In rabbinic
terminology this law is known as the law of *bar metzrah* and gives an
individual a legal claim upon the property that adjoins his if it is put up
for sale, for he can argue "I am your next door neighbor and therefore
your first obligation is to me."[38]

With their deep moral outlook, however, our Sages protected the
seller from having to sustain a loss or scant on his obligations to his

nearest relations because of the physical proximity of a neighbor. Hence, if one sells his property in order to pay funeral expenses or to support a widow or to maintain his daughters, he is not bound by his reponsibilities to his next door neighbor. Since his needs are urgent he can sell to anyone who is ready to buy first.[39]

The law of preference, as set by the Talmud, is: an urban neighbor has preference over a rural neighbor; in the case of a neighbor and a scholar, the scholar has preference.[40] Maimonides, however, rules that the adjacent neighbor supercedes everyone. "Even if the buyer is a scholar," he writes, "or a relation to the seller, and the owner of the adjacent field is an *am ha-aretz* and not a blood relation, the latter still has preference and can evict the purchaser."[41] The principle that one's primary obligation is to his next door neighbor is based upon the verse, "And thou shalt do what is right and good in the sight of the Lord."[42] This obligation, however, was not looked upon merely as a moral duty, but as a legal responsibility. If one sells his property to anyone other than his adjacent neighbor, the latter has a right of preemption; he can present the purchase price and evict the buyer. This law, in my judgment, is the most thoroughgoing application to be found in the literature of any people of the principle that every man has a legal responsibility and a moral obligation to his neighbors.

## MAN'S RIGHT TO PRIVACY AND PEACE

Our Sages were concerned not only with defining man's legal rights but also with formulating rules to insure that in the exercise of those rights one person did not infringe upon the privacy of another. They gave full recognition to a person's right to privacy. The dictum of the Rabbis is: "Damage caused to one by the slights of another is real damage."[43] They further declared that looking through one's window into the courtyard of another (where in ancient times much of one's private affairs were conducted) or observing from one's roof (which in ancient times was often used for living quarters) the activities on the roof of an adjoining house, is a breach of privacy and constitutes an act of damage.[44]

Significant in these laws is the acceptance of the principle that interference with one's privacy constitutes legal damage for which one can sue in court. Since, as a rule, penalties for damages or injuries are exacted by the court only when a clear act of injury or damage has been committed, the law that interference with another's privacy in itself constitutes a damaging act is unique. It is another outgrowth of the rabbinic concept of individualism.

Together with the right to privacy, the Rabbis recognized man's right to peace. They established rules and regulations defining the circumstances under which a man can legally claim that his peace at home is disturbed by the actions of others. This right to peace and rest is set forth in one mishnah in terms which take on contemporary significance:

> A man may protest against another man who opens a shop within the courtyard and say to him, "I cannot sleep because of the noise of them that go in and out." He that makes utensils should go outside and sell them in the market. But none may protest against another and say, "I cannot sleep because of the noise of the hammer, or because of the noise of the millstone, or because of the noise of children."[45]

"Noise of the children," the Talmud explains, does not refer to the noise which children make when they go into a store to buy things, and it certainly never occurred to our Sages that the noise made by children in the home could become a cause of protest by next door neighbors. According to the talmudic definition, the law concerning the "noise of the children" rules that while neighbors can protest the opening of a store in a residential courtyard because the traffic of the purchasers disturbs their peace, they cannot protest the opening of an elementary school in a residential courtyard by arguing that the noise of the children interferes with their sleep.[46] This is another illustration of the deeply rooted regard which the Rabbis had for the Torah scholar and the advancement of Torah learning. The obligation of educating children supersedes one's right to personal peace and rest. It is quite possible that this attitude, the Rabbis thought, was the only one that could truly ensure man's ultimate peace of mind.

The desire to protect man's privacy and well-being determined many talmudic laws. Thus, if a man wishes to build a wall in his courtyard, he must build it at least four cubits away from his neighbor's window in order not to obstruct the other's light. If the window is low in the wall, the owner of the house can force him to build the wall four cubits higher than the window so that no one can look into his house and infringe upon his privacy.[47] Here again, one's right to build on his property is not a license to disregard his neighbor's comfort or privacy.

Furthermore, since one must be considerate of his neighbors and townspeople, it is forbidden to establish a business which may create unpleasant odors and discomfort the people of the town. A tannery, the Mishnah says, may be set up only in the eastern part of the town, because the prevailing wind in Israel is from the northwest and the east wind is mild and reduces the discomfort produced by the tanning of hides.[48] Moreover, a person may not build a permanent threshing floor within his own grounds unless his property extends fifty cubits in each direction, ensuring that the wind will not carry the chaff and injure his neighbors.[49] It is the rabbinic view that while each man has certain inalienable personal and property rights, he cannot exercise these rights if they interfere, even if only indirectly, with another's privacy, comfort, and mental peace. One does not possess "ownership" over himself, nor does one possess complete ownership over his material goods, and one certainly does not possess ownership over another individual.

### THOU SHALT NOT DESTROY

This concept is reflected in the laws which deal with man's own property, not only in relation to other persons, but specifically in relation to himself. Just as an overabundance of self-love creates selfishness, so is self-hatred, expressed in damage done to one's own property and wounds inflicted upon oneself, a form of selfishness. Self-hatred implies that one's being and property are his possessions with which he may do as he sees fit. Furthermore, if a man is not concerned with his own welfare, he is certainly less concerned with the welfare of his fellow man. This concept is implicit in the precept, "Thou shalt love they neighbor as *thyself*."[50]

The following halakic concept bears on the point under consideration. The Torah states: "When thou shalt besiege a city a long time, in making war against it to take it, thou shalt not destroy the trees thereof by wielding an ax against them, for is the tree of the field man, that it should be besieged of thee?"[51] Obviously the law prohibits, in time of war, the destruction of fruit trees which are a source of sustenance for the inhabitants, but the Halakah sees in this law a principle of even greater import, classified under the negative command of *lo tashhit*—"thou shalt not destroy." The law is not limited to fruit trees nor to property which belongs to another. As Maimonides points out, "One transgresses the negative command of 'Thou shalt not destroy'... also when, with destructive intent, he breaks household goods, tears clothes, destroys a building, stops up a spring or destroys articles of food."[52]

The main objective of this law, then, is to teach that man has no right to destroy anything useful, even if it is his own property. A man has legal rights over his property as long as he uses it to benefit himself or others; he has no right to destroy it. Thus if a man rends his own garment unnecessarily, or destroys any of his utensils or any other useful object, he transgresses the negative precept of *lo tashhit*.[53]

If a man has no right to damage his own property, he surely has no right to inflict damage upon his body. In the words of the Torah, "Only take heed to thyself and guard life well,"[54] our Sages saw an exhortation to man that he do everything in his power to preserve his own life and not commit any act which may be injurious to his physical well-being.[55] Our Sages therefore attempted to so regulate the life of the individual that he should not endanger his physical well-being, forbidding, for example, the drinking of liquids left uncovered, for fear that they may have become contaminated by poisonous creatures.[56] As part of their religious instruction they taught that whoever endangers his life violates a positive precept in the Torah.

In recording this principle, Maimonides states, "If one says: 'I want to endanger my life, what concern is it to others?' disciplinary flogging is to be inflicted upon him."[57] More significant than Maimonides' statement that a man incurs bodily punishment for endangering his life, is his statement that a man cannot declare that his physical welfare is of no concern to others. Man does not possess ownership in his own being. Any act which endangers his life is a transgression of the will of God. Man's life is the possession of the Holy One blessed be He, and any act

which endangers a human life is a transgression of His will. The
Almighty entrusted life to man to "guard it well," not to endanger its
well-being.

## KIDDUSH HA-SHEM AND HILLUL HA-SHEM

A fundamental principle in Judaism, and one of the primary motives
for the observance of the Law, is man's continuous struggle to achieve
*kedushah*, a state of holiness. The Torah states: "Ye shall be holy, for I
the Lord your God am holy."[58] It is the duty of man to be holy, for in
reaching the state of holiness he imitates the nature of God, and *Imitatio
Dei* is the cornerstone of Judaism. One of the Sages interpreted the
above verse as follows: "What is the duty of a King's train?—to
imitate the King."[59]

God sanctifies man, but it is also the duty of man to hallow God: "I
will be hallowed among the children of Israel: I am the Lord who hallows you."[60] This most characteristic feature of Judaism, which asserts
that man, with all his limitations and faults, can hallow God, and that
God demands of man that he be ready to hallow His Name, is known in
rabbinic literature as *Kiddush ha-Shem*. Man hallows the Name either
by performing an unusual act, one which is not required of him, particularly in the sphere of Jewish-heathen relationships, or through an
extraordinary demonstration of his devotion to God.

The opposite of *Kiddush ha-Shem* is *Hillul ha-Shem*. Profanation of
the Name is expressed through deeds, major or minor, which demean
the name of God. *Hillul ha-Shem* is relative, often depending upon the
dignity and position of the individual. An act which may be considered
a *Hillul ha-Shem* in one person may be considered natural and in-
offensive if performed by another. The scholar, for instance, has to
conduct himself with greater dignity than does the average man, for he
bears the crown of the Torah. Thus the Talmud says, "Every student
of the wise who indulges in meals everywhere, profanes the name of
Heaven, the name of his teacher, and the name of his Father."[61] In
discussing the question of what act constitutes a profanation of the Name,
Rab, the founder of the first Babylonian academy said: "In my case, if
I should buy meat from the butcher and not pay for it immediately."

Rabbi Johanan said: "In my case when I walk four ells without Torah and Phylacteries."[62] These statements obviously imply that for those who are expected to attain a higher standard of morality and piety, deviation even in matters which are considered minor may be taken as profanation of the Name.

*Kiddush ha-Shem* and *Hillul ha-Shem* have their greatest impact on public acts, acts performed by an individual either with the community or in the presence of the community. The Jewish concept of community is most clearly delineated in those religious acts which require an *Edah* (a community) before they can be performed publicly in the synagogue, and through the similar concept of *Zibbur* (group) which constitutes a "religious community."

The synagogue, which from time immemorial was the center of Jewish religious life, embodied the religious consciousness of the community. The synagogue, as regards worship, is not a place for private meditation; it is the place for community worship. Public prayers, therefore, cannot be recited except in the presence of ten men, the minimum number required to constitute an *Edah*, for when "ten pray together the *Shekinah* is with them."[63] "Whence do we learn that a congregation is made up of ten? It is written concerning the ten spies sent to Canaan, "How long shall I bear with this evil congregation?" (Num. 14:27).[64]

The synagogue, the projection of the Jewish concept of community, served as a means of hallowing the holy Name. The Mishnah rules that those features which are peculiar to congregational worship require the presence of ten male adults.[65] The reason for this ruling, the Talmud declares, is that through synagogue worship, the name of God is hallowed, and since God's name can be hallowed only through those prayers in which a community participates,[66] a minimum of ten men is required. Hence the prayers of *Kaddish* and *Kedushah*, which proclaim the sanctification of God's name, are said only as part of congregational services, because His name can be hallowed only in the presence of the group.[67] As an individual, one may hallow the Name by extraordinary acts, but the Name can be hallowed by words of the mouth, by prayer, only in the presence and with the participation of the congregation.

This requirement of community presence was not limited to public worship alone. Often, the determination of whether a man's actions constituted *Kiddush ha-Shem* or *Hillul ha-Shem* depended upon whether or not his actions were performed in private or in public, that is, before ten or more men. This can be illustrated best by examples. As a rule, a man must be ready to lay down his life rather than commit one of the three cardinal sins—idolatry, immorality, and homicide.[68] If he chooses, even under duress, to save his life by committing one of these three sins, he is guilty of the highest degree of *Hillul ha-Shem*. On the other hand, laying down one's life to avoid committing such a sin is the highest degree of *Kiddush ha-Shem*.

Concerning all commandments other than these three cardinal sins, the Rabbis laid down the rule that a man may, or rather is required to violate the commandments in order to save his life. Thus, if a heathen attempts to force a Jew to violate the law in order to derive some benefit for himself, the Jew should not yield. If, however, the heathen's only purpose is to force a Jew to transgress the law of God, the law is that if there are not ten Israelites present, he should transgress the law rather than suffer death. If, however, the choice is put to him in the presence of ten Jews, he must suffer death rather than transgress, because the presence of the group imposes upon him the duty of hallowing the Name of God.[69]

In other words, where the three cardinal sins are concerned, a man must hallow the Name and die rather than transgress, whether faced with the choice in private or before a group. All other commandments a man may transgress in order to save his life if there are no others to witness his transgression. In the presence of the community, however, a man may not transgress *any* commandment, major or minor, even to save his life, because in public one must hallow the Name for any and every point of the law. Even Rabbi Ishmael, who differed with his colleagues and argued that under duress one should perform an idolatrous act rather than suffer death, would apply his ruling only where a private act was concerned.[70] He would not insist upon his opinion where an act performed in the presence of ten people is concerned.

This halakah not only teaches us something about the concept of *Kiddush ha-Shem*, it underscores a basic rabbinic view of the relation between man and society. A man is limited in his actions if he seeks to do that which can hurt or inconvenience others. Actions must be carefully considered because each act which a man performs must demonstrate his acceptance of responsibility for the community as a whole.

The Jewish community in ancient Israel, particularly after the destruction of the Temple, was never so secure that it did not have to fear sudden persecution and attack. In fact, midrashic literature is more an outpouring of the sorrow, pain, and difficulties of the Jewish communities than a record of the normal joy and gladness of a folk. The fact that an entire tractate, *Taanit*, was dedicated to public fasts, not including the fast of the Day of Atonement, is ample proof of the miserable plight of the Jewish people and their endless yearning for the help and salvation of God.

Besides the threats from external enemies, Palestine, an agricultural country, was under the perpetual threat of famine, a result, ironically and paradoxically, of either too little or two much rain. The Mishnah, however, asserts, "They sound the *shofar* because of any public distress—may it never befall—but not because of an abundance of rain."[1] The fasts were mostly public fasts in which the entire community participated. Indeed, a premium was placed on community solidarity, with great resentment expressed against individuals who did not participate in community prayers and joint pleadings before the Heavenly Father. One who isolated himself from the community was looked upon as one who refused to share in the common plights and hopes. What is even more, one who kept himself aloof from the community was regarded as one who did not consider himself a part of the *religious community* of Israel, for it was primarily the observance of the laws of the Torah that made of the Jewish people "one body and one soul."[2]

It was Hillel who first declared, "Separate not thyself from the community and trust not in thyself until the day of thy death."[3] Both of these statements are in reality but one, for when a person is too confident of himself he often thinks that he does not need to participate in the affairs of the community. The Talmud states:

When the people of Israel are sunk in distress and one of them keeps himself aloof, the two ministering angels who accompany every man approach and lay their hands on his head and say, "This one who has kept himself aloof from the sorrow of the community will not see the consolation of the community." In another place we learned: When the community is sunk in sorrow, let not a man say, "I will go to my house and eat and drink and peace be upon thee, my soul." Rather should a man participate in the distress of the community, for thus do we find it with Moses our master, that he distressed himself with the congregation, as it is said, "and the hands of Moses were heavy; and they took a stone and put it under him and he sat thereon" (Ex. 17:12). Did Moses then not possess one pillow or one mattress upon which to sit? But thus did Moses say, "Since Israel is sunk in distress I too will be with them in their distress." And whoever grieves himself together with the community is privileged to see the consolation of the community.[4]

Clearly, the Talmud attached great importance to community solidarity, particularly in times of suffering and distress.

It is worthwhile to note that the Talmud distinguishes between two distinct types of individuals who disassociate themselves from the community. One is *haporesh min hazibur*, that is, he who keeps himself aloof from the community and shows no concern for community affairs or troubles. The other is *haporesh midarkai hazibur* (he who separates himself from the way of the community), that is, one who does not live in accordance with the laws of the Torah, one who rebels against the theocracy of Judaism. The latter is included among those who remain in Gehenna eternally and have no share in the world to come.[5] Rashi maintains that there really is no need for a separate category for men who separate themselves from the ways of the community. The Talmudic text, which lists such a category, he says, is not a correct reading, and such men are counted as heretics and Epicureans since they rebel against the tradition and observance of the Torah.[6] Maimonides, apparently, recognized no distinction between *haporesh min hazibur* and *haporesh midarkai hazibur*, for he writes:

One who has separated himself from the ways of the community, *even if he does not commit a transgression* but only holds aloof from the congregation of Israel and does not fulfill the commandments in common with his people, who shows himself indifferent when they are in distress, *who does not observe their fasts* but goes his own way as if he were one of the heathens of the land and as if he were not one of them [the Israelites]—such a person has no share in the world to come.[7]

Moreover, in his enumeration of those who hinder the effect of repentance, he includes *haporesh min hazibur.*[8]

Particularly significant is the statement of Maimonides that if a Jew does not participate in and is not concerned with the suffering and distress of the other members of the Jewish community, he excludes himself from the religious community in its totality. By isolating himself he demonstrates that he does not consider himself a member of the Jewish people. In effect, Maimonides here seems to declare that a Jew who does not concern himself with the destiny of his co-religionists rejects the racial and religious heritage by virtue of which he belongs to the Jewish community and *excommunicates himself* from the people of Israel. Even though he does not transgress any of the commandments, even though as an individual he observes the law to the fullest extent, if a Jew turns his back on the community at large, if he refuses to make common cause with his brethren, then he excludes himself from the Jewish community and has no share in the world to come. No other Jewish authority has expressed such an uncompromising as well as such a deeply rooted loyalty to the community of Israel.[9]

## MAN'S RESPONSIBILITY FOR THE WORLD

The concept that an individual must act as a responsible member of the community is reflected in rabbinic literature not only in relation to one's moral and legal obligations, but also in the purely theological or philosophical realm, that is, in relation to the concept of an individual's contribution to what we may call "the merit for the existence of the world."

First, as discussed above, it is a rabbinic doctrine that the mere fact that the world exists is evidence that the world is at least equally divided between good and evil, between meritorious deeds and wicked deeds. Should the iniquities of the inhabitants of the world ever exceed their good deeds, the entire world will be destroyed, as were Sodom and Gomorrah. The same doctrine is applied to states, cities, and individuals.

Hence, the world is looked upon as a scale in which the balance between good and evil must be maintained if it is to survive, for as soon as the evil outweighs the good, the world can no longer exist. Our Sages declare:

A man should always regard himself as if he were half virtuous and half guilty. If he fulfills one commandment, happy is his lot, for he presses down by his action the scale of merit in his favor. If he commits a transgression, woe is to him, for he presses down by his action the scale of guilt against him. Concerning such an instance it is written, "And one sinner destroyeth much good" (Ecc. 9:18). Simon ben Eliezer says: Because the individual is judged in accordance with the majority of his actions, therefore, should a man always regard himself as half virtuous and half guilty. If he fulfills one commandment happy is his lot, for he presses down the scale of merit in his favor and in favor of the entire world. If he commits one transgression, woe is it to him, because by his action he presses down the scale of guilt against himself and against the entire world. Concerning such an instance it is written, "And one sinner destroyeth much good." Because of one single sin which he commits, he destroys much good for himself and for the entire world.[10]

This doctrine embodies the unique concept that one individual can by a single action, either good or bad, determine the ultimate existence of the entire world. Each human being, therefore, must weigh each of his daily actions not only for its effect on him, but also for its effect on the well-being of the entire world.

On this principle rests the rabbinic belief that the world may at times exist only through the merit of one righteous man, as it is written, "The righteous are the foundation of the world."[11] Statements expressing this view are legion: Even for the sake of one righteous man the world was created; No sooner does one righteous man depart from this world than another righteous man who is his equal is born; The Holy One Blessed be He foresaw that the righteous are few in number and He therefore planted them in each generation.[12] Rabbi Meir said: Great is the virtue of repentance; because of the repentance of one individual the entire world is forgiven.[13] The soul of one righteous man equals the entire world.[14] The world exists on one pillar and its name is the righteous.[15] Sometimes our Sages speak of thirty-six, sometimes of forty-five righteous men for whose sake the world exists;[16] in one place they declare: Because of thirty righteous Gentiles do the nations of the world exist.[17]

Through all these passages runs but one thought: were it not for the meritorious deeds of one or a few righteous individuals to counter-balance the wicked acts of the majority, the world could not exist.

Philo Judaeus, using almost the same terminology as the Rabbis, developed, in two fine passages, the same idea of the power of a single righteous man to maintain the world. In one place he writes:

Every wise man is a ransom for the fool, whose existence could not endure for an hour did not the wise provide for his preservation by compassion and forethought. The wise are as physicians who fight against the infirmities of the sick...we should try, as well we may, to save even those whom the evil within them is bringing to certain ruin, and follow the example of the good physicians who though they see that there is no hope for the patient, yet render their services gladly, lest others should think, in the event of some disaster which they did not expect, that it was due to the physician's neglect. For my part, when I see a good man living in a house or city, I hold that house or city happy and believe that their enjoyment of their present blessing will endure and that their hopes for those as yet lacking will be realized. For God, for the sake of the worthy, dispenses to the unworthy His boundless and illimitable wealth.... So when I see or hear that any of them is dead, my heart is sad and heavy. Not for them. They have reached in due course of nature the end we all must reach. They have lived in happiness and died in honor. It is for the survivors that I mourn. Deprived of the strong protecting arm which brought them safety, they are abandoned to the woes which are their proper portion, and which they soon will feel, unless indeed nature should raise up some new protectors to replace the old.... As then in the city good men are the surest warrant of permanence, so in the commonwealth of the individual composed of soul and body, the strongest force to ensure stability belongs to the aspirations of the reason to wisdom and knowledge.[18]

And again, commenting on the biblical verse, "In thee all the tribes of the earth shall be blessed,"[19] which he considered "a pregnant and significant" announcement, Philo wrote that "the righteous man is the foundation on which mankind rests" and called upon all men to "pray that like a central pillar in the house, there may constantly remain for the healing of all maladies the righteous mind in the soul and in the human race a righteous man."[20]

The theological doctrine of the power of the righteous to tip the balance in favor of an entire community and to intercede in behalf of his fellow men is frequently enunciated in the Bible and in rabbinic literature. The Torah tells us that Abraham prayed to God in behalf of Abimelech, and God healed Abimelech and his wife and his maidservants.[21] Moses too, constantly prayed in behalf of the Jewish community. Our Sages consider it a duty for one man to intercede with God in behalf of another, declaring, "Whoever is able to plead God's mercy for his fellow man and does not do so is a sinner."[22] In a similar vein, they say that whoever pleads God's mercy for another and is himself in need of the same thing, his need is granted first.[23] In fact, there is hardly a prayer in the Jewish prayer book which is merely a plea for one's own welfare. Nearly all prayers are phrased in the plural so that every person intercedes with God in behalf of the entire community.[24] Rabbi Joshua ben Hananiah was of the opinion that the standard prayers for the welfare of the entire community take precedence over the prayers for personal needs. Some rabbinic authorities were also of the opinion that even a solitary traveler on the road, when he prays for God's protection, should pray in the plural, "May it be thy will, O Lord our God, to lead *us* in safety."[25]

The belief in the efficacy of the prayers of the saint is based on the doctrine that a man of personal piety has a closer relationship with God, that God is more accessible to him and answers his prayers sooner. The most outstanding example of the power of the intercession of the saint is that of Honi the Circle-maker who lived in the last century B.C.E. Once, when he prayed for rain, his prayers were fulfilled and it began to rain, but only drop by drop. "Not for this rain have I prayed," he cried out, "but for rain that will fill the cisterns, pits and caverns." It then began to rain with violence. He then said, "Not for such rain have I prayed, but for rain of good will, blessing and graciousness," and it rained in moderation. His contemporary, and then head of the Sanhedrin, Simeon ben Shetah, felt that it was impudent and irreverent for Honi to address himself directly to God, and especially to swear by the Name and declare, "I will not stir hence until Thou have pity on Thy children." Therefore, the Mishnah relates:

> Simeon ben Shetah sent to him [saying]: "Hadst thou not been Honi [the great saint] I would have decreed a ban against thee! But what shall I do thee?—thou importunest God and He performs thy will, like a son that importunes his father and he performs his will; of thee Scripture saith: "Let thy father and thy mother be glad, and let her that bore thee rejoice" (Prov. 23:25).[26]

## ALL ISRAELITES ARE GUARANTORS FOR ONE ANOTHER

As indicated, not only do the righteous have the power to intercede in behalf of their fellows, it is in a sense their duty to do so. This duty, however, is not limited to the righteous. It is an accepted principle in the democratic theocracy of Judaism that all Israelites are perpetual sureties for each other and are responsible for one another's misdeeds.[27]

This principle of what may be called "spiritual surety" applies to cases where protesting against another's wicked deeds may prevent them from being committed. Failure to protest in such a case becomes tantamount to serving as an indirect cause of another's sin and makes one share responsibility for it:

> Whoever is able to protest against the transgressions of his own family and does not do so is punished for the transgressions of his family. Whoever is able to protest against the transgressions of the people of his city and does not do so is punished for the transgressions of the people of his city. Whoever is able to protest against the transgressions of the entire world and does not do so is punished for the transgressions of the entire world.[28]

This concept of responsibility is of course reciprocal. If the individual is responsible for the acts of the community, the community is responsible for the acts of the individual. On the verse, "And ye shall be unto Me a kingdom of priests and a holy nation,"[29] the Mekilta states: "It teaches us that they [Israel] are one body and one soul... if one of them sinned they are all punished, as it is written, "Did not Achan the son of Zerah commit a trespass concerning the devoted things and wrath fell upon all the congregation of Israel and that man perished not alone in his iniquity" (Joshua 22:20).[30]

The *Mekilta of Rabbi Ishmael* commenting on the verse, "I am the Lord thy God," places the enunciation of this principle at the Revelation of Mount Sinai:

This proclaims the excellence of Israel. For when they all stood before Mount Sinai to receive the Torah they were all of an equal mind to accept the reign of God joyfully. Furthermore, they pledged themselves for one another. And it was not only concerning the overt acts that God, revealing Himself to them, wished to make His covenant with them, but also concerning secret acts, as it is said, "The secret acts belong to the Lord our God, and the things that are revealed, etc." (Deut. 29:28). But they said to Him: Concerning overt acts we are ready to make a covenant with Thee, but we will not make a covenant with Thee in regard to secret acts lest one of us commit a sin secretly and the entire community be held responsible for it.[31]

According to this, the community is held responsible for the acts of the individual only when it is cognizant of such acts and can use its influence to prevent them. For acts committed in secret, however, the community bears no responsibility; in such cases the failure of the community to act cannot be considered a contributory factor in the misdeeds.[32]

Since, however, the group and the individual do bear a mutual responsibility, there are times when one man's wrongdoing can bring suffering upon the community, as in the case of Achan. It is, therefore, the duty of the individual to so conduct himself that his actions pose no danger for society at large. If it should happen that calamity overtakes a community, each member must carefully review his actions to determine whether his misdeeds have brought this suffering on the group. In fact, in times of great community distress, such as drought or plague, when a public fast was to be proclaimed, "The elder of the assemblage addresses them with words of admonition: My sons, let no one be ashamed because of his action. It is better that a man be humiliated in the presence of his fellow men because of his action, than that he

and his children be oppressed by starvation."[33] It was on occasions such
as these that public confession was urged upon the sinner,[34] for it was
taken for granted that the misfortunes of the entire community were
due to the sinful actions of the individual.

There is an interesting corollary to this principle of mutual responsibility which demonstrates how consequent the Rabbis were in applying
their religious principles to legal decisions and how organically related
these principles are. Mutual responsibility requires that one rebuke a
fellow man who is about to commit an offense, possibly preventing its
completion. At the same time, it is forbidden to circulate tales, even if
they are true, concerning the past deeds of a neighbor. The biblical
law, "Thou shalt not go up and down as a talebearer among thy
people,"[35] is applied in such instances. In innumerable passages the
Talmud stresses the seriousness of the offense of circulating an evil report
against another person.[36] Maimonides defines a "talebearer" as:

> One who carries reports, and goes about from one person to another
> and says: So and so said this; Such and such a statement have I heard
> about so and so. Even if what he says or reports may be true, the
> talebearer ruins the world. There is still a graver offense that comes
> with this prohibition, namely, the "evil tongue." This means talking
> disparagingly of anyone, even though what one says is true. But he
> who utters falsehood is called a slanderer. A person with an evil
> tongue is one who, sitting in company, says: That person did such a
> thing; So and so's ancestors were so and so; I have heard this about
> him, and he proceeds to relate malicious things.[37]

It is apparent, then, that circulating reports about another person, even
when they are true, with the intent of injuring his reputation, or even if
the intent is lacking but such is the result, is one of the most serious
offenses possible. In fact, our Sages liken it to the denial of the existence
of God.[38] Hence, while it is the duty of every individual to remon-
strate against wrongdoing, our Sages considered "witch-hunting" and
the destruction of a man's reputation, even of a man who has committed
a wrong act, in itself a far more serious offense than the original misdeed.

It is the responsibility of every man to help prevent wrongdoing, but
it is also the responsibility of each man to protect and respect the name
and reputation of his fellow man, an extension of the fundamental

belief in the sacred worth of the human personality. The accepted doctrine is that "all Israelites are guarantors for each other"[39] and are responsible for one another's actions. But the biblical verse, "Thou shalt surely rebuke thy neighbor" (Lev. 19:17) which teaches us that it is the duty of every man to return the erring person to the right path also declares, "Thou shalt not bear sin because of him." This means that one is not permitted to rebuke the sinner so as to cause him to change color.[40] Here again we have a demonstration of how fundamental to the rabbinic world-view is the principle of the sacredness of the human personality.

## THE MORAL RESPONSIBILITY OF THE HEADS OF THE COMMUNITY

The Talmud mentions various types of community functionaries: judges, the "seven best men of the city," heads of synagogues, "associates of the city," parnasim, who appear to have been lay heads of communities (though this title is interchanged with the term judges and kings),[41] gabaim, who administered the charity funds, and those who were in charge of distributing these funds. Two scholars were responsible for collecting the money for charity and three scholars were placed in charge of the distribution of the funds.[42] Rabbi Jose once proclaimed: "May my share of responsibility be among the collectors of the charity fund and not among its distributors," because, as Rashi explains, too often one may err in determining who deserves more and who deserves less help.[43]

With the exception of the gabaim shel zedakah and the mehalkai zedakah, the administrators of the charity funds and the distributors of such funds, it is difficult to determine the exact functions of the other officials. The judge seems to have occupied the most important position in the community because he was the scholar, the interpreter of the Torah, and the one who had to render decisions in accordance with the traditions of the Written and Oral Law. It is not the intention here, however, to discuss the structure and history of the Jewish community in Talmudic times.[44] The primary purpose is to define the moral philosophy of the Talmud in relation to the individual and the community.

The trend in all rabbinic sources is to emphasize the importance of scholarship and, above all, moral integrity for the judge, or, for that matter, for any other official of the community. Just as the Rabbis condemned the individual who isolates himself entirely from the Jewish community, so they condemned the community leader who uses his office for personal benefit or for self-glorification. The motive for one's engagement in public affairs must always be service for "its own sake," which in rabbinic terminology means for the sake of God. Thus, Rabban Gamaliel the son of Rabbi Judah the Patriarch said: "And let all who labor for the community labor for the sake of Heaven."[45] The community leader who uses his high office to arouse excessive fear in the hearts of the members of the community is classified among the "wicked in Israel" and perishes both in body and soul.[46] Maimonides places such a leader in the same category with those who separate themselves entirely from the community and have no share in the world to come.[47]

It is on account of three types of people, declare our Sages, that God sheds tears every day: For those who can afford to engage in the study of the Torah and do not, for those who cannot afford to engage in the study of the Torah and do, and for community leaders who treat the public arrogantly.[48] The last statement may be understood in its historical perspective. In ancient times it was the custom, particularly on the Sabbath, for lay members of the congregation to sit on the floor, literally, and listen to the discourse of the Interpreter of the Law. The Rabbis, therefore, level severe criticism at a judge who treats laymen with disrespect and forces his way through the holy congregation thus seated in order to reach his own seat. The Talmud characterizes such a judge as one "who steps over the head of the holy people."[49] Most eloquently does Maimonides set forth the respect which, in the rabbinic view, a leader should have for his community and the community for its leader:

> He is also forbidden to treat the people with light-mindedness. Though they may be ignorant, he should not step upon the heads of the holy people. Though they be ordinary people and lowly in their estate, nonetheless they are the children of Abraham, Isaac and Jacob. They are the hosts of God whom He brought forth out of Egypt with great power and a mighty hand. He should bear patiently the cum-

berance and burdens of the community, as did Moses our master, concerning whom it is said: "As a nursing father carries a suckling child" (Num. 11:12). It is also said: "And I charged your judges" (Deut. 1:16). This is an injunction to the judge to bear patiently with the community as does a nursing father with a suckling child... it is said... that God said to Moses and Aaron [you are to be leaders] with the full understanding that they will curse you and cast stones at you (*Sifre*, Num. 91, on Num. 11:11). Just as the judge is bidden to conduct himself in accordance with this commandment so is the community bidden to bestow honor on the judge, as it is said: "And I commanded you" (Deut. 1:18); it is an injunction for the community that the fear of the judge be upon them (Sanhedrin 8a).[50]

In general, Jewish tradition places great stress on the great democratic concept of respect—respect which the public functionary must have for the members of the community, and they for him. A study of rabbinic literature cannot help but impress one with these democratic principles which underlie the Jewish way of life. Our Sages never lost an opportunity to emphasize the moral responsibilities which the individual must feel for other human beings and for the community at large, and again, the reverence which the community, expressing itself through its leadership, must have for the ordinary man. These principles do not derive from social or political theories; they are direct outgrowths of the central Jewish concept of the sacredness of the human personality and its infinite worth.

### THE WILL OF THE COMMUNITY

Nowhere in rabbinic sources do we find reference to the present day method of preserving a democratic order, namely the selection of officers through the instrumentality of public election, by which process the elected officer becomes, in essence, an agent through whom the public will is expressed.[51] Nonetheless, it is to be recognized that there is hardly a democratic constitution which gives as clear and as firm an enunciation of the fundamental principles of a spiritual democracy as did the Rabbis of old in their theocratic approach to life.

In the Jewish social structure of old, the officers of a particular community, or the community at large, were not elected by popular vote requiring them to express the will of the community. In their private and official conduct the leaders had to express the will of God, which man can do only by practicing toward his fellow man the divine attributes of mercy and kindness. By vigilantly protecting the rights of every individual, regardless of how humble his station in life may be, the officers carry out this divine task. Man thus serves God by maintaining a moral relationship with his fellow men in the community through his devotedness to the divine disciplines. This is his acceptance of "the yoke of the Kingdom of Heaven."

But while in the democratic theocracy of Judaism the officers and judges of the community are guided not by the expressed will of the people but by the divine constitution, the attitude of the public was a deciding factor in the appointment of officers and judges, as it was in determining many religious and civil decrees which the Sanhedrin instituted. The Talmud states, "We do not appoint an officer in the community unless we first consult with the community."[52] This respect for the will and opinion of the community was accorded legal recognition of wide import.

The authority of the court, particularly the Sanhedrin which sat in the Chamber of Hewn Stones,[52a] was not limited to the interpretation of Biblical Law. It was vested with the authority of determining the accuracy of the oral traditions and instituting prohibitions which were in effect supplementary phases of the law and extensions of the principles behind it, even when such principles are not explicitly stated in the Torah. Such prohibitions were classified as *isurei derabbanan*, rabbinic prohibitions. In addition, when the exigencies of time, or, as the rabbis call it, the "need of the hour," demanded the temporary suspension of expressly stated laws of the Torah, this court did not hesitate to act, if in its judgment such acts would bring the community back to observance and stamp out religious laxity.[53] Then too, from time to time, the courts instituted general *takkanot*, innovations or decrees, which, though they did not have their origin in the law, were still not contrary to the traditional law. In the judgment of the court these decrees were a "fence for the law," that is, decrees which served to remove man from the danger of breaking the law itself.

A determining principle in framing general decrees instituted by the rabbis was laid down by Rabban Simon ben Gamaliel and Rabbi Elazar ben Zadok: "We do not issue a decree upon the community unless the majority of the community can stand up under it."[54] There is another rabbinic ruling, that a contemporary court cannot abolish the decree of an earlier court unless it is superior to the former in knowledge and in number,[55] but this principle, too, seems to have been applied only when the decree of the former court was accepted by the majority of the community.[56] Fundamental to this principle is the view that while the Sanhedrin has the power to institute decrees, the authority of its decrees cannot extend beyond the will or the ability of the people to accept them. This, of course, does not refer to a community which does not accept the authority of its court, but to a community which accepts the authority of the court but finds it impossible to fulfill its decrees. This approach truly reflects an essential principle in Jewish law: respect for the opinion of the public and care never to burden it beyond its capacity.

Needless to say, steps were taken to make this enligthened and ideal policy a realistic one. The people were trained in the law and taught always to respect the decisions and decrees of the courts of former genreations. Hence, even if the majority of the community failed to accept a decree, it still remained binding on the public until officially abrogated by the court. The authority of later courts to abrogate decrees which were not accepted originally by the majority of the community stems from the rabbinic dictum, "Every decree which the court ordains upon the community and which the majority of the community does not accept, has no force."[57]

Our Sages had such respect for public practice, *minhag*, that often, when they themselves were in a quandary in a particular matter concerning the proper halakic decision, they accepted the practice common among the members of the community as authoritative. Hence, the Talmud says: "If the halakah is undetermined in court and you do not know what its nature is, go forth and see what the community is accustomed to do, and then conduct yourself accordingly."[58]

In essence, this statement of the Jerusalem Talmud means that when the court is uncertain of the nature and application of a particular law, it can rely on the practice of the community, in the faith that such practice is based upon an ancient legislative source which is not known to the present court. It is, therefore, above all, an expression of faith in the community; that its practices are rooted in halakic sources, even though those sources are unknown to the present court. This is the authority of *minhag* as defined in a responsum by one of the leading rabbinic authorities of the Middle Ages, Rabbi Asher ben Jehiel, better known as Rosh or Asheri.[59]

A similar view is found in the treatise *Soferim*: "The statement that the *minhag* may supercede the halakah, has reference only to *minhag vatikim* (a custom of distinguished scholars), but a *minhag* which has no evidence in the Torah to support it is equivalent to an error in judgment."[60] According to this interpretation, custom *per se*, particularly in matters of ritual law, does not have binding force, unless practiced by distinguished scholars, which is *ipso facto* a legislative source.

Often quoted is the declaration by Rabbi Hoshiah, recorded in the Palestinian Talmud, that a custom can sometimes abolish a law.[61] Dr. Isaac Herzog has already noted that this statement deals only with civil law and therefore has no bearing on the legal authority of *minhag* in purely religious matters, where the consent of the individuals involved has no bearing.[62] Rabbi Hoshiah's words are directed at the Mishnah: "If one hired laborers and bade them to work early or to work late, he has no right to compel them to do so where the custom is not to work early or not to work late; where the custom is to give them their food, he should give it to them, and where the custom is to provide them with sweetstuff, he should provide it. Everything should follow the custom of the land."[63] Here the *minhag* establishes the presumption that even without any express stipulation, the intention of the laborers was to follow the common usage of the local community.[64]

The legal force of public custom manifests itself also in other instances. The Talmud records a disagreement between Rabbi Meir and Rabbi Eliezer ben Jacob, both outstanding rabbinic authorities. Generations later we find a difference of opinion among three Amoraim, appertaining to this controversy. One said the halakah was decided according to the opinion of Rabbi Eliezer ben Jacob, another one said that the *minhag* is according to the opinion of Rabbi Eliezer ben Jacob, while the third one said the people were accustomed to practice (*nahagu*) in accordance with the opinion of Rabbi Eliezer ben Jacob.[65] Similarly, concerning another dispute which Rabbi Meir had with his colleagues, Rabbi Johanan said, "The people were accustomed to practice in accordance with the opinion of Rabbi Meir."[66] It is apparent, therefore, that on certain occasions the community at large chose to conduct itself in accordance with the opinion of a particular sage. In such cases the *minhag* acquired authorative legal standing.

The Talmud makes this interesting observation concerning the legal force of the three catagories, halakah, *minhag*, and *nahagu ha-am*, mentioned here. If we say the halakah is like Rabbi Meir, then we teach it to the disciples, and we render decisions accordingly if people inquire. If we say the *minhag* is like Rabbi Meir, we do not teach it to the disciples, but if people inquire we tell them to conduct themselves according to the *minhag*. If we say *nahagu ha-am*, the people themselves are accustomed to practice like Rabbi Meir, then we neither teach it to the disciples, nor render decisions accordingly when the people inquire. Whoever conducts himself in accordance with that opinion, let him do so; we do not ask him to change his practice.[67]

This rabbinic analysis expresses a fundamental attitude of the Talmud towards the validity of public practice. If the law concerning a particular practice was decided by a learned court, then it is taught to the disciples in school so that they may know how to render a decision. If it is only a *minhag* then we may assume that it has authority and that at one time scholars probably rendered such a decision. Nevertheless, we do not teach it to the disciples as law because, after all, we do not have definite knowledge of the origin of the *minhag*. But if a practice prevails merely on the principle of *nahagu ha-am*, that is, the people on their own authority have taken a decision to conduct themselves in accordance with a particular opinion, then we do not interfere with their practice, but we do nothing to perpetuate it. The layman's decision or practice cannot serve as an authorative source for the court and therefore it is not taught to the disciples nor can the court sanction it officially if people inquire after the accepted practice.[68]

### PUBLIC SERVICE AND SCHOLARSHIP

In view of the great weight given to public opinion and practice, community leaders, if they are to lead and not be led, have to bring a weight of their own to their position. In the view of our Sages, there was no more weighty or overpowering force than knowledge and learning.

Superiority in scholarship was, in a sense, the main prerequisite for any officeholder in the community. The greatest resentment of our Sages was reserved for the appointment to any public position of a man who was not well versed in Torah learning. If our Sages recognized any form of aristocracy, it was the intellectual and spiritual aristocracy of scholarship "for the sake of Heaven."[69] The following passage from *Pirke R. Meir* demonstrates this rabbinic attitude:

> Whoever labors in the Torah for its own sake merits many things, and not only so, but the whole world is indebted to him: he is called friend, beloved, a lover of the All-Present, a lover of mankind; it clothes him with meekness and reverence; it fits him to become just, pious, upright and faithful; it keeps him far from sin, and brings him near to virtue; through him the world enjoys counsel and sound knowledge and strength, as it is said "Counsel is mine and sound knowledge; I am understanding, I have strength" (Prov. 8 : 14); and it gives him sovereignty and dominion and discerning judgment; to him the secrets of the Torah are revealed; he is made like a never failing fountain, and like a river which flows on with ever sustained vigor; he becomes modest, long-suffering, and forgiving of insults, and it magnifies and exalts him above all things.[70]

Our Sages found in the scholar the qualities of personal piety, humility, and wisdom which are required when dealing with other men. It is no wonder then that the rabbinic ideal was for every public functionary to be above all a scholar of distinction. It can be readily understood, however, that a serious scholar was always faced with a dilemma. Was it worthwhile to sacrifice scholarship for the sake of rendering service to the community? Thus, Rabbi Joshua ben Levi once complained that because he was occupied with the needs of the community he forgot a great part of his learning.[71] On the other hand, if the scholar were to divorce himself completely from the affairs of the community, the leadership of the community would ultimately fall into the hands of men who are not versed in the Torah and the cause of justice and piety would suffer.

Living in a society in which scholarship was a prerequisite for practical contributions to the well-being of the community, many a scholar in ancient times must have faced this problem. Should he isolate himself in an ivory tower and dedicate his entire life to the study of the Torah or should he apply his knowledge to public service? The question as to which takes priority was put on the agenda at the famous conference in Lydda during the Hadrianic persecution in this form: "Is studying more important or doing?"[72] Rabbi Tarfon was of the opinion that doing is more important; Rabbi Akiba said that studying is more important because "studying leads to doing." The conference voted unanimously in favor of Rabbi Akiba's opinion because it was the rabbinic notion that the "practical usefulness" of a person in the life of the community depends on his scholarship.[73]

Placing responsibility for public service in the hands of Jewish scholars was not limited to Palestinian and Babylonian Jewry. The Hellenistic Jewish community, too, followed this practice. Philo Judaeus and his brother Alexander were the two outstanding Jews in ancient Alexandria, the former because he was acknowledged as the outstanding Jewish philosopher of his time, the latter because he was the richest Jew in Egypt, if not in the world.[74] Except for the fact that his son became an apostate and served under Titus in the invasion of Jerusalem, we know nothing of Alexander's association with Jewish life, though Josephus gives him the official title of "Alabarch." Philo Judaeus, however, was dedicated to public service. At the time of the riots in Alexandria, which broke out because the Jews refused to place cult statues of Gaius in their synagogues, the philosopher was chosen as the head of the embassy to Gaius to plead with him not to force the Jews to do that which was contrary to their religious principles. One may accept Professor Goodenough's contention that while we have definite knowledge of only this single example of Philo's public service, drawn from his treatises *In Flaccum* and *Legatio ad Gaium*, yet his other writings bear ample evidence of the fact that much of his time was dedicated to the service of the Jewish community in Alexandria.[75] It is in the analytic writings of Philo, as nowhere else, that the inner struggle of the scholar, torn between his burning desire to devote himself exclusively to the world of scholarship and his sense of compelling obligation to be of service to the community, is most sharply delineated. In the introduction to his third book of *Special Laws*, Philo writes:

> There was a time when I had leisure for philosophy and for the contemplation of the universe and its contents, when I made its spirit my own in all its beauty and loveliness and true blessedness, by some God-sent inspiration, a fellow traveller with the sun.... Then I gazed down from the upper air, and straining the mind's eye beheld, as from some commanding peak, the multitudinous world-wide spectacle of earthly things, and blessed my lot that I had escaped by main force from the plagues of mortal life. But yet, as it proved, my steps were dogged by the deadliest of mischiefs, the hatred of the good, envy, which suddenly set upon me and ceased not to pull me down with violence till it had plunged me down in the ocean of political cares where I am still swept away, unable to raise my head above the water. Yet amid my groans I hold my own, for planted in my soul from my earliest youth, I keep the yearning for education which ever has pity and compassion for me, lifts me up and relieves my pain.... And if unexpectedly I obtain a spell of fine weather and a calm from political turmoils, I get me wings and ride the waves and almost tread the lower air, wafted by the breezes of knowledge which often urge me to come to spend my days with her, a truant as it were, from merciless masters in the shape not only of men but also the variety of practical affairs, which pour in on me like torrents from different sides.[76]

It would be hard to find another passage in Jewish literature which describes so poetically the never ending struggle of the scholar suddenly caught up in the maelstrom of public service, thirsting to continue his studies and researches in the Torah, and, in Philo's case, also in general philosophy.

Philo apparently was of the opinion that "studying is greater than doing." Ideally, Philo would have advocated for the scholar a life of highest individualism and complete isolation from society and all its turmoil, a life of unbroken absorption in the sacred writings of the

Torah and in general philosophy. Recognizing, however, that willy-nilly the scholar is a member of the community in which he lives, that this relationship imposes upon him distinct responsibilities, Philo felt that scholars should plunge into public service, but at the same time not permit themselves to be drawn into the rapids of practical affairs. Rejecting the opinion of some of his contemporaries who maintained that the scholar should become a recluse and spend his entire life in contemplation, the Alexandrian philosopher advised scholars to participate actively in public affairs. But he also warned them to exercise their right to retire from public service and dedicate the rest of their lives to study after having fulfilled their community obligations. To illustrate and support his position, he drew upon the law in the Torah which requires Levites to serve actively only until the age of fifty[77] after which they are released from practical service and can dedicate the remainder of their lives to study and contemplation.[78]

### SERVICE FOR THE SAKE OF HEAVEN

The Rabbis declared that the ultimate worth of any human action is determined by the motive which lies behind it. They therefore urged man to perform all his deeds "for the sake of Heaven." In similar manner does Philo, using his own philosophic terms, declare that practical service is not to be scorned as long as men "do as a good artist does, and engrave upon the material substance a form as good as possible, and thus accomplish a work which may win men's praise."[79] Addressing scholars and philosophers who divorce themselves from their practical environments and dedicate their lives to the study of philosophy or of the divine law, Philo wrote:

... state business is an object of ridicule to you people. Perhaps you have never discovered how serviceable a thing it is. Begin then by having some exercise and practice in the business of life both private and public; and when... you have become masters of each domain, enter now, as more than qualified to do so, on your migration to a different and more excellent way of life.... By taking this course you will well avoid the imputation of shrinking from it through sheer laziness.... And apart from this, it is a vital matter that those who venture to make the claims of God their aim and study should first have fully met those of men; for it is sheer folly to suppose that you will reach the greatest while you are incapable of mastering the lesser.[80]

Philo, primarily as a philosopher, advised his contemporaries on the course a scholar should steer between the ideal and the real, between the world of contemplation and the world of practical affairs, between the duties which man owes to his fellow man and the duties man owes to God. Our Sages in Palestine and Babylonia, primarily religious moralists, went a step further. They did not merely give advice; they laid down, in clear and simple terms, the duties and responsibilities a scholar has toward the community in which he lives.

On the verse, "The king by justice establishes the land, but he that exacteth gifts overthroweth it,"[81] our Sages made a most interesting comment. Playing upon the word *terumoth*, which may mean either "gifts" or that part of the tithes which is given to the priest and cannot be used by an Israelite, they excoriated the "scholar who separates himself from the community":

> "The man of *terumoth* overthroweth it" applies to a scholar who knows the *halakoth, midrashoth* and the *Aggadah*, but when the orphan and the widow come to him so that he may adjudicate their litigations, he answers them, "I am engaged in my study. I am not free." God says to him, "I impute it on you as if you had destroyed the world."[82]

In another comment on the same verse, which to their minds referred to a scholar who refused to meet his obligations of public service, our Sages declared, "If a man places himself in the position of the *terumah* which is set aside in the corner of the house and says 'What have I to do with the burdens of the community, what concern do I have with their adjudication? Peace be upon my soul,' such a man causes the destruction of the world."[83]

Our Sages condemned most severely the scholar who concerns himself only with his own studies and piety and does not fulfill his moral responsibility of serving the community, even as they castigated the layman who separates himself from the community and does not make its problems his own. "Whoever is engaged in serving the needs of the community is equal to the one who is engaged in the study of the Torah,"[84] is their dictum.

## PUBLIC SERVICE NOT A PROFESSION

As much as they stressed the importance of public service, and though they urged all qualified men to shoulder social responsibility, our Sages never regarded public service as a profession. In the ancient Palestinian and Babylonian communities, the judge and the other officials of the community received hardly any pay for their skilled services.

Quite probably it was precisely because public service was not looked upon as a "profession" that *Imitatio Dei* became one of the fundamental principles in Judaism. It became a man's duty to imitate the ways of God, and in a smaller measure to imitate the way of saints. The verse, "Behold, I have taught you statutes and ordinances, even as the Lord my God commanded me,"[85] teaches us, our Sages declared, that "As I taught you without remuneration so shall you teach without remuneration."[86] This dictum was not merely an idealistic homiletical saying; the entire structure of Jewish public service is based upon it. It was taken to apply not only to a teacher but also to a judge or any other public official. It also applied to any individual who suffered financial loss while fulfilling a moral or religious duty.

The Mishnah states: "If a man takes payment to sit as a judge, his judgments are void: if for bearing witness, his testimony is void; if for sprinkling [the sin-offering water] or for sanctifying [mixing] with water the ashes [of the Red Heifer], his water becomes as the water of caverns, and his ashes but the ashes of hearths."[87] The same holds true for the fulfillment of any *mitzvah*, because such acts must be performed for the "sake of Heaven."

Obviously, when the Mishnah asserts that the judgment of a judge who "takes payment to sit as a judge" is void, it is not referring to bribes. The statement simply prohibits the acceptance of remuneration for performing one's responsibilities as a judge. It is not expected, of course, that a man should forego his own livelihood and perform only *mitzvot;* his right to certain compensation is recognized. How the compensation to which he is entitled is determined is another demonstration of the Jewish understanding of man's responsibilities as a creature of God.

Completing its statement concerning all who may not accept payment for their work, the Mishnah continues: "Moreover he may be given such payment as [would be given to] a laborer."[88] Other texts read *kepoel batel* as an "idle laborer."[89] The Talmud defines the mishnaic term *poel batel* as "a laborer who is idle at the kind of work in which he was interrupted."[90] The exact implication of this ruling is not quite clear, and Rashi and Maimonides apparently disagreed over its meaning.[91] One thing is clear, however, a person engaged in public service cannot receive full payment for his work. He may be reimbursed for any loss sustained while engaged in performing a public duty, but only at a minimum rate. The same principle of payment, classified by the Talmud as *agar betala*, a term equivalent to *poel batel*,[92] applies in determining the honorarium for a judge or any other public officer.

The only judges who received a regular, though still meager, salary were the judges called *gozrai gezerot* who functioned when the Temple was still in existence. Their salaries were paid from the Temple treasury.[93] These judges apparently were not concerned with individual litigations. They divorced themselves from all private work or business and devoted all their time to establishing rules and regulations governing fines and civil laws.[94]

Maimonides does not mention the right of a judge to claim payment as a *poel batel*. However, in line with the thought expressed in the Mishnah that a man who performs a public duty may stipulate in advance that he be paid for the loss of money sustained while performing the *mitzvah*,[95] Maimonides states:

Any judge who takes payment for pronouncing judgment, his decisions are void. This principle applies if the payment is recognizable [as payment for judicial services]. But if he was engaged in his own employment and two men come before him for litigation, he may say to them, "Either supply me a laborer who will do my work until I shall have adjudicated your case, or compensate me for my interrupted labor." This is permissible, provided that he takes this compensation in equal shares from both litigants and in their presence.[96]

As stated, this principle was applied not only to judges but also to teachers. While it is evident from talmudic literature that teachers of elementary schools were paid, it is also made clear that they were paid not for the instruction which they gave in the Bible and Oral Law, a religious duty that falls upon every Jew, but rather in payment for watching over the children.[97] That is, they were paid for supervising the children in the classroom. The Rabbis preferred that the salaries of teachers who were fully engaged in their work be raised through a city tax,[98] and Rabbi Simeon ben Yohai attributed the destruction of the cities of Israel to the fact that they did not provide adequate pay for the teachers of the Torah and the Oral Law.[99] But if there are rabbinic statements favoring the payment of salaries to teachers, there are almost no rabbinic sources which favor paying wages to public officials, particularly to judges and city-administrators.

Recognizing that judges and other officers of the community were not paid and were forbidden to receive remuneration for their public services, we can now readily understand the constant admonitions of the Rabbis that men in public service should not neglect their obligations to the public because of preoccupation with their own affairs. Our Sages say: "As long as one is a scholar in private capacity and is not concerned with the affairs of the community, he is not punished. But as soon as one is appointed to serve as the head of the community and takes for himself the Talit [symbolic garment of leadership], let him not say: 'I am engaged with the things which are for my own benefit and I am not concerned with the public,' for all the burdens of the community rest upon him."[100] It is the rabbinic point of view that even though public service is not a profession and the leader or the officer of the community is not a salaried man, his responsibility for the public welfare is in no way minimized.

### SELF-CRITICISM OF LEADERS

According to rabbinic tradition, the degree of an individual's responsibility for the religious and moral welfare of the community depends to a great extent on his influence and position in the community. A man who can prevent the wrongdoing of an entire community and fails to take up such a responsibility, shares in the guilt of the entire community. One who holds an official position in the community and does not reprove the members of their community for their immoral actions, is punished with those who committed the crime. The text of the Torah, "Cursed be he that confirmed not the words of this law to do them,"[101] declares the Talmud, refers to courts which fail to enforce the law or reprove those who commit immoral actions, and to scholars who "observe the Torah, engage in good deeds," but do not concern themselves with the moral life of the community.[102]

Since the guilt for the wrongdoings of the community was shared by its leaders, we can readily understand the disillusionment of our Sages when, at times, their exhortations and attempts to prevent transgressions failed to achieve their objectives. Rabbi Tarfon declared it difficult to reprimand others, for if one says to the transgressor "Remove the mote from between thine eyes," he is immediately told, "Remove the beam from between thine eyes," and Rabbi Akiba showered love upon those who reproved him and thereby demonstrated the truth of the words of Solomon (Prov. 9:8), "Reprove not the scorner, lest he hate thee; reprove the wise man and he will love thee."[103] Such passages express the anguish of the leaders when they found moral dissolution in the Jewish community.

Some commentators claim that these and similar declarations found in the *Sifra* and the Talmud show that our Sages absolved themselves from the responsibility of admonishing the members of their communities. On the contrary, they reveal that each one in his own way attempted to find the cause for his failure to exercise a greater moral influence on the life of his time. The Sages were racked by their acceptance of a religious responsibility to admonish the members of the community lest they share in their guilt, on the one hand, and the partial failure of their admonitions, either to prevent contemplated wrongdoing or to bring the wrongdoer to repent for his immoral and irreligious acts, on the other. In this regard there is a most revealing passage in the *Sifra*:

Rabbi Tarfon said, "By the Temple Worship, if there is any one in this generation who is able to reprove." Rabbi Elazer b. Azariah said: "By Temple Worship, if there is anyone in this generation who is able to accept reproof." Rabbi Akiba said: "By Temple Worship, if there is any one in this generation who knows how to administer reproof." Rabbi Johanan ben Nuri said: "I call heaven and earth to witness that more than four or five times was Rabbi Akiba [censured] before Rabban Gamaliel because I complained against him; nonetheless he showered love upon me."[104]

All these Sages were struggling with the problem of community responsibility. Rabbi Tarfon found an answer to this spiritual dilemma in self-criticism, in admitting the existence of moral imperfections in the recognized leaders of the community. He therefore declared "Who is able to reprove!" He felt that before one can administer reproof, he must make it impossible for the one admonished to retort, "Remove the beam from between thine eyes." Rabbi Elazer b. Azariah, on the other hand, placed the blame on the members of the community, because they are not morally attuned to accept reproof. Rabbi Akiba also blamed the leaders, not for their moral imperfection, but for not knowing *how* to administer reproof; for failing to understand the frame of mind of the sinner and not finding the proper approach in reproving him. Rabbi Johanan b. Nuri was of the opinion that the head of the community is not obligated to reprove the perpetual sinner, the scorner who does not listen to reproof and who hates the one who attempts to correct his ways. He then related his own experience with Rabbi Akiba to illustrate the virtue of ideal admonition.

### HIS BROTHER'S KEEPER

While the community, as a whole, and its leaders are responsible for the moral and religious well-being of the members of the community, it is the responsibility of every individual in the community to be concerned with the moral life of his neighbor, for each Israelite is a guarantor for his brethren.[105] Uncontrolled, however, such responsibilities can themselves lead to immoral actions and abuses. Our Sages, therefore, formulated definite rules and delineated the circumstances under which a man is obligated to involve himself in the moral conduct of another.

The concept that all are guarantors for each other is drawn by the Talmud from the verse (Lev. 26:37), "and they shall stumble one upon his brother."[106] But in discussing the method and extent of reproof, the Rabbis based themselves on Leviticus 19:17; "Thou shalt not hate they brother in thy heart; thou shalt surely rebuke they neighbor, and not bear sin because of him." The Talmud and the *Sifra* interpret this verse as follows:

Our Sages taught: "Thou shalt not hate thy brother in thy heart." Perhaps the Torah meant only that one may not smite him, slap him, curse him? Therefore it says, *"in thy heart"*: it has reference to the hatred of the heart. Whence do we learn that if a man sees his neighbor commit something unseemly he is obligated to reprove him? It is said "thou shalt surely rebuke they neighbor." If he rebuked him, and the latter did not accept the rebuke, whence do we learn that he has to rebuke him again? The verse reads, "thou shalt *surely* rebuke," carrying forth in all ways. One might assume that he must rebuke him even though his face blanched, therefore it states, "thou shalt not bear sin *because of him.*"[107]

This passage leaves no doubt that our Sages understood the negative command of "Thou shalt not hate thy brother in thy heart" to apply particularly to hatred directed against a sinner, without doing anything to prevent his sinful actions. The Torah, therefore, commands one not to bear any grudges against the sinner, let alone inflict any injuries upon him. It stresses that while one is obligated to rebuke the sinner it should not be done with animosity. Reproof of the sinner must never be so administered as to bring the rebuker to sin. Just as one shares in the guilt of another if he does not reprove him for his action, so does the reprover bear sin if he puts the sinner to shame.[108]

Maimonides, elaborating in his *Minyan Hamitzvot* on the negative command contained in "Thou shalt surely rebuke they neighbor." clearly defines the concept that every Israelite is responsible for the moral conduct of his brothers: "It is indeed not right that one should say: Since I do not sin but another sins, why should I be concerned with his God? Such an attitude is contrary to the Torah. We are commanded neither to sin ourselves nor to forsake any of our nation who sins. If any one attempts to transgress we are obligated to reprove him and to bring him back [to the right path]. In this commandment is also included the duty to rebuke others, when they commit sins against their fellow men. But we must bear no grudge against the sinner in our heart, so that no sin accrue to the rebuker.[109]

In his *Mishneh Torah*, Maimonides gives extensive consideration to the text in Leviticus 19:17 and draws from it many injunctions in addition to the injunctions not to entertain hatred in one's heart against any man and not to harbor hatred against a sinner, whether he sins against man or against God. First, whoever is able to reprove a sinner and keep him from evil action, and does not do so, shares in the guilt of the sinner. However, to embarrass and shame an offender in public is as serious an offense as to shame any other man in public. Furthermore, in offenses committed against man, it is the Torah's objective that the injured party not harbor ill-will in his heart against the offender. Hence, to forgive the wrongdoer in place of rebuking him, when it is a fair assumption that the admonition will serve no purpose, is to go beyond the demands of strict law. To act in this way is to conform to the high moral standard of the saints. Ordinarily, however, the requirement of admonishing a wrongdoer applies only if there is hope that the offender will refrain from transgressing, or be influenced to return to the right path. Once, however, it is clear that reproof will in no way change the actions of the sinner, one is absolved from his duty to reprove and does not share in the guilt of the sinner.[110]

This entire position is effectively summed up in *Seder Eliahu Rabbah*: What is meant by "Thou shalt surely rebuke thy neighbor?" One would think that even if it is known to you that he is a wicked man, it is your duty to admonish him. Therefore it said, "Thou shalt surely rebuke *thy neighbor*," meaning, only your neighbor who loves you and who joins with you in the learning of the Torah and the fulfillment of *mitzvot*. You are not bound to reprove the wicked man who is your enemy. In such instance, moreover, you are forbidden to admonish him, as it is said: "He that correcteth a scorner getteth to himself shame; he that reproveth a wicked man, it becometh unto him a blot. Reprove not a scorner, lest he hate thee; reprove a wise man, and he will love thee."[111]

# 8. MAN AND HIS FAMILY

## PARENTS AND CHILDREN

In the rabbinic view, every human being who has a mind of his own is responsible for his actions. Before a court of man, no one can be held legally responsible for an act except he who performs it. Even one who indirectly causes the performance of another's acts is not responsible for them. The "laws of heaven," however, do hold a man responsible if he is the cause, even indirectly, of a criminal or immoral action of another. In consequence, one who is appointed head of a community assumes a moral responsibility for the acts of the individual members of the community. Hence, if through his non-action, the community strays, under the "laws of heaven," the leader is held responsible for the offense because his non-action was the indirect cause of their immoral act.

It is in this light too that we can understand the relationship between parents and children, and their mutual responsibilities.

The fundamental religious principle of the Jewish theocracy—the sacredness of the human personality—teaches that every man is the property of God, and therefore no man can become the property or chattel of another. The same philosophy governs the relationship of parents and children. In ancient Roman law the head of the house was considered the full master and undisputed owner of his own family. "By the laws of the Romans, a father had unlimited authority over his son," asserts Philo.[1] He then continues to define the Roman philosophy of parenthood:

Parents have not only been given the rights of exercising authority over their children, but the power of masters corresponding to two preliminary forms under which servants are owned, one when they are home-bred, the other when they are purchased. For parents pay out on their children sums of money many times the value of a slave, and for them to nurses, tutors and teachers, apart from the cost of their clothes, food and superintendance in sickness and health from their earliest years until they are fully grown. "Home-bred," too, must they be who are not only born in the house, but through the masters of the house, who have made the contribution enforced by the statutes of nature in giving them birth.[2]

In the ancient non-Jewish world, the father, as the head of the family, had complete authority over the lives of his children because, in a sense, children stood in the same relationship to their parents as slaves did to their masters. In Jewish law, however, the parent-child relationship was an entirely different one. Parents, particularly fathers, had legal rights over daughters, but only while they were minors, and even such authority was limited in scope. While in a certain sense, in the eyes of heaven, a son too, was considered the possession of his father until he reached his majority, legally, the father had no possessive rights over his minor son which could be enforced by law. When, however, children reached maturity, the age of thirteen years and one day for a boy and twelve years and six months for a girl,[3] parents retained no legal authority over their children.

The legal rights which the father had over his minor daughter, as stated explicitly in the Bible or as derived by our Sages from the biblical context, were three in number: a father could take a husband for his daughter—a right the Rabbis adduced from the biblical verse,[4] "I gave my daughter unto this man as a wife";[5] he could sell her as a Hebrew maidservant—a right explicitly stated in the Bible, "And if a man sell his daughter to be a maidservant";[6] he could annul her vow—also explicitly stated in the Bible, "But if her father disallow her in the day that he heareth, none of her vows, or her bonds wherewith she hath bound her soul, shall stand."[7]

In each of the three instances enumerated above, the authority of the father over his daughter differed, according to rabbinic tradition, with the age of the daughter. With reference to marriage, the father could betroth his daughter as long as she was a *ketanah*—that is, as long as she was under the age of twelve years or until she showed signs of puberty —or while she was a *na'arah*—that is, during the six months period between the age of twelve and her majority at the age of twelve and six months. With reference to selling her as a maidservant, the father could do so only as long as she was a *ketanah*, a minor.[8] With reference to annuling her vows, his authority was limited to the period when she was a *na'arah*, because prior to that age she was a *ketanah*, a minor, and the vows of minors are never valid.[9]

A daughter sold by her father while she was still a minor was set free as soon as she showed signs of puberty. The Bible further indicates that anyone who acquired a minor as a maidservant had a moral obligation to take her for a wife for himself or for his son.[10] A father should exercise his right to sell his minor daughter primarily in the hope that her master or his son would marry her before she reached maturity. Hence, according to rabbinic tradition, the father could sell his minor daughter as a maidservant only to one with whom, or at least with whose son, a legally valid marriage could be effected.[11]

In general, Hebrew slaves, male or female, were hardly "slaves" in the accepted sense of the term. In fact, one had to be more considerate of his Hebrew servant than of his own children. On the verse, "If thou buy a Hebrew servant, six years he shall serve,"[12] the Mekilta states:

I might understand this to mean in any kind of service, but it is said, "Thou shalt not make him to serve as a bondservant" (Lev. 25:39). Hence, the Sages say: A Hebrew slave must not wash the feet of his master, nor put his shoes on him, nor carry his things before him when going to the bathhouse, nor support him by the hips when ascending the steps, nor carry him in a litter or chair or a sedan chair as slaves do, for it is said, "But over your brethren the children of Israel ye shall not rule, one over another with rigor" (Lev. 25:46).

"Six years he shall serve." I might understand this to mean by doing any kind of work, whether it is humiliating to him or not. Therefore it says, "As a hired man" (Lev. 25:40). Just as a hired man cannot be forced to do anything other than his trade, so a Hebrew slave cannot be forced to do anything other than his trade. Hence, our Sages said: The master may not put him to work in a trade in which he has to attend upon the public, such as a wellmaster, a barber, tailor, butcher or baker. Rabbi Jose said if one of these was his trade, he must work at it for his master. "As a hired man and as a settler" (Lev. 25:40). Just as a hired man works only during the day, so the Hebrew slave is to work only during the day and not during the night. Rabbi Jose said: It all depends on what his trade is.[13]

This passage is quoted here in full to show that Hebrew slaves were not the property of their masters and that the latter did not possess any ownership over them. They were, in the full sense, employees; in order not to degrade them, masters often had to show them greater consideration than they did their own children. The Talmud states: "Because it will be good with thee" (Deut. 15:16)—with thee in food, with thee in drink; you should not eat white bread and he black bread; you should not drink old wine, and he new wine; you should not sleep on feathers and he on straws. Hence, they said, whoever acquires a Hebrew slave is as if he acquired a master for himself.[14] With all the great consideration shown to Hebrew slaves, the Rabbis still considered any form of slavery degrading. A woman could be sold as a maidservant by her father but, as stated before, the main purpose of such a transaction was to arrange a good marriage for her. Once a woman reached maturity, however, she could not sell herself as a maidservant nor could the court sell her as one, even in the event that she committed a theft.[15] Furthermore, a father had the right to sell his minor daughter as a maidservant only when he was reduced to such poverty that he did not possess a bed or movable object, or even a garment to wear. Moreover, even when he sold her he could be forced to redeem her.[16]

A father's consent was enough to contract a legal marriage for his minor daughter. Yet, our Sages said: "It is forbidden for a father to betroth his minor daughter until she grows up and says I want so and so as my husband."[17] In the Middle Ages, and even in later periods, it was customary for fathers to contract marriages for their minor daughters but, as the Tosafists explain, this was done primarily because of the unsettled economic conditions of the Jews in Europe, and "if a man is able to provide for his daughter a dowry at this moment he may not be able to afford it at a future date and his daughter may suffer the consequences of remaining in an unmarried state (*agunah*) for the rest of her life."[18]

Another consideration which dictated early marriages was the desire to protect the chastity of young girls, particularly when orphaned by the death of their fathers. In order that "people should not take liberties with orphans as they are accustomed to do with ownerless property,"[19] the Rabbis instituted a *takkanah* that the mother and brothers of an orphaned minor had the right to give her away in marriage. They reserved for her, however, the right to reject the husband chosen for her by her family when she reached maturity. The dissolution of such a marriage required no bill of divorcement; an oral rejection (*miun*) by the girl was sufficient to automatically dissolve the union.[20]

In short, the legal guardianship which parents had over their minor children had as its main purpose the protection of the young against abuses, and in the case of a minor daughter, to provide her with a husband. While the father had many legal rights over his minor daughter, she was not considered "property" over which he had unlimited authority. If, for example, a father injured his own minor daughter, he was legally responsible to pay her for the indignity inflicted, her pain, and the cost of medical treatment.[21] If she inherited property from her maternal grandfather, the father had no legal rights to her possessions.[22]

Maimonides, it is true, was of the opinion that "under the laws of heaven" minor children, whether male or female, are considered to be the possession of their parents. This, in his view, is the theological reason for the statement that minor children suffer death on account of the sins of their parents. On the verse, "The fathers shall not be put to death for the children, neither shall the children be put to death for the fathers; every man shall be put to death for his own sin,"[23] the *Sifre* comments, "Parents die for their own sins and children die for the sins of their parents."[24] There is no doubt that the *Sifre* here refers to the death of minor children, in accordance with the rabbinic tradition that God first punishes man for his sins through the loss of his material possessions[25] and then, if repentance does not follow, He punishes him with the death of his minor children.[26]

Maimonides characterized this as a "fundamental principle" in the concept of divine retribution and wrote: "In the case of certain sins, justice dictates that the sinner should be punished for his sin [by the divine court]... bodily or with the loss of material substance or with the death of his minor children, for minor children have no mind of their own and have not yet arrived at the age of assuming their own duties. They are like his property (*kekinyano heim*), and it is written, 'Every man shall be put to death for his own sin' (Deut. 25:16), which implies from the age that he becomes a man."[27]

This distinct view of retribution given by Maimonides is based upon

the Talmud and midrashim. Nevertheless, I have been unable to uncover any early sources which state that minors, who have no minds of
their own and therefore have not yet assumed their own legal and
religious obligations, are considered the property or quasi-property of
their parents, through whose loss the parents can be punished.

The question of whether parents have legal rights in the lives of their
minor children aside, it is the undisputed opinion of our Sages that once
a daughter becomes a *bogeret*, that is, reaches the age of twelve years and
six months, and a son becomes thirteen years and one day old, parents
no longer have any legal authority over them. The reason for this is
that at such ages children are held to have a mind of their own and must
take up their own responsibilities. To allow anyone, even parents, legal
rights over them beyond that stage would imply a sanction of possessive
rights in the personality of another individual, a form of *obligatio* in the
personality of another human being. The principle of individualism
works both ways, with concrete results—if in the eyes of the laws of
man, parents no longer have any rights or authority over their children,
they cannot be held legally responsible for their actions. Needless to
say, children bear no responsibility for the acts of their parents.

One might question whether such a society, in which the concept of
individualism was so greatly emphasized that even parents had neither
legal authority over their children nor legal responsibility for the acts
of their children, could actually exist. After all, the family is the foundation of the community in its totality and may be characterized as a
"miniature community." Where familial responsibility and authority
are so lax, can a normal community exist? Yet it is a fact that the ancient Jewish family was the source of public morality and many moral
problems which plagued the ancient world rarely arose in the Jewish
community.

The strength of the Jewish family rested on three religious principles:
(1) the responsibility of the father to teach his children, boys more in-
tensively than girls, the moral laws of the Torah; (2) the constant
awareness of the father that while under the laws of man he had no legal
responsibility for the actions of his children, under the laws of heaven,
as the head of the family, he was fully responsible for the actions of his
children. In other words, what the king is to the nation, the head of the

community to the community, parents are to the family; (3) the religious belief that the duty of honoring parents is equivalent to the duty of honoring God. This, above all meant that children, regardless of their age, owed obedience to their parents whenever such obedience did not contravene the moral and religious obligations which fall upon every individual.

One of the chief duties of a father is to teach his son Torah. This paternal obligation the Sages derived from the verses, "And ye shall teach them to your children, talking of them...that your days may be multiplied."[28] Rabbi Jose ben Akiba said, "From this verse they established the tradition that when a little child begins to talk his father begins to converse with him in the holy tongue and teaches him Torah. If he does not converse with him in the holy tongue and does not teach him Torah it is considered as if he had buried him."[29]

After many of the great Jewish saints, including Rabbi Akiba, met a martyr's death during the Hadrianic persecutions, the rabbinic seat of learning was established in the Galilean city of Ushah. There the rabbinic synod instituted, among other things, the *takkanah* that a man must bear with his child, if the child does not want to learn Torah, until the age of twelve. From that age on, however, he may use force to make him study the Torah.[30] This duty of teaching a child Torah is not to be compared with the modern concept of giving a child an "education." It meant, particularly, instructing a child in the moral and spiritual way of life, and required teaching not only moral theory but also the significance of practice. Rabbi Nehorai, therefore, said, "I would set aside all the crafts in the world and teach my son naught save the Law, for a man enjoys the reward thereof in this world and its worth remains for the world to come... for it guards him from all evil while he is young and in old age it grants him security and hope."[31]

It is the father's ability to inculcate in his child a love for Torah learning and Torah practice that ultimately determines the moral conduct of the child. It is no wonder that our Sages so greatly resented the *am ha-aretz*, the ignorant man. This resentment did not spring, as is commonly believed, from a Pharisaic "aristocracy of learning" which looked down upon the ignorant man. The fact is that the only means our Sages had of enforcing moral discipline was the study of the Torah, for it led ultimately to moral practice. In this they believed implicitly. If ignorance were countenanced, immoral generations could easily become the rule, particularly when children at the age of thirteen years were considered individuals and were not subject to the authority of parents. Therefore did Rabbi Nathan ben Joseph say, "Who is an *am ha-aretz*? Whoever has children and does not raise them in the study of Torah."[32] The study of the Torah was not a matter of "mental gymnastics." It was an indispensible necessity if an intellectual and moral way of life were to be established. Hence, though one be a scholar himself, if he does not train his children to study the Torah in order to practice it, he too may be classified as an *am ha-aretz*.

The second factor, no less important, in maintaining the solidarity of the family, is the fact that while parents cannot be held legally responsible for the acts of their children, in the eyes of heaven, they are responsible for their children's misdeeds, particularly if they fail in their duty of properly training them. This is the meaning of the rabbinic dictum, "Whoever is able to protest against [and thus prevent] the misdeeds of the people of his own home and does not do so, is punished for the deeds of the members of his family."[33]

Maimonides, in discussing repentance, classifies the great offenses for which the Holy One blessed be He does not offer the offender an opportunity to repent. Among them he lists the sin of causing a community to sin, which also includes preventing a community from fulfilling a religious duty. Leading people away from the right path to an evil path, of which the seducer and enticer[34] are examples, is as grave an offense as allowing one's son to fall into mischief without protesting against his action. This last is an offense of extreme weight, because had the father protested against his son's actions, the latter, still under parental control, would have obeyed and separated himself from his evil course. Since the father did not protest, he is held to have caused his son to sin.[35]

Morally, a child is always considered to be under the control of his father; therefore, if one does not check his son's immoral actions he is as responsible as if he had directly caused his son to sin. This is another application of the rabbinic religious philosophy which teaches that the laws of heaven hold a man responsible if by his action or non-action he is the cause for another's depraved deeds. In the case of a parent, who is morally responsible for the conduct of his son, non-action or his failure to check the evil ways of his own child makes him responsible in the eyes of heaven for the child's misdeeds. If, however, a parent does try to check the misbehavior of his child, even is he does not succeed, he is no longer held responsible for the latter's misconduct.

### THE LAW OF THE REBELLIOUS SON

It is in this light that we can properly understand the rabbinic approach to the law of the "rebellious son." Failing to grasp the fundamental rabbinic philosophy, many mistakenly claim that the Rabbis wanted to abolish the Biblical concept of *patria potestas*, or that in their "liberality" the Tannaim endeavored by juristic contortions to mitigate the severe penalty parents can, according to the Torah, impose on a misbehaving son. Our Sages, however, based their decisions not on such grounds but rather upon profound religious convictions as well as on established traditions. It is only in the light of their religious and legal philosophy that we can understand their interpretation of this law.

The law of the rebellious son is: "If a man have a stubborn and rebellious son, that will not hearken to the voice of the father and the voice of his mother, and though they chasten him, will not hearken into them; then shall his father and his mother lay hold on him, and bring him out unto the elders of the city, and unto the gate of his place. And they shall say unto the elders of the city, 'This is our son, stubborn and rebellious; he doth not hearken to our voice: he is a glutton and a drunkard.' And all the men of the city shall stone him with stones, that he die; so shalt thou put away the evil from the midst of thee and all Israel shall hear and fear."[36]

A careful reading of the text makes it obvious that parents did not have the authority to punish their children with death for disobedience. Therefore, this law has nothing in common with the concept of the ancient world that parents have full possessive rights over the lives of their children, including the right to put them to death. The Torah clearly demands that the child be brought before the court. It is the court that decides whether or not his actions constitute a criminal offense punishable by death. Furthermore, the Torah itself makes clear that the death penalty is imposed not because the child disobeyed his parents but because he was a "glutton and a drunkard."

In interpreting this law, our Sages first laid down the rule that the law does not refer to a minor. Since a minor has no mind of his own, he cannot be punished by court. Minors, as mentioned before, may, according to rabbinic belief, die by the hand of God for the sins of their parents, but never for their own transgressions. Hence the Mishnah says, "A minor is exempt since he has not yet come within the scope of the commandments."[37] According to this tradition, the law of a rebellious son applies from the time a child has reached the age of thirteen years and one day and produced two hairs until the time that hair has surrounded the entire membrane—at most a period of three months. During this time the child already possesses a mind of his own but is still under the control of the parents.[38] Since the rebellious son has not committed a capital offense punishable by death, the reason the court can punish him for his serious misbehavior is that his present conduct allows us to presume that he will eventually commit a capital offense. The Torah prefers that he die now before he can commit more serious offenses.[39] The Mishnah records the following conditions which must be fulfilled before one can be condemned as a rebellious son:

If his father was willing [to accuse him] and his mother was not willing, or if his father was not willing, but his mother was willing, he cannot be condemned as a stubborn and rebellious son; it applies only if both were willing. Rabbi Judah says, if his mother was not fit for his father, he cannot be condemned as a stubborn and rebellious son. If either of them was maimed in hand or lame or dumb or blind or deaf, he cannot be condemned as a stubborn or rebellious son.... They must warn him, and scourge him before three [judges]. If he again behaves evilly he must be tried before twenty-three [judges]. He may only be stoned if the first three judges are there, for it is written "This our son," to wit, this is he who was first beaten before you.[40]

With so many strictures applied to the law of a stubborn and rebellious son it is no wonder that the Talmud states that there never was a case of a stubborn and rebellious son who was condemned to death nor will there ever be one. The law was given, they continue, only so that we may "study it and receive reward."[41] Too many, however, fail to realize the fundamental principle underlying this law in the Mishnah and the Talmud.

Normally it is not the parents who bring accusations against an individual who commits a capital offense. In this law, peculiarly, they are the accusers. They are the ones who declare that the conduct of their child is so rebellious that if he is not punished now he will sooner or later commit capital offenses, causing injury to others and bringing down the death penalty upon himself. Since the parents are morally responsible for the conduct of their children, they here become the accusers. But in such a case the Mishnah lays down one fundamental rule—a son can be condemned as stubborn and rebellious only if the entire blame can be thrown upon the son and only if the parents in no way, either directly or indirectly, caused their son's behavior. Hence, if the father did not previously endeavor to check his son's misdeeds, the latter cannot be condemned as a stubborn and rebellious son. Again, if, as a result of physical defects the father cannot fully exercise his authority as a father, then the entire blame cannot be placed on the son. Similarly, a son cannot be condemned as a stubborn and rebellious son if the marriage of his parents was not a proper one; an unsuccessful marriage may often be the indirect cause of a child's misbehavior. If both parents are not ready to accuse the child, that is, if there is disagreement, then it is a sign that the entire blame is not the son's. In other words, parents can bring accusation against their son before a human court only if they can be fully absolved of any responsibility for their child's action in the eyes of heaven, and only if the home environment was congenial and permitted the full exercise of parental responsibility. Under such conditions alone can we assume that the child is fully responsible for his own conduct and that if he is left unpunished he will commit more serious crimes in the future.

It is in this light that we can understand an Alexandrian tradition pertaining to the law of a stubborn and rebellious son. To my knowledge, this tradition is not recorded in Palestinian sources; still it fully accords with the religious philosophy which guided the Rabbis in their approach to the law. Philo, in his discussion of the stubborn and rebellious son follows quite closely the halakic regulations laid down in the Mishnah, but adds the following point:

The son who is puffed up and carried away by his folly is denounced by his parents as "*This* son of ours," and it is in these words that they indicate his disobedience and recalcitrance. By using the word "this" in indicating him, they suggest that they have other children who are obedient either to one or both their parents.[42]

In another place, Philo states, "They say '*This* son of ours is disobedient,' and thus by the addition of "this" they show that they have other sons, strong-willed and self-controlling."[43]

The Mishnah, too, it will be recalled, places emphasis on the pronoun "this." In the Mishnah the pronoun was understood to give to the statement of the parents the sense of "this is the same son whom we have already reprimanded and rebuked but who still refuses to listen to us. We have, therefore, fulfilled our responsibility as parents and are blameless for his evil conduct." In the Alexandrian tradition, the pronoun was read so as to give the statement of the parents the following force: "*This* son of ours is disobedient but we have other children who conduct themselves properly, evidence that his misbehavior is not our fault for we have raised other children who practice self-control." Both readings, however, give the same result—parents cannot accuse their children of misconduct unless they can prove that they have faultlessly discharged their responsibilities as parents. Parents can accuse their children of serious laxity in behavior only if they can prove that they had no share in such conduct and that they did everything possible to guide their children properly.

But is it really possible for parents to be fully certain that in no way are they even indirectly responsible for the wrongdoing of their children? Can they really point a finger and say, "If this son of ours is disobedient, it is entirely because of his own bad character?" Our Sages thought this humanly impossible and, therefore, they declared that the law of the rebellious son was recorded in order to "study it and receive reward." Indeed, much reward may come to parents, and people in general, by studying this law, for above all it emphasizes the mutual responsibilities which are operative in the raising of a family.

## RESPONSIBILITY OF CHILDREN FOR THEIR ACTIONS

The great solidarity of the Jewish family was a result of the fact that parents considered themselves morally responsible for the actions of their children. Children, on the other hand, were held responsible for their own actions once they reached maturity, regardless of the environment in which they were raised. They could never before a court of man blame their parents for their offenses. On the other hand, children could not be held responsible for the immoral actions of their parents even before the divine court.

This whole question of responsibility hinges on the verse: "For I, the Lord thy God, am a jealous God, visiting the iniquity of the fathers upon the children unto the third and fourth generation of them that hate Me."[44] Tannaitic, midrashic and talmudic sources often raise the question, "Does not this verse seemingly contradict the statement in Deuteronomy: The fathers shall not be put to death for their children, neither shall the children be put to death for the fathers; every man shall be put to death for his own sin?"[45]

Many are the answers given to this question, but the one which seemed to be most widely accepted is the talmudic reply that the verse in Exodus applies to those children who "retain the deeds of their parents in their hands," whereas the verse in Deuteronomy applies to those children "who do not retain the deeds of the parents in their hands."[46] In other words, a child raised in a home in which serious offenses were committed cannot claim that it is his father's fault that he committed similar offenses. He cannot claim that his environment is responsible for his immoral actions for he has a mind of his own and he should have been guided by his own moral judgment. If, however, a child does not continue the evil deeds of his parents, then he cannot be held responsible for his parents' misbehavior even in the divine court.

It is interesting that Alexandrian Jews also endeavored to explain this verse in Exodus. The interpretation offered by Philo, while not exactly similar to the one given in the Talmud, is in consonance with the rabbinic concept that a parent is morally responsible for his child's immoral conduct if he is even indirectly, by his non-action, the cause of it. Though a parent may not be punished for his child's act because his relation to it was one of non-action, nevertheless, he is considered to have sinned in serving as the indirect cause for his child's wrongdoing.

In a striking allegorical interpretation of Noah's act of transferring the curse which was due Ham upon his son Canaan, as recorded in Genesis,[47] Philo writes:

It was Noah's son Ham who, from idle curiosity, wished to see his father naked, and laughed at what he saw and proclaimed aloud what it was right to leave untold. But it was Canaan who is charged with another's misdeeds and reaps the curses. For it is said: "Cursed be Canaan; a servant, a bondman shall he be to his brethren" (Gen. 9:25). What, I repeat, was his offense? Let us expound in full the inward interpretation. The state of non-action and the state of motion differ from each other. While the former is static, the latter is dynamic.... We speak not only of carpenters, but of practicing carpentry, not only of painters but of painting, not only of husbandmen, but of farming, not only of musicians, but of flute-playing, singing or some similar performance. Now which of the two categories is subject to praise or blame? Surely those who are actually engaged in doing something. They it is whose success or failure entail respectively praise or blame. Those who possess the knowledge and nothing more, and are not actually doing anything, remain in peace and find in their inactivity the privilege of security.... Ham the son of Noah is a name for vice in the quiescent state and the grandson Canaan for the same when it passes into active movement.... Now no legislator fixes a penalty against the unjust when in a quiescent state, but only when they are moved to action and commit the deeds to which injustice prompts them.... It is natural enough then, that the just man should appear to lay his curses on the grandson Canaan, for it is the single subject, wickedness, which is presented in two different aspects, non-action and motion. But rest takes precedence in point of age to motion, and thus the moving stands to stationery in the relation of the child to the parent. Thus it agrees with the verities of nature when Canaan is described as the son of Ham, or non-action, and this serves to show the truth of what is said elsewhere, "visiting the iniquities of fathers upon the children unto the third and fourth generation" (Exodus 20:5).[48]

In this significant passage Philo simply allegorizes an oral tradition which existed in Alexandria. The question which Philo raises is the same as that found in rabbinic literature: Why is it that though it was Ham who sinned, it was his son Canaan who was cursed? Why is it that the father commits iniquity and punishment falls upon the children? Philo's answer is that the father sinned by non-action, for which no court can punish, while the child sinned in his actions, a result of the quiescent sinfulness of the parent. Therefore, explains Philo, God visits the iniquities of the unpunishable acts of parents on the punishable acts of the children. In this respect it seems Philo retained the spirit of the Palestinian tradition that being the non-active cause for the wrong action of children is considered a sin of the parent.

Philo's view, however was apparently not shared by all Jews in ancient Alexandria. In his treatise on the *Nobleness of Birth*, Philo attempted to refute two erroneous theological concepts which some of his contemporaries accepted as truth: that the blameless lives of parents help to redeem the wickedness of children and that the iniquities of parents are charged against the children even if the latter live lives of moral excellence. Philo sums up his long treatise with the following words: "Must we not then reject the claims of those who assume as their own precious possession the nobility which belongs to others, who, different from those just mentioned, might well be considered enemies of the Jewish nation and every person in every place? Enemies of our nation, because they give their compatriots license to put their trust in the virtue of their ancestors, and despise the thought of living a sound and steadfast life. Enemies of the people in general, who even if they reach the very summit of moral excellence, will not benefit thereby, if their parents and grandparents were not beyond reproach. I doubt indeed if any more mischievous doctrine could be propounded than this...."[49] As evidence that children of moral excellence do not share in the iniquities of their parents, Philo points to Abraham, who attained the highest standard of moral nobility though his father was a polytheist worshiping the stars and planets. To illustrate that paternal moral nobility cannot save wicked children, he points to Adam who could not save Cain, to Noah who could not save Ham, to Abraham who could not save Ishmael, and to Isaac who could not save Esau.[50]

The Palestinian midrashim, which share Philo's views in these matters, use the same illustrations as Philo. Thus on the verse: "There is none that could save out of my hand,"[51] the *Sifre* comments, "Fathers do not save sons. Abraham did not save Ishmael, nor did Isaac save Esau."[52] The oft-repeated rabbinic dictum, "Fathers do not save sons" is also used by Philo: "Just parents are no help to the unjust, nor temporate parents to the intemporate, nor in general good parents to the wicked."[53] Similarly the Midrash states: When the Holy One blessed be He said: "He visits the sins of the fathers on the children," Moses declared: "Almighty, how many wicked persons give birth to righteous ones? Shall they share in the iniquity of the parents? Terah was an idol worshiper, and his son Abraham was righteous. So with Hezekiah, and so forth. Is it proper for the righteous to be punished for the sins of their parents?" The Holy One blessed be He answered, "You have convinced me. By thy life, I shall disregard my own view in favor of yours, as it is written: 'The parents shall not die because of their children, and children because of their parents'" (Deut. 24:15).[54] Thus there is full agreement between the rabbinic and non-rabbinic literature pertaining to the visitation of sins of fathers upon sons and the reverse.

### THE MERIT OF THE FOUNDING FATHERS

While Philo, like our Sages, held the view that the righteous parent cannot save the son, he firmly believed in *zehut abot*, "the merit of the fathers." Though in the life of the individual family this concept is of minor significance, the survival of the Jewish community and the nationhood of Israel is largely due to the merits of the founding fathers. The Jewish people collectively are the beneficiaries of the good deeds of the fathers of the Jewish race. Philo, who clearly reaffirms the Jewish belief in the eventual coming of the Messiah, stresses that the future miraculous ingathering of the Jews from all parts of the world will, in no small measure, be due to the intercession of the Patriarchs in behalf of the Jewish people. While he does not mention the founding fathers by name, he undoubtedly refers to Abraham, Isaac, and Jacob. Interestingly, the question of whether the good deeds of the Patriarchs still continue to influence God's dealing with the Jewish people or ceased to do so at a certain point in history, was a matter of speculation among our Sages.[55]

In two remarkable Philonic passages pertaining to the nationhood of Israel is the importance of "the merit of the fathers" expressed. In one Philo declares:

> One may say that the whole Jewish race is in a position of an orphan, compared with all the nations on every side... the Jewish nation has none to take its part, as it lives under exceptional laws which are necessarily grave and severe, because they inculcate the highest standards of virtue.... Nevertheless, as Moses tells us, the orphanlike desolate state of his people is always an object of pity and compassion to the Ruler of the universe whose portion it is, because it has been set apart from the whole human race as a kind of first fruit to the Maker and Father. And the cause of this were the precious signs of righteousness and virtue shown by the founders of the race, signs which survive like imperishable plants bearing fruits that never decay for their descendants, fruits salutary and profitable in every way, even though these descendants themselves be sinners.... [56]

In another place, speaking even more explicitly of the Messianic Age, he writes, "Three intercessors they have to plead for their reconciliation with the Father. One is the clemency and kindness of Him to Whom they appeal.... The second is the holiness of the founders of the race... [who] cease not to make supplications for their sons and daughters, supplications not made in vain, because the Father grants to them the privilege that their prayer should be heard. The third is one which more than anything else moves the loving kindness of the other two to come forward so readily and that is the reformation working in those who are being brought to make a covenant of peace."[57] Hence, according to Philo the uniqueness of the Jewish people, and their ultimate Messianic ingathering, is in good part a result of *zehut abot*, the merit of the fathers of the Jewish race.[58]

### LEGAL OBLIGATIONS OF MARRIAGE

The religious concept of individualism, which posits that one individual cannot acquire possessive rights in another individual, is also closely reflected in the understanding our Sages had of the duties which a husband and wife assume when they enter into a contract of marriage.

It is noteworthy that in the law of marriage, as recorded in the Torah, the obligations a husband owes his wife are explicitly stated: "Her food (sh'erah), her raiment, and her conjugal right (o'natah) he shall not diminish" (Ex. 21:11). On the other hand, the obligations of a wife are nowhere stated. For a general understanding of the institution of marriage, therefore, we are entirely dependent upon the oral traditions.

Apparently there was disagreement among the Tannaim concerning the interpretation of the word sh'erah. In Hebrew it may mean either "sustenance," that is food, or "flesh" or "body." The Mekilta states:

Sh'erah means her food, as it is said, "Who also eats the flesh of my people" (Micah 3:3), and as it is written, "He causes flesh to rain upon them as dust" (Psalms 78:27).... These are the words of Rabbi Josiah. Rabbi Jonathan says: "Her body, her raiment" (sh'erah kesutah) means raiment which is becoming to her body: if she is young, he should not give her garments worn by older people, and if she is old he should not give her garments worn by younger people. "And her time (o'natah may also be "timely" in Hebrew), meaning that he should not give her summer garments for the winter and winter garments for the summer. Whence do we derive that the husband must provide her with food? Is this not derivable through a syllogism (kal vahomer)? If he cannot deprive her of the things which are not essential for the preservation of life, is it not only just that he should not be able to withhold from her the things that are necessary for the preservation of life? Whence do we learn of her conjugal rights (derek eretz)? This, too, is a syllogism. If he cannot deprive her of the things for which she was not primarily married, is it not only just that he should not be able to deny her the things for which she was primarily married?[59]

This tannaitic passage reveals the humaneness with which our Sages treated the married woman and the psychological understanding they had of her needs, for which they made the husband responsible.

These obligations were held by our Sages to be m'deoraitha, that is, duties placed upon the husband by the Torah. The deep consideration which the Rabbis had for the welfare of the married woman is further revealed in mishnaic legislation:

> If a man vowed to have no intercourse with his wife, the School of Shammai says [she may consent] for two weeks. The School of Hillel says, for one week only. Disciples of the Sages may remain absent for thirty days without the consent of their wives while they occupy themselves with the study of the Torah, and laborers [may abstain] for one week.[60]

The Mishnah and the Talmud also set forth conditions under which, if a husband denies his wife her marital rights, she may force him to divorce her and claim her *ketubah*. This same obligation rests also on the woman; if she refuses to live with her husband she is considered a *moredet*, a rebellious wife.[61] The chief religious obligations of a married woman are to observe the laws of purity and chastity and conduct her home in such a way as not to cause her husband unintentionally to violate the laws of the Torah.[62]

The deep respect and appreciation which the Rabbis had for the natural sensitivity of women is further indicated by the following statement in the Mishnah:

> And these are the persons whom the court can force to divorce their wives: he that is afflicted with boils, or that has polypi, or that collects [dog's excrements] or that is a coppersmith or a tanner, whether these defects were in them before they married or whether they arose after they married. And of all of these Rabbi Meir said: Although the husband made it a condition with her [to marry him despite his defects] she may say, "I thought that I could endure it, but now I cannot endure it." But the Sages say: she must endure him [if she originally consented to the condition] against her will, save only if he is afflicted with boils because she will enervate him.[63]

In regard to the other obligations and legal rights which fall to the husband upon marriage, a sharp distinction is drawn between *de'oraitha* and *derabanan*, between the laws of marriage as stated in the Bible and the many *takkanot*, innovations which were instituted by the rabbinic courts throughout the ages. The Rabbis increased the rights of the husband over the wife but in return demanded that he assume greater obligations towards her.

The Rabbis declared that biblically, *m'deoraitha*, the husband has almost no legal rights over his wife excepting those which come with the mutual obligation assumed by husband and wife to live with each other, and the obligation of the wife to conduct herself in accordance with the laws of purity and chastity. The husband has no legal rights, for instance, over a woman's earnings, or as it is called in the Talmud "the work of her hands," nor can he force her to work for him. Anything that a wife finds is her legal possession. Any property that she brings with her as her dowry, or whatever she inherits during her marriage, or inherited prior to her marriage, is her own property over which the husband has no legal rights.

The right of a husband to inherit his wife *m'deoraitha* (according to biblical rule) was a matter of controversy in the Talmud[64] as well as among later rabbinic scholars. These differed over the question whether, according to the Torah, a husband is a legal heir of his wife. Maimonides maintained that the right of the husband to inherit his wife was established by an enactment of the Scribes, giving him priority over everyone else. But according to Mosaic law, Maimonides held, the husband is not considered an heir.[65] Rabbi Abraham ben David, however, disagreed and ruled that a husband's legal right to inherit his wife is affirmed by Mosaic law.[66]

Rabbinic enactments bestowed upon the husband many rights which might be considered possessive rights. But though these enactments may have limited the independence of the woman, they were instituted basically for her ultimate protection. The Rabbis decreed, for instance, not only that the earnings of a wife belong to her husband, but that she is legally bound to do all domestic work. Deeply concerned with "peace of home," our Sages ruled so because they felt that the husband, held legally responsible for the support of his wife by the Torah, might come to resent his wife's retention of her earnings and eventually cause domestic difficulties.[67] Since the purpose of this enactment was primarily to protect the woman, she is always free to declare, "I choose not to be supported by my husband, and do not allow him to acquire the right over my work."[68] A husband, on the other hand, is bound by the laws of the Torah to support his wife, and therefore is not given the option of declaring, "I choose not to support her and relinquish my rights over her work."[69]

A declaration by a woman that she prefers to keep her own earnings and forego her right to be maintained by her husband, according to many rabbinic commentators, not only permits her to keep any earnings she may acquire outside her home, but also relieves her of her legal obligation to perform the duties of a housewife.[70] This view, however, is opposed by Rabbi Nissim Gerondi who argues that such a declaration applies only to her outside earnings, and not to the normal domestic obligations of a wife. These she must fulfill even if she does not wish to be supported by her husband.[71]

The reason for obligating a woman to carry out the household duties and outlining the type of work she is to perform, particularly if she is supported by her husband, is stated in the Mishnah:

These are the works which a woman does for her husband: grinding flour and baking bread and washing clothes and cooking food and giving suck to her child and making ready his bed and working in wool. If she brought him one servant she need not grind or bake or wash; if two, she need not cook or give her child suck; if three she need not make ready his bed or work in wool; if four she may sit all day in the chair. Rabbi Eliezer said: Even if she brought him a hundred bondswomen he may force her to work in wool, for idleness leads to unchastity.[72]

The Talmud explains that the Mishnah did not mean to impose upon a woman heavy work, such as grinding: "She does not grind but attends to the grinding."[73]

Domestic chores in ancient times differed little from those which are expected of a woman in any agricultural community in modern times. The Rabbis, who strongly scorned idleness in a man, were even more strongly opposed to idleness in women, for they believed that idleness leads to moral deterioration. The Rabbis also decreed that things found by a woman belong to her husband.[74] The reason given in the Talmud is to prevent hostility between husband and wife.[75]

By rabbinic enactment a husband acquired the right of usufruct in property which his wife brought with her as part of her dowry, or which she inherited, without becoming responsible for any depreciation of its value. This type of property is called *niksai melug*, that is, the husband has the right to "pluck it," to use its income. Property for whose depreciation the husband assumes responsibility is called *niksai zon barzel* (lit. 'sheep of iron). The husband has the usufruct of it, but should he later divorce his wife he is answerable for any loss in its value whether through deterioration or damage.

The purpose of this enactment was to make the husband legally responsible for ransoming his wife in the event she was taken captive, a not uncommon occurrence in ancient times. The Rabbis enforced this obligation upon him by granting him the right to use the income from her property.[76] The obligations in marriage are summarized by Maimonides:

> The husband assumes in accordance with the laws of the Torah three obligations, namely food, raiment and marital relations. Seven additional obligations were placed on the husband by the enactment of the Scribes. He also acquires by marriage four benefits and all of them were enacted by the Scribes, namely, the earnings of her handwork, the things which she found, the usufruct of her property, and the right to inherit her in the event of her death.[77]

Our purpose here is not to discuss in detail the various responsibilities marriage throws on husband and wife. Rather, our concern is to illustrate that in the legislation of the Talmud, in accordance with the laws of the Torah, marriage gave the husband almost no legal rights over his wife where monetary matters were concerned. The concept of individualism, in its many phases, prevailed here too.

It has been often averred that women are given almost no status in the Bible. On the other hand, it is also possible to claim that the Rabbis in their interpretation and definition of a woman's legal rights reached "ultramodern" concepts of "suffrage" or freedom. In truth, neither of these statements is correct. The Bible is concerned with safeguarding the rights of women, but only out of moral and religious considerations. In the Torah it is the man who assumes legal obligations toward his wife because it is the man who is the stronger of the two. As the property owner he obligates himself financially, through his property, to support his wife and provide for her needs. The woman, as a rule, is not the property owner. Therefore, to allow her husband to acquire possession, *m'deoraitha*, of her future earnings or things that she found, or property which she inherited, would be tantamount to giving him possessive rights in her person. This would be a form of slavery and contrary to the entire religious and moral philosophy of the Torah. Thus the Torah imposes upon a man legal responsibilities toward his wife but denies him the automatic acquisition of possessive benefits through marriage.

The Rabbis followed a similar line of thought. They sought to protect the woman—to insure that her husband support her without grudge or rancor, ransom her if she is taken captive, provide her with medical care in case of sickness, take care of her burial in case of death, and provide her with an income in case of his death. It was to achieve this aim that they instituted a number of enactments which, if they seemingly diminished her independence as a married woman, gave her increased protection in case of emergencies. Since these enactments were promulgated solely for her benefit, she was free to decline the protection they offered in favor of preserving her independence—the birthright accorded every human being by the Torah's philosophy of the sacredness of the human personality. Moreso, even when the enactments of the Rabbis were in force, husband and wife preserved their individuality. The husband was not held responsible for the acts of his wife, nor did he, by the act of marriage assume full possession over her personality, for she was not "owned" by him. The Roman law of marriage under *manus*, which meant the complete subjugation of the wife to her husband both in person and property, was unknown in Judaism, for Judaism stands upon the religious principle that no human being can become the real property of another.

# 9. MAN: HIS INTENTION, WORD AND ACTION

Our Sages recognized three stages in man's conduct: intention, articulation and action. By intention is meant the motive or purpose that impels a man to action, by articulation, the oral announcement of an intention or desire, and by action, the purposeful performance of a deed.

As a rule, man is held responsible for his actions only when they are intentionally performed. In the performance of religious acts, particularly those which are devotional, *kavanah* or *mahshabah*, intention or thought,[1] is of primary significance. Thus, a man who reads the *Shema*, that most important of all enunciations in which is expressed the unity of God, fulfills a religious obligation by his reading only if it is his intention to fulfill that obligation and only if he directs his heart toward its fulfillment. A reading of the first verse of the *Shema* without such *kavanah* or intention is not accepted as fulfillment of the obligation of prayer.[2] In fact, for the Rabbis it is this direction of one's mind toward heaven which gives the act of prayer its significance. There was disagreement among tannaitic scholars whether every religious act requires such intention,[3] but all were agreed that prayer, the most devotional of all acts, requires complete concentration of mind. In the words of Maimonides, "Any prayer uttered without mental concentration is no prayer.... And what is meant by mental concentration? It means that a man should clear from his mind all extraneous thoughts and realize that he is standing before the Divine Presence (*Shekinah*)."[4]

Philo Judaeus emphasizes that whoever performs a good action without a voluntary desire to perform it loses the merit of its performance. He writes: "Those, too, who perform any other right action without the assent of their mind or will, but by doing violence to their inclination, do not achieve righteousness."[5] Professor Wolfson has proved from many Philonic quotations that by "assent of mind" Philo meant the joy which one experiences in performing the right action.[6]

Some of our Sages, however, were of the opinion that the performance of a good deed, regardless of its motive, purpose or intention, constitutes a righteous act, particularly when it is performed in behalf of a fellow man. Thus it is ruled: "Whoever says, 'this *selah* I give to charity so that my son may live or that I may have a share in the world to come,' he is a thoroughly righteous person."[7] This view obviously implies that it is the act itself, and not the motive behind it, which is of primary importance. It is interesting, however, that some texts do not read "he is a thoroughly righteous person, (*zaddik gamur*), but "it is a proper charity (*zedakah gemurah*)"[8] stressing the act, rather than the motive of the person.

In any case, it is a principle of Judaism that while good actions merit a reward, the hope of a reward, whether in this world or the world to come, should not be the motive for their performance. The desire to fulfill the will of God and the joy which comes with doing His bidding should be the primary motive for serving not only God but also one's fellow man, which is but another form of service before God. Such an attitude Antigonus of Socho, the next in succession to Simeon the Righteous, urged all men to develop: "Be not like servants who serve their master for the sake of receiving a reward; rather be like servants who serve their master not for the sake of receiving a reward."[9]

Our Sages did not take the extreme position of Philo that a good action does not constitute a righteous act unless it is performed purely and for its own sake. They did constantly emphasize, however, the importance of carrying out the will of God. There is no better proof, they maintained, of purity of motive and intention in the performance of a good deed then its joyful execution. To describe this attitude they coined the phrase, *"simha shel mitzvah,"*[10] the joy of fulfilling a commandment. This, too, is the rabbinic intent in their declarations: "The Presence of God does not rest in man's grievous mood but in his joyful mood through the fulfillment of a *mitzvah,"*[11] and, "The Torah teaches proper conduct, and that is that when one fulfills a commandment he should do so with a joyous heart."[12]

Our Sages did not find it anomalous to speak of "the yoke of the Kingdom of Heaven" and at the same time teach that the acceptance of the sovereignty of God is the greatest of all joys. This may be gleaned from their characterization of the prophet Isaiah: "Isaiah differed from all other prophets in that he accepted the yoke of the Kingdom of

Heaven with greater joy than the others."[13] In short, the religious ideal taught by our Sages was that man should not look upon the duties imposed upon him by God as an onerous burden which he is compelled to take up. Man should always accept the *mitzvot* with love and fulfill them with unmotivated and pure intentions, for there is no greater joy for man than to lovingly and freely submit to the will of God.

## UNFULFILLED INTENTION

Man is given freedom to choose between right and wrong and therefore he is held accountable for his voluntary acts. But man is judged not only by his acts but also by his intentions. Moreover, even those intentions which are not translated into action may determine a man's worthiness. Thus, if a man intends to do a good deed but is prevented from doing it by unavoidable circumstances, God "joins intention to deed,"[14] and accepts his good intention almost as if it were a good deed actually performed. This, however, is not true of evil deeds. If a man contemplates evil but does not perform it, he is not punished for his evil intentions.[15]

Rabbi Akiba did not subscribe to this opinion. He ruled that a Jew who voluntarily eats a piece of swine's meat, only to discover that the meat was not that of a swine, or a woman who knowingly violates a vow she took upon herself only to discover that her husband had unbeknownst to her dissolved her vow,[16] is in need of atonement and forgiveness.[17] Rabbi Akiba apparently reasoned that while evil intention by itself does not constitute sin, an evil intention translated into action is a sin. Thus, even if an accident should render the act permissible, its performer is considered to have already committed a sin, and though the act is not punishable in court it does require atonement and forgiveness.

The Talmud states that Rabbi Akiba interpreted the verse, "Then he shall make void her vow which is upon her ... and the Lord will forgive her,"[18] to mean that a woman who intentionally transgresses her vow without knowing that her husband has dissolved it, needs divine forgiveness. Whenever Rabbi Akiba read this verse, the Talmud reports, he used to shed tears exclaiming, "If a man who intends to take swine's meat and it so happens that it is lamb's meat, needs atonement and divine forgiveness, how much more so does one require divine forgiveness if he intends to take hold of swine's meat and it is swine's meat!"[19] It is quite apparent that it was Rabbi Akiba's purpose to drive home the point that in the eyes of the Torah intention and motive are all important, particularly when a man is ready to purposefully carry out an improper intention.

### UNREVEALED INTENTION

The Talmud considered human intention important not only with regard to right and wrong actions, but also with regard to the relations between one man and another, particularly where property transactions are concerned. This is illustrated in a story recorded in the Talmud. There was a man who sold his property with the intention of emigrating from Babylonia to the land of Israel but at the time of sale he did not express to the vendee his reason for the sale. It then happened that he was prevented from making the trip and he sought to void the transaction. Rabba, the famous Babylonian Amora, rendered the decision: "Intentions hidden in the heart are of no consequence."[20] The undisputed opinion in the Talmud is that legal transactions, to be valid, require *da'at*, intention or willingness. It was therefore ruled that had the vendor made an oral stipulation at the time of the sale that the transaction was conditional pending his emigration to the land of Israel, the sale would automatically have become void. It was the fact that he kept his intentions hidden that made them of no consequence. Behind this law lies the principle that no human being can be held responsible for understanding "the language of another's heart." Hence, while we believe the reasons given by the vendor for the original sale, nevertheless the sale is ruled to be valid because the seller did not express them in terms which the purchaser could have understood.

It is worth noting that whereas in transactions between man and man, unspoken and unrevealed intentions are of no significance, the Talmud declares that if a man resolves in his heart to offer a sacrifice or give a material object for the use of the Temple, his intention alone becomes an act of transaction. Combining the two verses in the Torah, "That which goes out of thy lips thou shalt observe and do,"[21] and "Take ye from among you an offering unto the Lord, whosoever is of willing heart, let him bring it,"[22] the Talmud states that a gift to God does not require an oral pledge. If "he completed his resolution in his heart," that in itself already makes the gift a part of Temple property.[23]

The difference between the secular and the sacred is not difficult to discern. In financial transactions between man and man, unarticulated intentions are in no way binding for the thoughts of the heart are unknowable to man and therefore unable to obligate him. However, in things which relate to God, before Whom nothing is hidden and Who can read the hearts of men, a resolution of the heart is no less binding than the spoken word and has the same force as a legal mode of transfer in human transactions.

Legal transfer in Jewish law requires acquiesence on the part of the vendor and faith on the part of the vendee, both of which must be openly expressed through a legal mode of transfer. Lacking such a mode of transfer, or without a contractual obligation, the mere intention of one of the parties, or even a spoken word, does not constitute an irrevocable determination and does not consumate a transaction. In secular, human transactions only an act can legally transfer property from the domain of one person to another. In sacred matters, such as gifts to the Temple, man's resolution is sufficient. Some rabbinic authorities would even consider charity to be a sacred matter. In the words of the Mishnah, "The word of the mouth to the Most High is equivalent to an act of conveyance in secular transaction."[24] This distinction is not merely a technical matter; it is a symbolic affirmation of the principle that in the eyes of God man's intentions and words are sacred and that before the Most High human intentions are as binding as legal acts.

Though our Sages ruled that intentions are not binding upon man, they considered it one of the fundamental virtues enjoined by the Torah for a man to honor his intentions even when they were hidden, if they affect his fellow man. Rabbi Simlai, the famous Aggadic teacher and preacher of the third century, taught that God gave Israel 613 commandments—248 positive commandments, corresponding to the number of limbs in the human body, and 365 negative commandments, corresponding to the number of days in the solar year.[25] Elaborating upon this he continued: In Psalm 15, David distilled the 613 commandments into eleven all-inclusive fundamental virtues.[26] Among these virtues is the one which reads, "He that... speaketh truth in his heart."[27] To illustrate what is meant by "speaking truly in the heart," the Talmud cites R. Safra.[28] R. Safra had an article he wished to sell. One day while he was reciting the *Shema*, a man presented himself before him and said, "I will give you so much money for the article." Not wishing to interrupt his prayers, R. Safra did not acknowledge the offer. Taking his silence to mean that R. Safra wanted a higher price for the article, the buyer increased his offer. When he had completed his prayers, R. Safra announced that he would sell the article at the price first mentioned. Since it had been his original intention to sell at that price, he felt morally obligated to honor his unspoken resolution.[29] Thus, while in financial transactions the intentions and resolutions of the heart are not legally binding, it is nevertheless a virtue to honor them. In the eyes of the higher law resolutions of the heart constitute moral obligations.

It is interesting to note further that, without exception, all of the cases cited by the Talmud as illustrations of the eleven virtues enumerated by David deal not with the observance of the letter of the law, but rather with the higher law which lies "beyond the boundaries of strict justice." For example, the verse, "nor doeth he evil to his fellow,"[30] our Sages tell us, does not appertain to refraining from bringing direct and actual harm to another, but rather to desisting from harming one's neighbor even indirectly by not encroaching on his trade.[31] The virtue of "He that putteth not his money in usury"[32] is attained by one who does not charge interest even when it is legally defensible to do so, as for example, when lending money to a heathen.[33]

The verse, "nor taketh he a bribe against the innocent,"[34] if taken literally, could hardly represent an exalted virtue. Our Sages, therefore took it to refer to a judge who is so scrupulous that he turns away from anything which might suggest even a shadow of indebtedness to a litigant. As men who attained such virtue, the Talmud points to Rabbi Ishmael ben Jose and Rabbi Ishmael ben Elisha. The former had a tenant farmer whose custom it was to bring Rabbi Ishmael ben Jose fruit from his own garden every Friday. Once the farmer brought him the fruit on Thursday. When Rabbi Ishmael asked him why he had brought the fruit a day earlier, the tenant farmer replied that since he had to come into the city that day to appear before Rabbi Ishmael in a litigation, he had brought the fruit with him to save himself a trip into the city on the morrow. Rabbi Ishmael refused to accept the fruit saying, "I will be disqualified from adjudicating your case." The other example cited by the Talmud concerned Rabbi Ishmael ben Elisha who was a priest as well as a judge. A man once presented him with a gift legally and properly due to a priest, but Rabbi Ishmael refused it lest "I become disqualified to act as a judge in your lawsuit."[35]

In selecting such examples our Sages obviously wanted to teach us the important lesson that in the eyes of the Torah one does not become virtuous simply because he complies with the law as it is enforceable in court. The truly virtuous man is not concerned merely with legal technicalities. He searches always for the higher purpose of the law and strives to attain that ethical perfection which comes through living up to the spirit as well as to the letter of the law.

### DESIRING THAT WHICH BELONGS TO ANOTHER

Neither for the Sages of the Talmud nor for Philo did evil intentions constitute a sin punishable in court. However, some of the Palestinian Tannaim, as well as Philo and later Maimonides, did consider the evil intention which a man has when he desires to misappropriate that which belongs to his fellow man to be a violation of a negative command. In fact, according to them such an intention is a violation of one of the Ten Commandments.

The fact that the tenth commandment, "Thou shalt not covet," is given in Hebrew as "*lo tahmod*" in Exodus,[36] and as "*lo titaveh*" in Deuteronomy,[37] led some of the Tannaim to consider it a dual prohibition. It forbade not only such covetousness which leads one to appropriate property of another without the owner's consent but in fact the very essence of covetousness itself; that is, the mere desire or lust to own the property of someone else. The difference between covetousness and robbery is that in the former the coveter is ready to pay full value for the article he desires, whereas the robber would forcefully deprive another of his property without compensating him for it. Analyzing the difference between the two readings in the tenth commandment, the Mekilta writes:

Here [in Exodus] it says, "Thou shalt not covet" (*lo tahmod*), and there [in Deuteronomy] it says, "Thou shalt not desire" (*lo titaveh*), in order to make one doubly culpable for desiring and coveting [a thing which belongs to another]. How do we know that if one desires a thing which belongs to another, he will ultimately covet it? It is said, "Thou shalt not desire" (*lo titaveh*), and "thou shalt not covet" (*lo tahmod*). How do we know that if a man covets a thing which belongs to another, he will ultimately commit robbery? It is written, "And they covet fields and they rob them" (Micah 2:2). Desire is in the heart, as it is said, "Thou mayest eat flesh after all the desire of thy soul" (Deut. 12:20), and coveting is in action, as it is said, "Thou shalt not covet the silver and the gold that is on them and take it unto thee" (Deut. 7:25).[38]

This same interpretation is found in other tannaitic midrashim.[39] There were quite a few Tannaim, therefore, who held that merely to desire in one's heart to possess that which belongs to another is a violation of the tenth commandment. The reason for this prohibition is also clear. There is a great danger that if one permits himself to entertain desires for that which does not belong to him he ultimately will be led to covet it and will attempt to obtain it. At first he may adopt less extreme methods, but if these should fail, his covetousness will finally lead him to the even greater transgression of robbery. Maimonides, following this tannaitic tradition, and citing the story of Ahab and Naboth (I Kings, Chap. 21) as an example, thus warns of the danger of covetousness: "Desire leads to coveting, and coveting to robbery.... Furthermore, if the owner will stand up against the coveter in order to safeguard his property or prevent him from committing robbery, it may lead to bloodshed."[40]

In this connection it is of interest to note the remarks of Philo Judaeus. As we have seen, he believed that evil intentions which are not translated into action are not transgressions, yet he begins his discussion of the tenth commandment thus:

The last commandment is against covetousness or desire, which he knew to be a subversive and insidious enemy. For all the passions of the soul which stir and shake it out of its proper nature and do not let it continue in sound health are hard to deal with, but desire is hardest of all. And therefore, while each of the others seems to be involuntary, an extraneous visitation, an assault from outside, desire alone originates from within ourselves and is voluntary.[41]

Obviously, it was Philo's intent in this statement to modify his previous stand. Often, evil intentions are not a part of man's willingness to do wrong but rather an irresponsible and involuntary impulse. Desire, however, particularly the desire to acquire things which belong to another, is a voluntary wrong for which a man is responsible. Such desires of the heart, Philo feels, echoing the tannaitic opinion, are in fact transgressions of the negative commandment, "Thou shalt not covet," even without a physical act of appropriation.[42]

In another place, using a phraseology almost identical with that of the Palestinian Sages, Philo calls desire "the fountain head of evils" and "the progenitor of plunderings and robberies and repudiations of debts and false accusations and outrages, also seductions, adulteries, murders, and all wrong action, whether private or public...."[43]

Hence we can readily see that there was unanimity among Jewish thinkers on this point. While evil intentions, from the strictly legal point of view, do not make one a transgressor, desire, which often is nothing more than a form of intention, if it is a lust to acquire things belonging to another, is definitely a transgression of the tenth commandment.

## THE INVIOLABILITY OF A MAN'S WORD

We recall that the Talmud cited the act of R. Safra as an example of virtuous conduct. As exemplified by this sage, the highest degree of ethical perfection is reached when one abides by the resolutions of his heart. The second degree of moral perfection is reached when one honors his words in matters of transactions. Legally, every transaction, in order to become valid, requires a formal mode of transfer. If, however, in matters of sale, a person reneges on a verbal understanding, though he is legally clear, he is called a *mehusar amanah*, one who is lacking in honesty.[44] Similarly, a man who promises to give another a gift and does not fulfill his promise is also characterized as a person who lacks honesty.[45]

There is, however, a more serious kind of breach of the divine code of virtuous behavior. If two parties agree upon a sale and settle on price and all the other matters pertaining to the sale, but before they can consummate the sale with a legal mode of transfer a third party intervenes and buys the property for himself, that third party is denounced as a *rasha*, a wicked person. The Talmud compares this kind of conduct to the act of a man who rushes forward to grab a forgotten sheaf of grain for himself before another poor man, who had waited for the removal of the stock of grain to claim whatever is left over, is able to pick it up. While legally, both men, being poor, have the same right to the forgotten sheaf, the person who waited at that particular spot for a longer time has a moral right to it. He who comes later and snatches it from him is morally a wicked man. Similarly, the man who first negotiates for the purchase of property has, when all other things are equal, a moral claim to its acquisition, even though no legal act of transfer has as yet taken place.[46]

The most serious ethical offense in transactions is for a man, after he has agreed to a sale and a mode of transfer has taken place, to take advantage of the fact that the particular mode of transfer used was not legally binding and retract on his original agreement. In this case, since the oral promise was followed by an act, a clear indication was given by him of his intention and determination to consummate the sale. If he retracts now, the most serious sanctions available to the court are directed against him. Let us illustrate this with an example.

To become legally binding, any sale or purchase requires a *kinyan*, a tangible mode of acquisition. An oral agreement to sell or buy an article, called *kinyon debarim*, a verbal mode of transaction, is not binding on either party and both can retract. Different modes of acquisition are required for movable objects and immovable objects. For instance, *kesef*, money which the purchaser gives to the seller, does not constitute a *kinyan* for *metaltelim*, movable objects; as long as the purchaser has not taken possession of the article through the *kinyan* of *meshikah*, drawing it out from the vendor's domain, both parties have the legal right to retract. If therefore, two people agree to a sale of movable objects, and the vendee turns over a sum of money to the vendor, the latter has a legal right to void the sale. Morally, however, it is considered dishonest for him to retract after he has entered into a verbal agreement and a *kinyan kesef* has taken place, even though in this case, it is not a binding mode of acquisition.

In such cases, the Sages did not merely inform the retractor that he had committed a moral wrong; they scathingly informed him of his status in the eyes of God. The Mishnah rules:

If the vendee had drawn the *perot* [the movable object] into his possession from the vendor but had not yet paid him money, neither may retract; but if he had given him money, but had not yet drawn the movable object from the vendor's into his own possession he may retract. They, however, have said: "He that exacted punishment from the generation of the Flood (Gen. 6:13) and the generation of the Dispersion (Gen. 11:9) will exact punishment from him who does not abide by his spoken word."[47]

When the Mishnah states, "if he had given him money, but had not yet drawn the movable object," it does not necessarily mean that he paid him in full. The law applies even if he had given him only a token payment for the sake of a *kinyan*. Morally he should not retract because one must stand by his word.

In the Talmud there is a disagreement between the two great Babylonian Amoraim, Abaye and Raba, as to the meaning of the *mi-she'para*, the formula, "He that exacted punishment, etc.," mentioned in the Mishnah. Abaye said that the one who retracts his spoken word is informed in general terms of the divine punishment which awaits such retractors, but the court does not pronounce the formula in the form of a curse. Raba, on the other hand, maintained that the court actually pronounces a curse on the retracting party in the form stated in the Mishnah.[48] Raba's opinion became the accepted halakah, and significantly this is the only instance in rabbinic literature in which sanctions were instituted in the form of the pronouncement of a curse.

The above analysis of the laws of retraction serves to underscore the sacred worth which our Sages placed on a man's word. The entire rabbinic judicial structure was built on trust in a man's word, once given. On the trustworthiness of the words of two witnesses a man could be exonerated or found culpable, subjected to corporal punishment or be made to pay money to others, set free or put to death.

Jewish courts never required an oath of witnesses. A man's spoken word was sufficient evidence for the court. The very authenticity of the Torah-tradition was based upon oral transmission and rested on the faith placed in the spoken word of those who transmitted it. It is therefore easy to understand how deeply our Sages were concerned with the sacredness of the spoken word and why they took the extreme measure of pronouncing a curse on one who breaks trust and retracts from his verbal agreement.

## THE SPOKEN WORD

The fact that in legal transactions an oral agreement or promise creates only a moral obligation does not mean that the spoken word cannot create legal obligations. On the contrary, there is probably no other legal system in the world which gives the spoken word the legal force it has in rabbinic law.

It has already been pointed out that gifts to the Temple and, according to some authorities, gifts to charity do not have to wait upon formal modes of transfer to be consummated. In such cases, a man's verbal declaration is sufficient to effect an immediate transfer and bind him legally. The very equation between gifts to the Temple and charity is significant of the Jewish attitude in these matters.

Behind this law is the principle that only in transactions between one man and another is an act of acquisition necessary, but in the case of a gift to *hekdesh* [the Sacred], a man's word by itself constitutes an act of transfer, for God needs no *kinyan*. "A verbal pledge in relation to the Most High is equal to the act of transfer to human beings."[49] In fact, some rabbinic authorities state that in ancient times when sacrifices were offered in the Temple, the *korban* [offering] could be invested with *kedushath haguf* [sanctity] only by word of mouth. Only a man's word can make the secular sacred. A *kinyan*, which is a commercial form of transaction, cannot effect such a change. In matters of *hekdesh* the word of mouth is not a mere "vow." With the utterance of a man's word his property instantaneously passes from his possession into the possession of the Most High, from the secular to the sacred.

The Talmud, it would appear, included charity among the sacred things. The Talmud tells of a man who received a minor injury and sued the culprit in the court of Rabbi Joseph. The latter made the culprit pay half a *zuz* in damages. Said the injured: "Since it amounts only to half a *zuz*, I do not desire to accept it; I give it to the poor of the town." Then he retracted and said: "I will take it and will cure myself." But Rabbi Joseph ruled that he could not retract because "the poor have already acquired possession of it, for we are the hand [the agents] of the poor men."[50]

The interpretation of this passage was the subject of great controversy among the leading scholars of the Middle Ages. Both Rabbi Isaac Alfasi and Maimonides are of the opinion that a promise to give charity has the same legal force as an act of transfer in a business transaction.[51] The Talmud asserts that charity "is analogous to sacrifices."[52] Maimonides, going even further, states that while in accordance with rabbinic law one cannot by means of a *kinyan* transfer things which are not in existence, insofar as charity and consecrated things are concerned, a man's mere word is sufficient transfer. Continuing, Maimonides writes:

> There are some Gaonim who disagree with the above and say that the poor can acquire possession only in the same manner that a private person can. Therefore they cannot acquire possession over a thing which has not yet come into existence even if he had agreed previously to do so; he is compelled to fulfill his promises in matters of charity or consecrated things, just as he is compelled to fulfill a vow.[53]

Since an oral promise to give charity is equivalent to an actual transfer in a financial transaction, an oral pledge, according to rabbinic law, creates an obligation on one's estate and in case of death the charity can be collected from the heir.[54]

As stated, a man can consecrate an object to the Temple by word of mouth, for with the mere utterance of his intention the property is automatically transferred to the Temple. In this light, we can understand many other instances in rabbinic law in which a spoken word becomes a powerful legal instrument. The most striking example of the sacredness and legal power of the spoken word is the principle of *hefker* under which a person may renounce his ownership over property simply by saying, "Let this thing become *hefker*." Once this formula is pronounced, any one may take possession of the ownerless property through a simple act of acquisition. Dr. Isaac Herzog makes the following cogent observation:

> The express declaration by the owner totally releasing his property, whether *karka* or *metaltelim* [real or movable goods], from his ownership, setting it free for whomsoever would be first to take it, is effective in Jewish law.... An interesting phenomenon this—that a few words uttered without ceremony in favor of an indeterminate individual or individuals to be made determinate by mere chance, should divest the owner of his title![55]

While I fully agree with Dr. Herzog's observation, I see no evidence for his theory that *hefker* was originally a form of charity.[56] If anything, it appears to me that the laws of *hefker* deepen our insight into the rabbinic principle that a man's word is both sacred and legally binding.

Legally speaking, there is a fundamental difference between *hefker* and *mekirah*, a sale. In a sale, which involves the transfer of property to a particular individual or group of individuals, the buyer does not acquire title to the property unless and until he completes a formal mode of acquisition. As long as the vendee has not taken legal title to the property, the spoken word of the vendor does not bind him legally, even though he is morally obligated to fulfill his word. In the case of *hefker*, however, the owner does not transfer his property to any particular individual; his action, therefore, is not dependent upon someone else's act of acquisition. Since he merely renounces his own rights to the property no formal mode of transfer is required, his spoken word being sufficient to render the property ownerless.

We can therefore understand why the School of Hillel held that *hefker* is valid only when the property is released unconditionally, but if acquisition of the property is restricted to a particular group of people the *hefker* is void. The Mishnah states:

> The School of Shammai says: If a man proclaims a thing ownerless (*hefker*) for the benefit of the poor alone, it is legally ownerless property. The School of Hillel says that the property does not become ownerless unless it is proclaimed ownerless even for the rich.[57]

It was obviously not the aim of the School of Hillel to safeguard the interests of the rich. What they meant to say is that *hefker* is valid only when one proclaims his property ownerless without any conditions attached and without setting any restrictions on who can claim it for himself. *Hefker* means simply that the owner completely renounces any rights he has over the property and thus makes it available to all. As an example of *hefker* the Hillelites cite the law of the Sabbatical year when the produce of the fields becomes ownerless and every person is free to take as much of it as he pleases.

The legal reasoning of the School of Hillel is clear. If one declares his property to be *hefker* for a limited group of people only, then it is not a complete renunciation of his rights but rather an act of transfer, a gift given to a group of people. As such, the spoken word unaccompanied by a formal act of transfer has no legal value. To permit a man to declare his property *hefker* and still retain the right to choose the person or group to whom it should be given would be to go contrary to the very principle of *hefker*, which in reality means a renunciation of all of one's rights over his property.

Maimonides, with profound insight, explained the principle of *hefker* in the following words: "*Hefker*, though it is not a *neder* (a vow), is still equivalent to a *neder* in that he is forbidden to retract. What constitutes *hefker*? That is when a man says: My property is *hefker* for all."[58] Many great scholars and commentators have attempted to explain Maimonides' apparent equation of the principle of *hefker* with the principle of *neder*, but they all missed the point. It was Maimonides' intent merely to relate the principle of *hefker* with a similar principle which allows a man, simply through the power of the spoken word, to cede all rights and benefits he enjoys in his own property. It was not his intention to equate the two.

According to the tannaitic definition of *neder*, a man may by a spoken word forbid upon himself any benefits from his own property. Once he utters the formula of a *neder* he no longer has any right of benefit in his property. Similarly, declares Maimonides, by means of the spoken word in *hefker*, one can relinquish all rights to his property, and he is not permitted to retract. Should he retract and claim the property as his own after someone else acquired possession of it, or refuse to permit another person to claim it, he infringes upon another's rights and lays claim to property which is not his own. Never, however, did Maimon-

ides mean to rule that *hefker* and *neder* are one and the same and that he
who retracts in a case of *hefker* violates the command in the Torah,
"When a man voweth a vow, or sweareth an oath to bind his soul with
a bond, he shall not break his word, he shall do according to all that
proceedeth out of his mouth."[59] Rather, a distinction is noted: when
one violates a vow his transgression is between himself and God, but
when one retracts his pronouncement of *hefker* he trespasses on the
rights of his fellow men for he denies them their right to claim ownerless property. His retraction, therefore, is void.

Just as through the spoken word a man can legally renounce all rights
over his property, so can a person through the spoken word assume
obligations upon himself and his property. Thus, a surety legally binds
himself merely by stating that he takes on the responsibility of an *oreb*
(a surety); and if the debtor does not pay his debt the creditor can
legally collect his debt from the property of the surety. In fact, there
are numerous instances in rabbinic law where a "word of mouth" becomes a legally binding instrument.[60] In short, "word of mouth" in
Jewish law creates not only moral obligations but constitutes a powerful
legal instrument in depriving oneself of property rights and benefits,
and in the assumption of numerous legal obligations. In matters of
transactions, however, agreement by *parlor* is not legally binding because the vendee can establish his right to the property only through a
legal act of acquisition; as long as the property remains in the domain of
the vendor, an oral understanding creates only moral obligations.

## ACTION: DIRECT AND INDIRECT

In the rabbinic legal system, there are two ways by which a man may be
penalized for his immoral or criminal acts; he can be punished by a
human court, or he can be punished by the divine court, that is, "in
accordance with the laws of heaven." Hence, though the Torah is the
revealed word of God, the punishments which the Torah authorizes a
human court to mete out differ from the punishments inflicted by the
divine court.

A human court can hold an individual legally responsible only for
acts actually performed by him, whereas the divine court holds a person

responsible even for merely having caused a criminal or immoral act to have been performed. In the eyes of the laws of heaven a person who is instrumental in bringing a criminal act into being is responsible for the act and its consequences, even though he himself has not performed that act.[61] Thus, Rabbi Josiah said:

There are four offenses which a man commits for which he is not liable under the laws of men but for which he is liable under the laws of heaven: he who breaks down a fence which encloses his neighbor's animal so that it goes out and causes damages; he who bends another's standing corn towards a fire; he who hires witnesses to testify falsely; he who has the knowledge to give testimony in behalf of another and keeps silent.[62]

In the four instances enumerated by Rabbi Josiah, the man did not commit a criminal act; he merely provided others with the opportunity to commit a criminal act. He therefore cannot be punished by a human court. In rabbinic terminology such an act is classified as *grama*, that is, serving as the indirect cause of damages or injuries to another person. The Torah makes one legally responsible only for injuries and damages directly inflicted, not for damages and injuries indirectly caused. In the same way, the Mishnah states that if a man entrusts fire to a deaf-mute, an imbecile or a minor, who in turn set off a fire which damages property, he is not culpable by the laws of man but is culpable by the laws of heaven.[63]

There are rabbinic authorities who maintain that in cases where the penalty is money indemnity, setting in motion an act which as an indirect cause will unquestionably result in loss, makes one subject to legal actions. Such an act they classify under the principle of *garmi*. On the other hand, an act which in itself may or may not inflict damage, even if ultimately it does cause someone a loss, is not subject to claim before a human court. The latter constitutes merely a *grama*.[64]

The distinction between *garmi* and *grama* does not apply in capital offenses. A human court can punish only a man who actually commits an act of murder, not one who is the indirect cause of a murder, even if his act made the death of the victim inevitable. If, for instance, one person binds another and leaves him to be killed by wild beasts, or hires another to commit murder, he cannot be held accountable before a human court, but he is punished by the divine court.[65] Maimonides, therefore, states, "If one hires an assassin to kill his fellow man, or sends his slaves to kill him or binds him up and leaves him in front of a lion or another beast and the beast kills him... he has earned death at the hands of heaven, but in such cases capital punishment cannot be inflicted at the hands of the court."[66]

There can be no more inevitable, albeit indirect causes of homicide than the illustrations given by Maimonides. None the less, according to Jewish legal tradition, the murderer cannot be punished by a human court because he did not directly commit an act of murder. He is liable, however, before the divine court because morally he committed a homicide.

This principle of legal and moral liability affects the entire system of rabbinic jurisprudence. A man is legally liable in a human court only for offenses directly committed, not for offenses for which he was the indirect cause. In the latter case he is subject only to the laws of heaven. The rabbinic distinction between direct actions and indirect causes may not be very tenable in the modern, and particularly secular, view. If, however, we bear in mind that in the Jewish theocracy the belief in divine reward and punishment is not a mere theory but a reality, and that the laws of heaven actually exist, the Rabbis' position is clear and understandable. They never feared that their legal philosophy, particularly in regard to capital punishment, would lead to a demoralization of human conduct. They merely transferred such cases from one type of a court to another, quite possibly a more effective court.

This rabbinic attitude casts light upon one of the controversies between the Sadducees and Pharisees about which much has been written but which has not been adequately explained.

According to biblical law, if witnesses are proven to have given false testimony, "then shall ye do unto him as he had proposed to do unto his brother."[67] The rabbinic interpretation of this law is that witnesses can be condemned for having given false testimony only if another pair of witnesses state in court: "How can you testify so, you were with us that day in such a place."[68] In this wise the testimony of the second pair of witnesses incriminates the first witnesses themselves, but does not in any way touch upon the criminal act which is in question before the court. This negation of testimony is called *hazamah*. If, however, two pairs of witnesses contradict each other in their testimony on the act itself, so that one pair testifies that one man killed another and the second pair says, "How can you testify so when he [the murderer] was with us that same day in such a place," then the evidence of neither is accepted and neither pair suffers any penalty, because there is no way of determining which pair is testifying falsely. This denial is called *hakhashah*.[69]

In talmudic annals there seems to be no controversy over what constitutes false testimony. The line of distinction between *hazamah* and *hakhashah* is clear. The Mishnah, however, does record the following disagreement between the Sadducees and Pharisees:

False witnesses are put to death only after the judgment has been completed [i.e. the sentence pronounced]. For the Sadducees used to say: Not until he [who was falsely accused] has been put to death, as it is written, "a life for a life" (Deut. 19:21), meaning, his brother [the accused] is still alive. If so, why is it written "a life for a life?" One could think that as soon as their evidence is received [and found false] they [the witnesses] are put to death, therefore the Scripture says "a life for a life." They are not put to death until the judgment [of the court] is completed.[70]

Josephus reports that, as a rule, the Sadducees were more severe in punishing offenders than the Pharisees.[71] Yet, here, in the only reference in the Mishnah to a disagreement between the Sadducees and the Pharisees with reference to penalties, the former appear to have been more lenient.

It is my opinion that this disagreement between the Sadducees and the Pharisees is more than a mere difference over the interpretation of verses. This controversy reflects a basic disagreement between the Pharisees and the Sadducees over the power of the courts to inflict punishment. The opinion of the Sadducees, it appears to me, is a direct outgrowth of their severity in punishing offenders.

The Sadducees interpreted the verse "then shall ye do unto him as he had proposed to do unto his brother," to mean that false witnesses are punished not because they committed a crime in bearing false witness, but because through their evidence they indirectly caused an innocent

person to be put to death.  According to the Pharisees, on the other
hand, the crime of false witnesses lies in their having given false testimony.  Since the Sadducees held that false testimony is a crime only because it causes an innocent person to be put to death, they ruled that
only if the death sentence has already been executed can the false witnesses be held to have committed an act of murder.  If, however, their
testimony is refuted before the accused is put to death, their testimony
effects nothing and they are free from all penalties.  For the Pharisees,
however, the fact that a man is put to death by the false evidence of
witnesses does not constitute an act of murder punishable in court.  The
false witnesses are at most an indirect cause of the death of the accused,
and for serving as an indirect cause of homicide a man can be punished
only by the laws of heaven and not by a human court.

False witnesses, in the Pharisaic view, are punished primarily for
having given false evidence, and their punishment must be commen-
surate with what they had "proposed to do unto his brother."  Hence, if
by their false testimony they had intended to deprive one of his property, they should suffer that penalty, and if they testified falsely to a
murder, then for their false testimony they should suffer the same penalty
which would have been inflicted on the accused.  The Pharisees required
that the court sentence be pronounced before the law of *ed zomeim*
was applied.  Only after the testimony was officially completed could
the witnesses, when disproved, be declared guilty of having given false
evidence.  Once, however, the accused was put to death the court ruled
the case closed.  It refused to accept testimony of other witnesses who
came to incriminate the first set.  The court simply assumed that the
testimony of the first set was true.

The logic of this Pharisaic position is clear.  If the court were to permit the refutation of testimony even after the execution of the death
sentence, no case could ever be closed.  There would always remain the
possibility that a third pair of witnesses would arrive to incriminate the
second set, and a fourth set to incriminate the third set, and so on,
leading perhaps to the death of many innocent men.  The Pharisaic decision was, therefore, that after either the accused or the first set of in-
criminated witnesses suffer death, the case is officially closed and removed from the court's calendar.

It is, therefore, my opinion in analyzing this controversy, that the Sadducees maintained that legally a man can be held liable by human courts for being the indirect cause of a criminal act. This principle, as is well known, was also extant in ancient Roman law and its influence can be seen even in our contemporary common law. The Pharisees, however, with their firm religious belief in the laws of man and the laws of heaven, ruled that a person could be made legally responsible before a human court only for those acts which were direct criminal offenses. For an act of murder one is liable in a human court; for having indirectly caused the death of another, a man can be truly judged and punished only by the court of heaven.

The position of the Pharisees is a very consistent one if we remember their unshakable belief in particular providence and divine reward and retribution. Thus, if it should happen that witnesses succeed in deceiving a human court and cause the execution of an innocent man, there is always a Higher Court before which they will have to stand trial. As our Sages put it, "before heaven the truth is revealed." False witnesses will ultimately be punished by the laws of heaven for having been the indirect cause of a man's death,

## ARTICULATION AND ACTION

The Pharisaic stand asserts that in Judaism, man's intentions, motives and purposes, whether for good or evil, are of great significance. It is intention, say our Sages, which gives meaning to and determines the validity of an act. Intention by itself, however, if it does not express itself in action, plays almost no role in determining the merit of an individual action. Actions alone determine the status of man, and by them alone is he judged for good or evil. In fact, the accepted halakah is that a man can be punished in court only for those violations which involve a physical action.[72] Maimonides lists only three cases in which the spoken word constitutes a transgression for which a man may be punished by flogging.[73] Morally, as our Sages often declared, transgression through an "evil tongue" is one of the most serious offenses,[74] but legally, in nearly all cases, offenses committed by the spoken word are not acts of transgression and are punishable only by the hand of God.

Philo Judaeus gave expression to this fundamentally Jewish thought in a very significant passage:

Practically, cases both of sinning and achieving righteousness fall into three classes, thoughts and words and deeds. And therefore, in his Exhortations, Moses, when he is showing that the acquisition of good is neither impossible nor hard to pursue, says, "Ye need not fly up to heaven, nor go down to the end of the earth and sea to lay hold of it, but near (and in the words that follow immediately he shows the nearness as if it were nearly visible to the eye) is every word to the mouth and heart and hands."[75] In these three words he figures *words*, *thoughts* and *intentions*, and *deeds*[76]... since righteousness and sinning are found in these places, heart, mouth and hand... wrong thinking and intending is the least serious, and actually carrying out injustice the most serious, while saying what we should not _tands midway between the two.... It is easy to see why wrong-speaking is a graver matter than wrong-thinking. A man's thoughts are sometimes not due to himself, but come without his will... But speaking is voluntary.... But unjust action is a more grievous sin than any speaking, for the word is the shadow of the act, men say, and if the shadow is harmful, the act must be more harmful. And, therefore, Moses exempts mere intention from accusation and penalty.... But all that issues through the mouth he requires to make its defense and stand its correction on the principle that the speech is our own power. But in these trials words are judged more leniently, culpable actions more severely, for he appointed great penalties for the authors of great misdeeds, those who carry into actual execution what their ill-intended intentions have planned or their reckless tongues have uttered.[77]

It is apparent from this passage that Philo maintained that a man cannot be held responsible for his wrong and evil intentions because thoughts are difficult to control. For his spoken words, however, a man is held fully responsible, and while he may not be punished for wronging another by means of spoken words, he is called upon to defend his spoken word and "stand its correction."[78] Philo as well, as the Rabbis, recognized the deep significance of the Biblical adage: "Guard that which comes from thy lips" (Deut. 23:24).

## UNLAWFUL ACTIONS UNDER DURESS

According to talmudic law, a man is held responsible for his actions only if by his own free will he chooses to perform such actions. If, however, against his will he is compelled to commit an unlawful act he is neither legally nor morally responsible. The Rabbis deduced this principle from Deuteronomy 22:26 which declares that if a man rapes a betrothed woman he is punished by death. "But unto the damsel thou shalt do nothing; there is in the damsel no sin worthy of death," the damsel was a victim of force. The verse concludes with the words, "For as when a man riseth against his neighbor, and slayeth him, even so is this matter," equating an act performed under duress with an act performed under threat of death.

It is important to delineate the talmudic law of duress. If a man is told to violate a negative command—such as to bear false witness—or else his money will be taken away, the halakah is that this is not considered *duress* to absolve him of responsibility for the unlawful act. A man must be willing to sacrifice all his worldly possessions rather than transgress the law. Hence the Mishnah rules: "If witnesses [attesting to the valitidy of their signatures on a legal document] said 'this is indeed our handwriting, but we acted under compulsion'... they may be believed."[79] The Talmud, in defining the law of the Mishnah, states: "They are believed... only if they said 'we were compelled by reason of threats to our lives'; but if they said, 'we were compelled by reason of threat to our money,' they are not believed because one cannot incriminate himself."[80]

According to the Talmud, then, a man is under no circumstances permitted to give false testimony to save his money. To do so is to violate the negative commandment, "Thou shalt not bear false testimony against they neighbor";[81] and the halakah is that a man cannot incriminate himself by revealing that he committed an act of wickedness. This Talmudic passage is the source for the decision of later rabbinic authorities that one is not permitted to commit a criminal act, or for that matter to transgress any negative command, even if he is under threat of losing all his money. The decision is, "Let him lose all his money but not commit an unlawful act."[82]

### INFORMING UNDER DURESS

While a man may commit unlawful actions in order to save his life, apparently a distinction is made between all other transgressions and that of robbery. The Talmud states: "If they forced him and he pointed out to them his fellow's property, he is not liable to make restitution to the owner. If, however, he takes the property with his hand and surrenders it he is liable to make restitution."[83] The distinction between pointing out where one's fellow's property is, and taking the property with one's own hand and surrendering it, is clear. In the former case the man commits no act of transgression. Indirectly he may be responsible for the loss of his fellow's money, but, since he acted under duress, to save his life, he is not legally liable to make restitution. However, if he takes the property with his own hand, he commits an act of robbery; thus, though under duress to save his life, he is legally liable to make payment.

It is striking that the halakah is that even when he takes the property in his own hand and surrenders it, he does not violate the prohibition of "Thou shalt not rob him,"[84] since he does so under duress; and yet he must compensate the owner for his loss. This halakah can be understood in two ways. Either the requirement of compensating the victim of a robbery is independent of the crime or sin involved and therefore even a permissible act of robbery does not exempt one from making compensation, or since the offender used another's property to save his life, he is legally bound to compensate the owner for his loss. The latter view was accepted by Maimonides who ruled that "whoever saves his life through the property of another, must repay it."[85]

Vows and oaths[86] were endowed with great force and sanctity in rabbinic law. This is understandable, surely, in view of the great value and sacredness attached to the spoken word, as touched upon above. It is permitted, however, to violate vows and oaths pronounced under duress. But here again there is consistency in the halakah. For an oath or vow to be valid, "the words of the mouth and the intent of the heart must be alike."[87] Hence when a man takes a vow under compulsion, to save his life or his money, his heart and mouth are not at one and therefore he does not bind himself with his words.[88]

## NON-ACTION UNDER DURESS

So far we have discussed actions performed under duress, and noted that a man must be ready to sacrifice all his worldly possessions rather than commit an unlawful action and transgress a negative command. But apparently the Rabbis recognized a difference between action and non-action under duress. If, to save his money, a man does not perform a good action (i.e., a positive command of the Torah) does he thereby commit a transgression through his non-action?

There is obviously, a distinction between committing an unlawful act under duress to save one's money and failing to perform a good action for the same reason. In the latter case the halakah seems to be more lenient.[89]

As noted, under duress a man may transgress any of the negative commands in order to save his life. Going even further, Maimonides ruled that no one has the right to give up his life in order to avoid violating a negative command. He writes: "When one is enjoined to transgress rather than suffer death, and suffers death rather than transgress, he is guilty of causing his own death."[90] This is a consequent application of the principle that a man's life is not his personal property which he can, even in a spirit of piety, offer up as a supreme sacrifice. Acts of supererogation and saintliness are limited to going beyond the requirements of the strict law in dealing with one's fellow man, or for that matter in matters relating to God. They do not however give a man license to cause his own destruction. It is the will of God that man should violate the law rather than to cause his own death; man cannot choose to set that will aside.

Maimonides' decision was accepted by Nachmanides[91] but the Tosafot school held the opinion that one is permitted to surrender his life for the sake of not violating a negative command.[92] Remarkably both Tosafot and Nachmanides, who hold contrary opinions, base their decisions on a statement in the Jerusalem Talmud. The story is told there that a certain R. Abba bar Zemina was engaged as a tailor by a non-Jew in Rome. His employer brought him forbidden food and said to him. "Eat!" R. Abba answered him: "I shall not eat." The employer then said: "Eat or I will kill you." R. Abba replied: "If you wish to kill me, do so, for I will not eat *nebelah.*"[93]

From this talmudic story the Tosafot deduced the principle that a man is permitted to demand of himself greater devotion to God, and not violate the law even at the cost of his own life. Nachmanides, however, quoted the concluding statement in the Talmud to the effect that if R. Abba bar Zemina had known that it is permitted to violate the law to save one's life he surely would have eaten.

### THE THREE CARDINAL SINS UNDER DURESS

There are, however, transgressions which a man should not commit even under threat of death. During the Hadrianic persecution the halakah was set that in the matter of the three cardinal transgressions, idolatry (*abodah zarah*), adultery or incest (*gillui arayot*), and homicide (*shefikat damim*), one must suffer death rather than sin.[94] Later rabbinic authorities pondered what the halakah would be in the event a man under duress did commit one of these three cardinal sins? Does he, by such an act, commit a capital offense punishable by death or not? Is the halakah to be understood that in these three cases, a threat of death does not constitute an act of compulsion (*ohnes*), but that nevertheless, in view of the seriousness of their transgressions, one should sanctify the name of God and suffer martyrdom. If the interpretation that martyrdom is preferable but not mandatory is accepted, it means that if a man chooses to transgress rather than die he is not condemned as would be a man who deliberately commits such transgressions. This was the view of Maimonides, who ruled that in such cases one who suffers death rather than transgress sanctifies the name of God, and that "If this act of martyrdom took place in the presence of ten Israelites, he sanctifies the name of God in public, like Daniel, Hananiah, Mishael and Azariah, Rabbi Akiba and his colleagues. These are the martyrs who suffered by royal decree, and no person has attained a higher rank."[95]

On the other hand, Maimonides continues, if one is enjoined to suffer death rather than transgress, and he transgresses, he profanes the name of God, and if at the time of his transgression there are ten Israelites present, he profanes the name of God publicly. However, since the transgression was committed under duress, he does not suffer the penalty of stripes nor, in the case of homicide, does the court sentence him to death. The death penalty and the penalty of stripes are inflicted only if one transgresses of his own free will in the presence of witnesses and only after he was forewarned.[96]

It was Maimonides' opinion that no one can be held legally responsible, even in the case of the three cardinal sins, for a transgression committed to save one's life. The ruling in these three sins: "let him die and not transgress" is rather a demand that each man should sanctify the Name and avoid the profanation of the Name. The first is a positive and the second a negative precept, but for transgressing these the court cannot inflict punishment. Nachmanides sided with Maimonides in this decision, while other rabbinic authorities disagreed. These latter rendered the decision that wherever the Talmud states "let him die and not transgress" a man has no choice and if he transgresses to save his life, he is treated as if he had committed the transgression of his own free will.[97]

## MAN IS ALWAYS FOREWARNED

As we have seen, the general rule in rabbinic law is that a man is held responsible for actions only if they are performed of his own free will, but not if they are performed inadvertently or under compulsion. This principle is certainly true if one commits unlawful actions for which the court of man must enforce penalties. In case of damages the Mishnah states: "A man is always forewarned (muad) whether he acts inadvertently or willfully, whether he is awake or asleep. If he blinded his neighbor's eye or broke his vessel he must repay in full."[98] To this the Talmud, in the name of Tanna de be-Hizkiah, adds that a man must pay full damages "in case of compulsion as in the case of willfulness."[99] In the name of Rabbah, however, the Talmud makes a distinction between injuring a person wilfully and injuring a person inadvertently or under compulsion. In the former case compensation must be made for five separate outgrowths of the injury: (1) damages, (2) pain, (3) medical care, (4) enforced idleness and (5) humiliation. In the last instance, however, one has to pay only for damages caused by the injury. Hence, if a man, as a result of a wind of unusual strength, falls from a roof and injures another, he pays only for the damages, and is not liable for the other four counts.[100]

It appears from the above that the talmudic understanding of the Mishnah is that in instances of injuries committed inadvertently or under compulsion, one has to pay damages to the injured party even as one pays damages for destroying another's property. But the laws of "compensation" (which apply particularly to injuries) are in effect only when such injuries are committed wilfully, in full knowledge that an unlawful action is being committed. Hence the laws of the Mishnah and the Talmud, that one must pay in full "whether he acts inadvertently or willingly," and "in case of compulsion as in the case of willfulness," apply only to the legal obligations which result from committing damages, whether these be to property or human beings. This singular principle does not apply to any legal obligations resulting from committing injuries. There is a fundamental difference between injuring another person and damaging another's property. In the case of injury, one not only causes damage, he commits a crime against the human personality. Hence, if one man injures another but the damage done amounts to less than a *perutah* (which requires no compensation), he does not have to pay, but he has committed a crime and is subject to corporal punishment. Our Sages derived this principle from Deuteronomy 25:2 which limits corporal punishment to forty stripes. The exact phrase is "he shall not exceed" and on it the *Sifre* comments: "If the messenger of the court exceeds in punishing the offender, he violates the negative command of "he shall not exceed."[101] The Talmud thereupon states that if by inflicting additional physical injury not sanctioned by the Torah to a wicked man, one violates a negative command and commits a criminal act, how much more is one liable for committing a criminal act if he smites an innocent man.[102]

In other words, if a man injures another inadvertently or under compulsion, the laws pertaining to crimes of "injuries to another" do not apply because there was neither knowledge of nor intent to injure another. The legal obligation to pay for damages on the other hand, is not measured by one's intention or wilfulness. In fact the Talmud does not ever characterize damaging one's property as a criminal offense. It limits its discussion merely to the legal obligations which fall on a man to pay for damages done to another's property, whether caused by him or by his possession. This does not mean of course, that our Sages considered it permissible to damage another's property. They were, however, concerned with insuring that restitution would be made to one whose property was damaged. However, being prepared to pay, does not give one permission to damage another's property. Maimonides specifically declares, "One is forbidden to cause damages willfully, with the intention of paying for the damage he caused."[103] At the same time he declares in another place: "If one commits *injury* against another person, he may not be compared to one who *damages* another's property. For in the latter case, atonement is effected for him as soon as he makes the required compensation. But if one wounds another, atonement is not affected for him even if he paid all the five courses of payment, or even if he has sacrificed the rams of Nebaiot, for his sin is not forgiven until he begs forgiveness of the injured person and is forgiven by him."[104] The thief, the robber, as well as the one who inflicts bodily injuries even of a temporary nature on another, all commit crimes against men and sin against God. Therefore, even when the criminal makes compensation he still needs repentance, and the primary purpose of such compensation and penance is to win the pardon of the person against whom such offenses were committed.

The seriousness of criminal actions depends on whether they are committed with intention or unwittingly, whether willingly or under duress. On the other hand, man is responsible for damages which he commits regardless of whether he inflicts them willfully or inadvertently. It is the duty of man to guard himself against doing any damages to another, for as the Mishnah states, "Man is always forewarned." Hence, even if he does damage inadvertently or under compulsion he is liable.[105]

To sum up, the legal obligation to pay for *damages* is not measured by one's criminal intent or by one's willfulness to commit such action. It is governed rather by the principle of negligence, even if the act itself was committed inadvertently. Therefore when one injures another inadvertently or under compulsion, the rules of money indemnity which apply belong not under the laws of injuries (*Hobel*) but rather under the laws of damages, (*Mazik*).

### KNOWLEDGE OF THE LAW

There is a fundamental difference between general law and Jewish law. The former looks upon law as the chief concern of the jurist, the attorney, and the specialist in jurisprudence. The latter, which has its origins and is deeply rooted in religious convictions, looks upon law as a moral guide and as a means of learning how to obey the divine word of God. It is this attitude that explains Judaism's insistence, probably unparalleled in any other legal system, that every Jew must be versed in the law of the Torah and its oral traditions.

The duty to study the Torah falls upon every Jew regardless of his financial status or his physical condition. The rich and poor, the strong and sick, the young and old, the single and married, are all under obligation to study the law, "to meditate therein day and night."[1] Nor is this study pursued for any immediate or "practical" end. The great men in Israel never made their learning a "career"; they did not study to become "judges" or "attorneys." In the words of Maimonides: "The great sages of Israel, some of them were woodcutters, some drawers of water, while others were blind. Nonetheless they engaged in the study of the Torah by day and by night and they are included among those who transmitted the oral traditions in a direct line from Moses our teacher."[2] The study of the Torah is a religious obligation of the highest rank, and the Mishnah tells us: "These are things whose fruits a man enjoys in this world and the capital [full reward] is reserved for the world to come: honoring father and mother, deeds of loving-kindness, making peace between man and man—and the study of the Torah equals them all."[3]

The study of the Law has a double significance. First, since the law is the divine word of God, there can be no better way of worshiping God than by studying the commandments given by Him. The study of the law communicates religiosity and by such study one communes with God. Hence, our Sages constantly emphasized the importance of studying the Torah not for self-seeking motives but "for its own sake," for the sake of piety and a better understanding of its contents. True, they also encouraged the study of the Torah for motives that were less pure, but only on the sound theory that "out of doing it not for its own sake comes doing it for its own sake."[4]

Second, the study of the law is of prime importance because the law deals with practice, with the observance of the duties man owes God and his fellow man. It is impossible for man to live in accordance with the law if he does not have a full knowledge of it. Our Sages frequently quote the verse, "Thou shalt meditate therein day and night, that thou mayest observe to do according to all that is written therein,"[5] with great stress on the last half of the verse.

Josephus, copying Philo verbatim, writes in his apologetic treatise, *Contra Apionem*:

Indeed most men, so far from living in accordance with their own laws, hardly know what they are. Only when they have done wrong do they learn from others that they have transgressed the law. Even those of them who hold the highest offices admit their ignorance: for they employ professional legal experts as assessors and leave them in charge of the administration of affairs. But should anyone of our nation be questioned about the laws, he would repeat them all more readily than his own name. The result, then, of our thorough grounding in the laws from the first dawn of intelligence, is that we have them, as it were, engraved on our souls. A transgression is a rarity; evasion of punishment by excuses an impossibility.[6]

An apologist, Josephus, like Philo, exaggerates the knowledge of the law the average Jew had, but in principle his statement is correct. The duty of studying the law rests on every Jew, for in Judaism the law is not a closed precinct restricted only to professionals or a handful of specialists in jurisprudence; it is the province of all.

### STRICT JUSTICE AND THE HIGHER LAW

There is another significant aspect of rabbinic law which differentiates it from other laws, both modern and ancient. The latter, concerned primarily with the protection of society and finding a *modus vivendi* which will allow people to band together without usurping one another's rights, are not concerned so much with ethics and morality as with the functional part of law. Of course, every legal system seeks to establish rules of conduct which are binding upon the community and may be enforced in court, and it is true that a legal system must reflect the broad moral principles of the society which evolved it. It is also true, however, that the primary purpose of nearly all legal systems is to protect society as a whole, even if in the process injustice is done to individuals. The court must deal with realities, it cannot concern itself with ideals. It is, in fact, impossible for any judicial system, regardless of its high moral standards, always to bridge the gap between the enforcement of the law for the good of the community at large and the extension of ideal justice to individual members of the community.

Furthermore, it is the prime function of law to protect rights and dispense justice. It would, therefore, be going out of its domain were it to concern itself with such principles as kindness and mercy which one individual may extend to another but which lie beyond the proper limits of law itself. It is the duty of the judge in a civilized society to enforce justice and protect human rights; he certainly cannot be expected to legally enforce mercy and kindness. Such matters are left to the conscience of the individual, or, to put it another way, are conceived as the peculiar concern of the spiritual and religious sphere of life.

Jewish law, however, which is primarily an expression of the Jewish concept of individuality as it affects man's relations with his fellow man, is more concerned with individual morality than with the protection of society. Furthermore, since rabbinic law is not a purely secular law, but is regarded as a divine way of life and a guide for every man in his daily life, the law, as rendered and enforced by the court, is not always the highest ideal to which a man should aspire. There are times when the law of the courts, though necessary in court, is not the ultimate ideal for man.

## THE LINE OF THE LAW

Every Jew has a duty to study the Torah and its oral tradition so that he may know not only how to live "within the line of the law," but also how to fulfill the higher law, how to live "beyond the line of the law," though the court itself cannot force him to do so. The observance of this injunction to man that he live in accordance with a higher moral standard which cannot always be enforced in court, is not left entirely to the kindness of the heart of the individual. Just as the judge is enjoined to render his decisions in accordance with the strict letter of the law, man is instructed to live "beyond the line of the law."

"And thou shalt teach them the statutes and the laws, and shalt show them the way wherein they must walk, and the work that they must do."[7] The Mekilta comments that in this verse "the work" means that men must regulate their lives in accordance with justice, but that "they must do" in accordance with the higher law; they must practice a way of life which is beyond the line of the strict justice (*lifnim meshurat hadin*).[8] The Talmud therefore records: "Rabbi Johanan said: Jerusalem was destroyed because they adjudicated their disputes in accordance with the law of the Torah (*din torah*). Should they then have followed the practice of untrained arbitrators? No, but they permitted their adjudications to stand on the strict law of the Torah and did not conduct themselves beyond the line of justice."[9]

The criticism here expressed obviously was not directed against the courts, which are bound to render decisions in accordance with the strict concept of justice. It was directed against the people as a whole for their failure to practice the higher law, for preferring to live in accordance with the strict *din torah* and refusing to live in accordance with the greater ideals which are not enforceable in court.

The principle—that while it is the duty of the court to render decisions in accordance with the strict justice of the Torah, it is the duty of the individual to conduct his life, where his fellow man is concerned, in accordance with the higher moral law—is founded upon the rabbinic concept of the sovereignty of God. The two main attributes of God are justice and mercy. According to the oral tradition the name "Lord" stands for strict justice while the name "God" denotes mercy and graciousness. Commenting on the verse, "And the Lord God made earth and heaven,"[10] the Midrash says that God deliberated: "If I create the world in my attribute of divine mercy alone, sin will be abundant. If I create it in my attribute of strict justice, how can the world endure! I will create the world in both of my attributes, justice and mercy, and thus will it endure."[11]

## JUSTICE AND MERCY

In God, Whose essence is unity and oneness, all attributes are not only reconcilable; they are one. It would be unthinkable and a great heresy to assume that the attributes of justice and mercy are separate powers within God. Even to identify God with mercy alone, or with goodness alone, may approach heresy, for it implies that justice flows from another power or another authority.[12] God, in His divine wisdom and goodness, created and governs the world in justice and mercy simultaneously. But man, even in his unity, is essentially a duality, composed of body and soul, of separate impulses of good and evil, of a sense of justice and a feeling for mercy. In man, therefore, justice and mercy are two separate and often irreconcilable virtues. How then can man imitate God in His attributes of justice and mercy?

The ways of God are often beyond man's understanding and it is not a duty of man to involve himself in theological speculations over how the attributes of God work harmoniously. All we know is that God, by means of all His attributes of action, sets the moral structure of the universe. But mortal man often finds it impossible to exercise both strict justice and mercy at the same time.

How then can man imitate God? The answer is that God, through His revealed will as expressed in the Torah, instructs that strict justice, dispensed in accordance with the concepts of justice as defined in the Torah, is the particular province of the court. Indeed the court is forbidden to allow its decisions to be influenced by the great virtue of mercy. The individual, however, should try to raise himself above the principle of strict justice, beyond the strict requirement of *din*. In his relations with his fellow man, every person should guide himself by the principle of supererogation. By doing this he will truly imitate God's attribute of mercy and fulfill to the highest degree the will of God.

The judge, in his official capacity, therefore, rendering decisions in accordance with the concepts of justice as expressed in the Torah, symbolizes God's attribute of justice. In this light we understand the accepted tannaitic interpretation, also embodied in the Targum, that the verse "Thou shalt not revile God,"[13] is a prohibition against reviling a judge.[14] Our Sages would certainly not have bestowed upon any human being the title of God. What they actually meant, of course, is that since the name of God stands for strict justice, the judge who dispenses strict justice is, in that respect, a personification of the Name of God. Our Sages call upon man in his private capacity to imitate God in His attributes of mercy, graciousness, and loving kindness. Should, however, a judge, attempt to temper his decisions with mercy he will fail his office and render unjust decisions.

This principle is forcefully illustrated by two tannaitic statements. The Mishnah notes: "If one died and left a wife, a creditor, and heirs, and he had goods on deposit or a loan in the hand of others, Rabbi Tarfon says: The property should be given to the one who is under legal disadvantage. Rabbi Akiba said: Mercy has no place in dispensing justice."[15] Involved in this mishnah is the rabbinic law that a creditor cannot legally collect his debt from the movable property which heirs inherit. Morally, however, heirs have an obligation to repay their father's debts out of the movable property which they inherit. Rabbi Tarfon therefore felt that the deposit should be turned over to the creditors, for once the heirs collect it, the creditors will be at a disadvantage. Rabbi Akiba argued that while such a decision would be an act of mercy, the property legally belongs to the heirs and the court must govern not by mercy but by strict justice. In other words, an act of mercy by the court in behalf of a party who has no legal claim constitutes an unjust or illegal act toward the other party. The court must abide by the rule of strict justice, but an individual must live in accordance with a higher moral law even when such law is not enforceable in court.

Similarly, on the verse, "Thou shalt not respect the person of the poor nor favor the person of the mighty, but in righteousness shalt thou judge thy neighbor,"[16] the *Sifra* comments that the judge must not say to himself: "This man is poor. Inasmuch as this rich man is under obligation to support him, I will give judgment in favor of the poor one to enable him to support himself honorably."[17] It is the judge's duty to render decisions in accordance with strict justice, for an act of mercy toward one party is an injustice to the other.

### DIVINE WILL AND HUMAN CONSCIENCE

These higher standards set by our Sages are, in a sense, divine duties which a man should practice. It would be incorrect to regard acts performed *lifnim meshurat ha-din* merely as non-required good deeds executed by a man under the dictates of conscience, kindness or reason. Just as strict justice is the minimum requirement of the law, so is it the duty of the individual to live up to the standards of the higher law.

In fact, our Sages considered those good acts of a man which are not required of him by the law of the Torah to be of lesser merit than required acts. However, those acts which are obligations and are performed beyond the line of the law (*lifnim meshurat ha-din*) were considered most meritorious. Thus Rabbi Haninah taught that the reward of one who performs meritorious acts which are required by the Torah is greater than the reward of one who performs good acts which the Torah does not require of him.[18]

When one performs good deeds which are obligatory his motive is to obey the will of God, and obedience to the will of God is the foundation of the moral structure of Judaism. Good deeds which are not required by the Torah, while undoubtedly meritorious, are performed primarily at the spur of one's conscience and reason. Such good deeds, are not equal in merit to those good deeds performed to meet the will of God. Thus, when a Gentile observes the seven commandments, six of which, according to tradition were dictated by God to Adam and one to Noah,[19] he performs meritorious deeds, for they are divine laws given to all mankind. But a Gentile who engages in the study of the Torah, while certainly meritorious, does not receive as great a reward as does a Jew who engages in such studies.[20] The latter, by studying Torah bends to the divine will as it applies to the Jewish people, the former, who has no obligation to study the Torah of Israel, does so under the prodding of his own reason. Led by his own will, he does not meet a divine obligation and therefore his reward is smaller.

Maimonides similarly notes that "a woman who is engaged in the study of the Torah will be rewarded, but not to the same degree as a man. This is because she was not commanded to engage in the study of the Torah. One who performs a meritorious act which is not obligatory will not receive the same reward as does one upon whom it is incumbent and he fulfills it."[21]

In short, in dealing with a fellow man, those deeds which are motivated by the principle of *lifnim meshurat ha-din* are the most meritorious because the law of the Torah requires of man to live "beyond the line of law."

### DEGREES OF HIGHER LAWS

There is one fundamental difference between one's duty to live "in accordance with *din*," that is, the strict law of justice, and one's higher duty to live "beyond the line of the law." Strict justice puts all people on the same footing: "Ye shall have one manner of law, for the stranger as for the native."[22] But the duty to live in accordance with the higher law is not always equal for every one; there are degrees in the higher law. The obligation of a man to follow these higher standards of morality is often dependent upon his own standard of piety and his status in the community. People who assume leadership and are renowned for their learning must set for themselves a higher standard of morality, and serve as examples for others.

There are cases, however, where the duty to live in accordance with a higher law applies to all alike. This is particularly so in cases of unjust acts in which a court cannot enforce penalties in accordance with the strict law of justice.[23] Thus, if one frightens another person by shouting behind him or by suddenly approaching him in the dark, thereby causing him to become ill, the court cannot exact compensation, since the offender did not come into actual contact with the victim and inflict an injury through a physical act. But if the human court cannot make the offender legally liable for money indemnity, the higher law, the law of heaven, does make him responsible for compensation.[24]

The higher law is invoked in a similar instance concerning witnesses. If witnesses fail to testify in a case, causing the case to be dismissed because of lack of evidence, they are considered to have caused the claimant a loss of money, but only by indirection. The court of man cannot force the witnesses to make compensation for the loss. In accordance with the higher law, however, the witnesses are liable and must make good the claimant's loss.[25] Thus the duty to live in accordance with the higher law falls on all men, and if anyone causes a loss to his fellow in these and similar ways, the laws of heaven demand that he make compensation. The expression in the Tosefta in all such cases is: "And heaven does not forgive him until he makes payment;"[26] since the human court cannot take action in such cases "his judgment is entrusted to heaven."[27]

At times, one's duty to fulfill the higher law is expressed in the Talmud by the words, "If he comes to fulfill his duty to Heaven he should make payments."[28] This statement is used in a case in which an individual, of his own free will, declares that he owes money to one of two people but is not sure to which one. In such instance, if he desires to fulfill his duty to heaven, he should make full payment to both parties.[29] This act would be a moral act of much higher degree than those to which reference was made above.

There is, however, a still higher degree of morality, required of the teacher of the law. The oft-cited story of the two great Babylonian teachers of the law, Rabbah bar Hanah and Rab, may serve as an illustration. Rabbah bar Hanah hired carriers to transport a cask of wine. In transit the cask was broken in circumstances which made the carriers legally responsible to make restitution. Rabbah impounded their garments to cover his loss and the carriers summoned him before Rab. The latter ordered Rabbah to return the garments. Rabbah then asked: "Is this the law?" Rab answered, "Yes, for it is written 'thou shalt walk in the ways of the good,'"[30] and Rabbah returned their garments. The men then complained to Rab that they were poor, that they had worked a whole day and had nothing to eat, whereupon Rab told Rabbah to pay them their day's wages. Rabbah asked again, "Is this the law?" Rab answered, "Yes, as it is said, 'and keep the paths of the righteous.'"[31]

There is no doubt that when Rab decided that Rabbah bar Hanah should pay wages to the carriers for their work, though they had caused him a loss, he ruled that a noted teacher of the law must live in accordance with the highest standard of morality; that his conduct must be exemplary. To a distinguished scholar like Rabbah, the highest standard of *lifnim meshurat ha-din* becomes simple law which he must put into daily practice.

At times our Sages set standards for "living beyond the line of the law" by placing one person's welfare above another's. Thus the Mishnah states that if a man searches for his own lost property and that of his father's, his own takes priority.[32] The Talmud, however, declares that while this is the rule for one who seeks to live up to the letter of the law, a person who desires to rise above the mere letter of the law must give priority to the return of another's property.[33] The Talmud further states that whoever gives priority to his own welfare over the welfare of another will eventually find himself dependent upon the charity of others.[34] Maimonides defined the higher law which helps man imitate God in His attribute of mercy, in terms of the verse, "And his mercies are over all His works" (Psalms 145:9), and concludes his statement by declaring that "whoever has compassion will receive compassion, as it is said: 'And He will show thee mercy, and have compassion upon thee and multiply thee.'"[35]

### THE MISHNAH OF THE PIOUS

Living in accordance with the higher law is often characterized as *middat hassidut*, a measure of saintliness. The Jerusalem Talmud calls this kind of action, "the Mishnah of the Pious," the law of the pious. It appears that even long before the tannaitic period, there were men of great piety who set for themselves a code of conduct, a *Mishnah*, to conform with the principle of supererogation, by which their relations with both God and man were governed. Thus, the Mishnah states that the earlier *Hasidim* used to contemplate for an hour before they said their prayers in order that they might direct their hearts properly toward their Father in heaven.[36] It seems that they were so scrupulous in their relations, not only toward God but also toward others, that occasionally what others would perform as a religious duty, the law of piety prevented them from doing.

The Talmud tells the following story about Rabbi Joshua ben Levi, a most esteemed Haggadist and a man of great piety. A Roman army once besieged the city of Lydda and demanded, under the threat of destroying the town, the surrender of a certain Ulla bar Kosheb. In order to save the city and its inhabitants, Rabbi Joshua ben Levi exerted

his influence on Ulla to surrender himself voluntarily. From then on
Elijah the prophet ceased to communicate with Rabbi Joshua. But
after much penance Elijah again appeared to Rabbi Joshua saying, "Am
I supposed to reveal myself to informers?" Rabbi Joshua answered: "I
acted in accordance with the Mishnah." Elijah answered: "This is not
the Mishnah of the Pious" (*Mishnat Hasidim*).[37]

The point of this story is that the Roman army gave the ultimatum:
"Either surrender Ulla or all will be destroyed." According to the
halakah which was accepted by Rabbi Joshua, it was the religious duty
of the people to surrender Ulla because he had been specifically named
by the Roman army.[38] But Rabbi Joshua, who lived in accordance
with the laws of the Pious, had no right to exert his influence on anyone
to surrender himself to certain death, even in order to save an entire
community. What is accepted as a legal requirement or moral law for
everyone else is not necessarily the proper rule or mode of conduct for
one who desires to live in accordance with the "Mishnah of the
Pious."

### PEACE AND JUSTICE

The attempt to reconcile the demands of strict justice with the ideal of
the higher moral law is especially evident in the rabbinic understanding
of the functions of a court. In order to create order and establish legal
forms of discipline to maintain peace in society, general law concerns itself primarily with justice as determined by the court. As a rule, however, strict justice in civil cases does not result in peace and harmony
between litigants. Each litigant considers himself right. Rare is the
loser who looks kindly upon either the judge or his victorious opponent.
Our Sages, as noted above, therefore interpreted the verse, "Thou shalt
not revile God," as a prohibition against reviling a judge. With their
true understanding of human psychology they asserted:

It happened that a certain man had litigation with another and he
came to the judge for adjudication. The latter decreed him to be
right, then the one who succeeded in the litigation went forth and
said, "There is none like this judge." At a later time the same man
had another litigation and came to the same judge who pronounced
him guilty. He then said: "There is no other judge as stupid as this

judge." One said to him: "Yesterday the judge was praiseworthy and today he is stupid?" Therefore Scripture asserts, "Thou shalt not revile God."[39]

Our Sages were aware of how difficult it may be at times to hew to the line of strict justice. In the terminology which is uniquely theirs, they expressed this feeling in the phrase "Let justice pierce the mountain,"[40] that is, as difficult as it may be and regardless of the fact that he may well meet with bitterness if not enmity, it is the duty of a judge to follow the rules of strict justice. He must not allow himself to be influenced by the human relationships involved in the cases which come before him.

On the other hand, our teachers regarded the establishment of peace and harmony among men at least as important as dispensing strict justice. Indeed, they were acutely alive to the eternal conflict between *mishpat*, justice, and *shalom*, peace. The Rabbis constantly emphasized that Moses and Aaron were equal in virtue,[41] yet in rabbinic literature, Moses symbolizes uncompromising *justice* while Aaron is the symbol of *peace*, the archetypal promoter of peace between man and man. Hillel the Elder, who took Aaron as his ideal, said: "Be of the disciples of Aaron, loving peace and pursuing peace, loving mankind and bringing them nigh unto the law."[42] Following in Hillel's footsteps, Rabbi Meir, the famous Tanna, was willing to suffer the greatest indignities if his humiliation could help bring peace between man and wife or effect a reconciliation between enemies.[43]

Whether it should be the aim of the judge, in following the divine law, to achieve peace among men and follow in the footsteps of Aaron, or follow the line of strict justice, and, like Moses, "let justice pierce the mountain," was a matter of serious dispute between Rabbi Eliezer ben Jose ha-Galilli and Rabbi Joshua ben Karha, Tannaim of the fourth generation. It should be emphasized that this disagreement related only to judges, for there never was any doubt among our Sages that it was the duty of everyone in his private capacity to strive for peace and harmony among men. After all, Moses himself, the prototype of strict justice, was a lover of peace.[44] Is not peace one of the attributes of God,[45] and does not the Mishnah state that Elijah will come "neither to remove afar nor to bring nigh but to bring peace into the world?"[46]

Moreover, the words chosen to close the Mishnah, this great code of law, are: "The Holy One, blessed be He, found no vessel that could contain Israel's blessing but peace, for it is written, 'The Lord will give strength to His people; the Lord will bless His people in peace! (Psalms 29:11).'"[47]

The dispute of our Sages, concerning the relationship of justice and peace, therefore centered on judges and revolved particularly around one point. Since strict justice and peace may be regarded as conflicting principles, what should be the primary responsibility of the judge? Is it his duty to try, with the consent of the litigants, to make peace through compromise, or is it his duty to concern himself only with what is strict justice in the case? Should a judge stand as the symbol of uncompromising justice or of compromising peace?

Rabbi Eliezer ben Jose was of the opinion that the judge must never introduce the idea of compromise between litigants, for as a judge his duty is to be like Moses, to "let justice pierce the mountain." Of course, if the litigants appeal to the court to arbitrate between them, then upon the learned court, as upon any ordinary individual, falls the moral and religious duty of making peace between man and his neighbor. Rabbi Jose ben Karha, however, was of the opinion that the court is duty-bound to use its good offices from the very first to have the disputants agree to a compromise, so that both justice and peace be served simultaneously. If, however, the litigants insist on strict justice, it is the duty of the judge to "let justice pierce the mountain."[48]

The halakah is that the court must always endeavor to temper justice with peace by means of a *pesharah*, a compromise. Litigants who agree to arbitration may change their mind and ask for a decision of strict justice, for justice is the first consideration of the court. If, however, both agree to a *pesharah* and bind their consent with a *kinyan sudar*, a legal form of transaction by which one's word becomes irrevocable, the *kinyan* obligates them to accept the decision of the judges even though it does not accord with strict justice.[49]

### EQUITY AND PEACE

Our Sages often felt that the ultimate goal in the performance of certain *mitzvot* is the attainment of peace among men. On Exodus 23:5, which requires a man to help release an animal lying under its burden even if it belongs to his enemy, the Midrash comments:

"Thou hast established equity."[50] Rabbi Alexandri said: Two ass-drivers, who hate each other, travel on the road. The ass of one of them falls under its burden and his companion by-passes him. But then he says to himself: it is written in the Torah: "If thou see the ass of him that hateth thee lying under its burden, thou shalt forbear to pass by him, thou shalt surely release it with him."[51] He immediately turns back and helps his fellow to reload. The other ass-driver then begins to meditate in his heart, saying, "This man is really my friend and I did not know it." Both then enter an inn, eat and drink together.[52]

Philo, too, perceives the purpose of this law to be the reconciliation of enemies, and writes that by fulfilling it, "You will benefit yourself more than him: he gains an irrational and possibly worthless animal, you the greatest and most precious treasure, true goodness. And this, as surely as the shadow follows the body, will be followed by a termination of the feud. He is drawn toward amity by the kindness which holds him in bondage. You, his helper, with a good action to assist your counsels, are predisposed to thoughts of reconciliation."[53]

### HER WAYS ARE WAYS OF PLEASANTNESS

At times, when our Sages wish to determine a doubtful halakah, they accept as a guide Proverbs 2:16, "Her ways are ways of pleasantness and all her paths are peace," in their complete acceptance that one of the aims of the Torah is to regulate the life of the people in the spirit of peace and pleasantness. Hence, if a man dies leaving a wife and child, and later the child dies, the widow is no longer required to marry her late husband's brother in accordance with the law of levirate marriage. It would not be "the way of pleasantness and of peace" for a woman, who at the death of her husband was free to marry anyone she wished, to be limited to levirate marriage at the time of her second tragedy.[54]

Applying this principle of "all her paths are paths of peace," our Sages instituted many laws aimed at avoiding discord among men.[55]

One such innovation was the recognition of one's *arba amot* (four cubits) as a mode of acquiring property. In order to avoid disputes among people who come across an ownerless object, the Rabbis ordained that a man acquires possession of such an object if it is found within the radius of four cubits of the place where he stands. But this mode of acquisition is not valid in a public domain where many people are crowded into the radius of four cubits.[56] The Mishnah also records numerous laws which our Sages instituted for the sake of maintaining peace between Jew and non-Jew,[57] in their firm belief that one of the main objectives of the Torah is to sustain peace and good will among all men.

## HALF SLAVE AND HALF FREE

Among the many ennobling principles propounded by our Sages was the concept of equity. In certain situations this concept required more consideration for the human personalities involved in a case than for the money at stake. The law of "the half slave and half free man" clearly illustrates this. In ancient times the institution of slavery, particularly that of Canaanite slaves, was sanctioned by law. If a slave was set free by one of two partners who owned him jointly, he became a "half slave and half free man." The Mishnah raises the question: what is the status of the half slave? and declares:

If one is a "half slave and half free man," he should work one day for his master and one day for himself. These are the words of the School of Hillel. The School of Shammai say: You have decreed well for the interest of the master, but for him you have not decreed well. He can neither marry a bondwoman nor a freewoman; shall he remain fruitless? Was not the world created for fruition and increase, as it is written, "He created it not to waste; He formed it to be inhabited." As a precaution for the general good the court should compel his master to set him free and he should write his erstwhile master a note of indebtedness for half his value. The School of Hillel then changed their mind and taught according to the opinion of the School of Shammai.[58]

The earlier opinion of the School of Hillel accorded with the strict letter of the law. The School of Shammai, however, based its decision on considerations of equity, seeking to insure fair treatment for each human personality. The life of a man half slave and half free, they realized, is impossible and it is not the wish of the Torah that a man should remain unacceptable either in the society of freemen or in the society of slaves. Hence, despite a temporary monetary loss to the owner, since the slave has no money with which to redeem himself, the master is forced by the court to emancipate his slave. In turn, the half slave, now granted complete freedom, gives his former master what corresponds to a "promissory note."[59] The School of Hillel bowed before the nobility of this concept of equity and accepted the halakah rendered by their opponents. The moral principle behind this decision is that it is juster that the master suffer a financial disadvantage than to deny the half slave the natural rights which God granted every human being.

### COURTS OF MAN AND COURTS OF HEAVEN

A study of the entire structure of Jewish law, as recorded in early rabbinic sources, cannot help but impress one with the great concern our Sages had for the protection of the life of the individual. The Rabbis took every precaution to eliminate the possibility of condemning an innocent man. The Mishnah records how witnesses were admonished by the court before they testified in capital cases:

Know ye, that capital cases are unlike non-capital cases. In noncapital cases a man may pay money and thereby make atonement but in capital cases the witness is answerable for the blood of him [that is wrongfully condemned] and for the blood of his posterity to the end of the world. So have we found it with Cain who slew his brother, for it is written, "the bloods of thy brother cry."[60] It says not "the *blood* of thy brother" but "the *bloods* of thy brother"—his blood and the blood of his posterity.... Therefore but a single man was created in the world to teach that if a man has caused a single soul to perish, Scripture imputes it to him as though he had caused a whole world to perish. If any man saves the life of a single soul, Scripture imputes it to him as though he had saved a whole world.[61]

Philo also expresses this Jewish concept of the infinite worth of the individual. He points out that the Ten Commandments were pronounced in the singular for three reasons: to teach "that each individual when he is lawabiding and obedient to God is equal in worth to a whole nation... even to the whole world"; to give the commandments added force, since every person will understand that they were addressed directly to him; and thirdly, to teach "that He wills that no king or despot, swollen with arrogance and contempt, should despise an insignificant person.... For if the Uncreated, the Incorruptible, the Eternal Who needs nothing and is the Maker of all, the Benefactor and King of Kings and God of gods could not brook to despise even the humblest, but deigned to banquet him on holy oracles and statutes, as though he should be the sole guest, as though for him alone the feast was prepared...what right have I, a mortal, to bear myself proud-necked, puffed-up and loud-voiced toward my fellows?"[62]

Many passages in rabbinic literature declare the infinite worth of the individual. Perhaps one of the most far-ranging applications of this principle is the presumption that a person is innocent unless it is proven otherwise beyond any shadow of a doubt. Neither hearsay, nor circumstantial evidence were admitted in court, particularly in capital cases.[63] Even if two witnesses saw a criminal act committed, the offender could not be condemned to death unless the witnesses had forewarned the accused that if he should commit the crime the penalty would be death. The accused had to "surrender himself to death" by saying "I know full well the consequences, nevertheless I will commit [the crime]."[64] We can readily understand that under such strict court procedures criminals could only with difficulty be condemned to death. In fact Rabbi Tarfon and Rabbi Akiba said, "If we had been in the Sanhedrin none would ever have been put to death."[65]

Leniency in punishing offenders was not limited to capital offenses. As we have stated before, a person was held legally responsible for homicide, damages, and injuries only if he, himself, committed the acts. If, however, he was only the instigator or the indirect cause of such acts he could not be held legally liable in court. If a person violated any of the positive precepts by action or non-action, no penalty was inflicted by the court. As for the transgression of a negative precept, a culprit had to be forewarned of the exact penalty awaiting him, otherwise he was not liable to any penalty. Similarly, for the transgression of negative precepts by non-action an offender incurred no penalty.[66]

When Rabbi Simeon ben Gamaliel heard the statement of Rabbi Tarfon and Rabbi Akiba cited above, he declared that "they would multiply murders in Israel." Some might take this as an apt evaluation of the entire penal code evolved by and put into effect by our Sages. The fact remains, however, that during the period when the Sanhedrin was in existence, and even after the destruction of the Temple when its authority to inflict penalties and fines in accordance with the laws of the Torah was weakened, the Jewish community lived a highly disciplined life.

We may ask: what could so motivate a community to live in harmony and accept upon itself such strong moral discipline when there was but little fear that penalties would be inflicted? The answer to this question is provided by two factors: one, the unique position of the judiciary, and the other, the profound moral influence our Sages exerted on the individual members of the community. These two features made possible the moral uniqueness and superior standards of the ancient Jewish community.

### THE PREROGATIVE AND HIGHER LAW OF THE JUDICIARY

It has been demonstrated that in the life of the individual there exist two standards of moral conduct. A man has to live in accordance with the strict letter of the law and follow the rigid principle of justice in his relationships with his fellow men. This duty of man to live in accordance with *din* is clearly spelled out in the Torah and in the oral tradition as recorded in rabbinic literature. There is a second standard by which man has to live. He must live in accordance with the higher law, strive for a loftier moral perfection, and be motivated by considerations of mercy and kindness. The duty to live *lifnim meshurat ha-din* cannot always be regulated by codes because living "beyond the line of law" depends upon special circumstances. Surely it is most difficult to define duties in which one must permit himself to be motivated by the qualities of mercy and loving-kindness. All we know is that there are occasions when the Torah requires us to accept higher moral standards and guide ourselves by a nobler mode of conduct.

The responsibility of the court to render decisions, convict criminals and inflict penalties was particularly defined by two such standards: the standard of the strict law of the Torah, and the standard set by specific circumstances. The latter was also sanctioned by the Torah and may be characterized as the extra prerogative of the court. It is evident upon analysis that the penal code of the Torah, as interpreted by our Sages, is determined by the rules of court procedure found in the Torah. The fact that the Torah, as expounded in the oral tradition, greatly restricts the court in imposing penalties, made both bodily punishment and capital punishment rare phenomena. If, however, the court, particularly the highest authoritative court in the land, should discover that as a result of laxity in punishing offenders people fail to observe the laws of the Torah, that with the fear of punishment gone the structure of Torah morality begins to disintegrate, what is it to do? Must the court ignore the demoralization and continue to follow the line of penal justice laid down in the Torah? The answer to this is that, under such circumstance, it is the duty of the court to resort to the second standard granted it by the Torah and avail itself of the prerogative given it. The court must perforce institute all necessary penalties and restore the community to the observance of the law.

The Talmud records isolated instances in which heavy penalties were inflicted on offenders not because according to the law of the Torah they deserved severe penalties, but because it "was the need of the hour."[67] Rabbi Eliezer ben Jacob relates the tradition that under certain conditions it is the prerogative of the court to inflict heavy penalties "which are neither in accordance with the halakah (the common law) nor in accordance with the laws of the Torah."[68]

It is on this account that our Sages instituted "corporal punishment for disobedience," used when a man fails to fulfill positive precepts.[69] There is no doubt that such punishments were administered only as emergency measures, especially when the court could not procedurally convict a murderer because of technical restrictions placed on it by the Torah. In such instances, as already discussed above,[70] the court could sentence the criminal to life imprisonment.[71]

The extra powers, particularly the power to inflict penalties unauthorized by the Torah, declares Maimonides, are "granted to the court not with the intention of violating the law, but in order to build a fence around it whenever the court sees that people generally abuse the law.... But whatever measure it adopts is only temporary and does not acquire the binding force of law."[72] It is not our intention to enter into a technical discussion of the extensive powers which the courts enjoyed. One thing is certain, that in addition to the duty of the courts to pronounce judgment and inflict penalties in accordance with the strict law of the Torah, the courts had the prerogative, and often the duty, which we may characterize as the *higher law of the judiciary*, to institute emergency measures and severe penalties for the purpose of preserving the moral and religious discipline of the community.

How often the courts found it necessary to avail themselves of this prerogative is a moot question. We can assert, however, without any hesitation, that our Sages did not for ulterior motives take advantage of this prerogative granted the courts. They did not seek extra and extensive power. Their primary aim was to preserve the penal law of the Torah which places great technical restrictions on the court, and their goal was to insure that the courts would never have to use the granted prerogatives, for their use would announce a deterioration of the moral standards of the community. The more people were inspired to live in accordance with the law of the Torah, the less need would there be for the court to avail itself of its extensive powers. The more men lived in accordance with the strict letter of justice and conducted their lives according to teachings of the higher law, the less need would our Sages find to invoke the higher law of the judiciary. Our Sages considered it their primary responsibility to teach the people a divine way of life. Through their teaching, rather than through their judicial power, were they able to guide the moral life of the community.

## MAN AND THE DIVINE COURT

We must bear in mind that while our Sages served as judges in the courts of ancient Israel, they were by no means professional judges, in the modern sense of the term. They were, above all, "teachers of the law." Their main goal in life was to study the Torah and to teach the people how to live in accordance with the will of God. The authority and the extensive powers of the court of man were greatly responsible for the preservation of moral order in the community. But if they helped to preserve Torah morality, they did not inspire it. The moral and religious discipline of the Jewish community did not derive from the ability or inability of the court of man to punish individuals for the commission of unlawful acts. Rather, the moral life of the community was the result of the inspired teaching of our Sages that there is a much higher court than the court of man (*dinei adam*) and that this court, the court of heaven (*dinei shamaim*), is a court which knows the innermost secrets of man's actions.

The court of man may acquit a criminal because it lacks unimpeachable evidence of intent in his crimes; before the court of heaven there is nothing unknown. The court of man may not be able to inflict penalties or make one liable for money indemnity for indirect damages or injuries, but in the court of heaven conviction is absolute; before it a wrongdoer is held liable for damages and must compensate for injuries.[73] Moreover, if a man instigates another to commit a homicidal act he cannot be punished by the court of man. But in the eyes of the court of heaven he is a murderer and will ultimately be punished as such.[74]

The great structure of Jewish morality rests on the religious principle of divine judgment, which holds that man is accountable to God for his acts and that the courts of heaven are even more real than are the courts of man. In every way did our Sages endeavor to inspire a moral and disciplined society by making each individual conscious of the fact that his actions and non-actions, for both good and evil, are judged by the highest court—the court of heaven.

The rabbinic term *dinei adam*, literally translated, reads "laws of man"; it must not, however, be taken to mean man-made law. On the contrary, this term is used for the laws revealed in the Torah, all of which are, in a sense, the laws of heaven. What is significant in *dinei adam* is that though the law entrusted to a court of human beings is revealed law, it may differ from the laws of heaven. The court of man must, above all, protect the individual and be his defender. But the court of heaven, before whom all secrets of the human heart are known, pronounces and enforces penalties for all sins and crimes committed by a man.

This distinction between human courts and divine courts was also known among the Hellenistic Jews in ancient Alexandria. Philo often speaks of human courts and divine courts, "the two courts...which nature has."[75]

The verse, "But the soul that doeth aught with a high hand...the same blasphemes the Lord"[76] is translated by the Septuagint as, "Whoever sets his hands to do anything with presumptuousness, the same provokes God." Philo interprets this verse to refer to the extremely arrogant who consider themselves "neither man nor demigod, but wholly divine."[77] With such men, he writes, "the laws deal admirably in not bringing them to be judged by men, but handing them over to the divine tribunal only.... Why is this? First arrogance as a vice of the soul is invisible save only to God. Chastisement is not for the blind to give but for him who can see."[78] Similarly, speaking of the punishment of Cain, Philo says:

> What then could be done to him by which he would pay the penalty he deserves, he who in single action included everything that is violent and impious? Slay him, perhaps you will say. That is man's idea—a man who has no eyes for the great court of justice—for man thinks that death is the determination of punishment, but in the divine court it is hardly the beginning.[79]

Thus, according to Philo, the most fitting punitive actions against man are determined by a divine court of justice which does not necessarily follow the standard of justice set by the courts of men. Furthermore, a murderer may by his skillfulness escape the death penalty in the court of men, but he is arraigned and condemned in the divine court, which Philo sometimes calls the "court of nature," meaning the court of God. The law pertaining to the unintentional murderer uses the phrase, "But God delivered him into his hand."[80] This Philo takes to mean that God utilizes the unintentional murderer as a minister of divine justice to punish an intentional murderer who escaped conviction by the court of men. But the unintentional murderer himself must have committed in his life sins of lesser proportions, for "He would not wish that any one whose whole life is stainless and his lineage also, should set his hand to homicide, however justly deserved."[81] Our Sages, too, interpret the phrase "But God delivered him into his hand," to mean that God often uses a person guilty of lesser offenses as an instrument of justice to punish a criminal of greater magnitude.[82]

Remarkably then, according to both Philo and the Tannaim, the punitive actions of the divine court do not always accord with the standards of justice followed by a human court. Moreover, even when the court of man fails to inflict punishment on criminals, God often uses as His ministers of justice men whose life is not stainless to inflict the necessary punishment. Nevertheless, a distinction exists between the rabbinic and Philonic understanding of the divine courts or courts of heaven. The Rabbis attached a dual significance to this heavenly court. First, they believed that while a guilty man may escape punishment in the courts of men, he stands convicted in the courts of heaven and that God in His own way will mete out the necessary punishment. Second, and above all, the rabbinic sources teach the equally important lesson that if an offender stands convicted before the courts of heaven he is morally and legally obligated to correct the wrongs he committed. When by the standards of the courts of heaven man is liable, heaven does not forgive him unless he makes restitution. In order to discharge his duty towards heaven it is incumbent upon him to right his wrongs. Hence, according to our Sages, the courts of heaven require of man to live by a higher standard of law. If he fails to obey these laws, and to live by these divine standards, the court of heaven will enforce its decisions in a manner known only to God.

This concept of the "higher divine standard" by which a man must live is not apparent in the Alexandrian sources. The Hellenistic Jews spoke of the divine court in the purely theological sense, that an offender will not escape punishment even if he cannot be convicted by the human court since the divine tribunal will convict him and mete out the necessary retribution. Apparently they did not arrive at the concept of a higher moral code. Only our Sages formulated a code of higher law which instructs man in what the court of heaven requires of him. Living by this code, man can gain forgiveness for his acts of omission and commission towards his fellow men; recognizing this standard of morality he knows what he has to do in this world to fulfill the will of the supreme, the divine court.

LOVE OF GOD THROUGH TOTAL COMMITMENT

Just as in man's relationship to man there is a level of justice which a man must practice, and a concept of higher laws towards which a man must strive, so also in the relation of man to God there is a higher law, a higher measure of worshiping Him. The minimum requirement in attaining a proper relationship with God is to *fear* Him; the greater ideal is to *love* Him. Our Sages, Philo, and the later Jewish philosophers, have expressed themselves clearly on the question of what constitutes love of God, and their views should be studied.

Man's duty to love God is declared in Deuteronomy 6:5, "And thou shalt love the Lord thy God with all thy heart, with all thy soul, and with all thy might." The Mishnah, commenting on this verse, states:

Man is required to bless God for his misfortune even as he blesses God for benefactions, for it is written, "And thou shalt love the Lord thy God with all thy heart, with all thy soul, and with all thy might." *With all thy heart*—with the good and evil impulse. *With all thy soul* —even though He taketh away from thee. *With all thy might*—with all thy worldly possessions. Another explanation is: *With all thy might*—whatever measure He metes out to thee, be thankful to Him.[83]

This mishnah posits two ways in which man reveals his love for God: by totally committing his life, not to speak of his worldly possession, to the service of God, and by accepting in the spirit of thankfulness, the judgment of God under all conditions. Over this second point, there seems to have been a dispute among the early Tannaim. The Mishnah records:

The same day Rabbi Joshua b. Hyrcanus expounded: Job served the Holy One blessed be He out of pure love, for it says, "Though He slay me I will trust in Him."[84] Rabbi Joshua (ben Hananiah) cried out: Who will clear away the dust from thine eyes, Rabban Johanan ben Zakkai, who didst teach that Job served God only out of fear, for it said "And that man was perfect and upright and one that feared God and shunned evil"[85] and here is Joshua (ben Hyrcanus), thy disciple's disciple, teaching that he served God for the sake of love.[86]

There was then, apparently, disagreement over whether accepting

God's punitive judgment with undiminished faith was in itself an act of loving God.

Rabbinic literature recognized that the command to fear God, drawn from the verse, "The Lord thy God thou shalt fear,"[87] is fulfilled even when one serves Him in hope of being rewarded. One loves God, however, when his actions are directed not by the hope of reward but solely by the desire to love him.

The entire discussion in rabbinic literature concerning the fear and love of God seems to be an extension of the declaration by Antigonos of Socho: "Be not like servants who serve their master for the sake of receiving reward; rather be like servants who serve their master not for the sake of receiving any reward. And let the fear of heaven be upon you."[88] Antigonos expresses here the thought which pervades rabbinic literature, that serving God without the expectation of reward constitutes love of God.[89] The *Sifre*, commenting on the phrase, "To love the Lord your God."[90] also instructs, "Whatever you do, do it not for the sake of receiving award, but for the sake of loving Him."[91] Thus, according to our Sages, man worships God best when he is moved by the desire to honor Him, not the desire of reward. Our Sages did not deny that there is an ultimate reward for a good deed, for this is a part of the teaching of the Torah. They only emphasized that a man's first motive should not be a hope of reward, but the yearning to honor God and fulfill His will.

Philo, too, in a number of places, leans towards the rabbinic distinction between love of God and fear of God. He differentiates between serving God out of fear of punishment and in the hope of a reward, and serving Him solely for the sake of honoring Him. Philo declares that some men are incapable of achieving a clear vision of God, and obey His commands only because they fear punishment. Echoing the saying of Antigonos of Socho, he declares that those who serve God out of fear of punishment are "foolish slaves who receive profit from a master who frightens them, for they fear his threats and menaces and thus involuntarily are schooled to fear." On the other hand, he continues, there are those who attain the highest degree of loving God, and serve Him not out of fear, but out of pure love. He concludes his discussion with the observation "that all the exhortations to piety in the law refer either to our loving or our fearing the Existent. And thus to love Him is most suitable for those in whose conception of the Existent no thought of human parts or passions enters, who pay Him honor meet for God for His own sake"[92]

It is thus apparent that for Philo, as well as for our Sages, "to love God" means to serve Him not out of fear and not for the sake of reward, but only to honor Him for His own sake. Actually, Philo seems to recognize three stages in the service of God. There are those who serve God for His Own sake, out of love; there are those who serve God in the hope of receiving a Heavenly reward; and there are those who serve God because they fear his punitive powers. In Philo's view all find favor before God, Who declares, "I accept both him who wishes to enjoy my beneficial power and thus partake of blessings and him who propitiates the dominance and authority of the Master to avoid chastisement. For I know well that they will not be worsened, but actually bettered through the persistence of the worship and through practicing piety pure and undefiled...since they have one aim and object, to serve Me."[93]

Obviously Philo considered the man who serves God for the sake of reward as next best to the one who serves Him for His own sake. Lower than these is the one who serves Him because he fears punishment. In fact, in another place Philo says that God asks nothing of man that is difficult; He desires only that man loves Him as a benefactor or, failing this, fears Him as a ruler and Lord.[94] Philo emphasizes that one who is moved by fear of punishment can attain only the lowest level of serving God. The higher degree of the love of God can be attained only by fulfilling the law, even if one's chief motive is the hope of winning His benefaction.

In one passage Philo seems to imply that one should not expect any reward for fulfilling his obligations to God for such acts are in themselves the greatest reward. As concerns one's duties to his fellow man, however, one may expect rewards, both in this world and in the world to come. Answering the question: Why is it that in the Ten Commandments the promise of reward is given only in conjunction with the fifth commandment, that of honoring parents, and not in all the others, Philo writes:

The refusal to acknowledge other gods or to deify the works of man's hands, or to commit perjury, needs no other reward. For surely the practice of such abstinence is in itself the best and the most perfect reward.... For wisdom is itself the guerdon of wisdom, and justice and each of the other virtues is its own reward....[95] Again, the experience of those who keep the Sabbath is that both body and soul are benefited.... So too, indeed, he who shows respect for his parents should not seek anything further, for if he looks, he will find the guerdon in the action itself. However, since this commandment, in as much as it is concerned with mortal things is inferior to the first four heads whose province is nearer the divine, He gave encouragement with the words, "Honor thy father and thy mother that it may be well with thee and that thy time may be long." Here He names two rewards: one is the possession of virtue... the other in very truth is immortality....[96]

In this remarkable passage Philo seems to imply that in the fulfillment of those duties which man has to God, the very acts themselves offer the greatest rewards for they enrich man spiritually. Hence the Torah found it unnecessary to mention particular rewards. Nevertheless such rewards are to be taken for granted because by fulfilling the duties which he owes to God, man is already rewarded; in their very fulfillment lies their reward, the reward of performing virtuous acts.

The duty of honoring parents, however, is regarded by Philo as the "borderline commandment between the sets of five." The first five deal with man's duties to God, and the other five, the negative commandments, deal with man's duties to his fellow man. By honoring parents one serves both "the immortal and the mortal side of existence."[97] Therefore, since man, by honoring parents, fulfills a duty "concerned with mortal things" which he owes to his fellow men, the reward is announced in the Torah. The intention of the Torah, however, is not to record the specific reward given for honoring parents; its purpose is rather to record in general the reward which accrues from meeting one's duty to his fellow beings, it therefore occupies the borderline position. One may inquire what the rewards for the fulfillment of one's duties to one's fellow men are. Philo lists three: one, the act of virtue in itself is a reward—this is the meaning of the phrase "that it

may be well with thee";[98] two, immortality of the soul; three, prolonged vitality of life, promised in the phrase "thy days may be long."

In the Talmud there seems to be disagreement over whether the
verse "and thy days may be long, and that it may go well with thee,"
implies a promise of reward in this world or in the world to come.
Rabbi Jacob said, "there is no reward in this world for the fulfilling
of a *mitzvah*." He therefore interpreted the verse in this fifth commandment to mean "that it may go well with thee in the world which
is wholly good and that thy day may be prolonged in a world which is
wholly lasting"[99] The Mishnah, in the beginning of the tractate *Peah*,
however, includes honoring parents among those good deeds "whose
fruits man enjoys in *this world* and whose principal is secured for him in
the *world to come*." This would seem to imply that the opinion of Rabbi
Jacob was an isolated one and was not accepted by our Sages.[100] They,
like Philo, maintained that God grants reward during man's earthly
existence, though the ultimate reward can come only in the immortal
world.

## LOVE THROUGH KNOWLEDGE

Our Sages believed that "love of God" is expressed through an observance of the *mitzvot*, motivated by a desire to obey the will of God without thought of a reward. Thus "fear of God" and "love of God" result
from the same action, with only the motive determining whether a
man is God-fearing or God-loving.

Some ancient allegorist interpreters of the Torah held the view that
love of God is the result of greater knowledge of God. The *Sifre*,
commenting on the verse in the Torah: "To love the Lord your God,
and to walk in all His ways and to cleave unto Him,"[101] records in the
name of the *Dorshei Reshumot* the following interpretation: "If thou
wishest to know Him Who by His word created the world, study the
Aggadah, for in this manner you will know the Holy One blessed be
He and cleave to His ways."[102] In other words, only through knowledge of God the Creator, a knowledge which is acquired through the
study of the Aggadah, a study much more theoretical than the Halakah,
does man truly learn to love God.

Maimonides, too, defines love of God primarily in terms of knowledge of God. He writes that "a person [who] contemplates His great and wonderous works. . .will obtain through them an understanding of His wisdom which is incomparable and infinite, he will immediately love, praise and glorify Him and crave exceedingly to know His great name."[103] This distinction between fear of God and love of God is made even more explicit by Maimonides in his philosophic work:

God declared in plain words that it is the object of all religious acts to produce in man fear of God and obedience to his word.... That this end is attained by certain acts we learn likewise from the phrase employed in this verse: "If thou wilt not observe to do. . .that thou mayest fear."[104] For this phrase clearly shows that the fear of God is inculcated when we act in accordance with positive and negative commandments. But the truth which the law teaches us, the knowledge of God's existence and unity, creates in us a love for God as we have shown repeatedly.... The two objects, love and fear of God, are acquired by two different means. The love is a result of the truth taught in the law including the Existence of God, whilst the fear of God is produced by the practices prescribed in the law.[105]

According to Maimonides then, the Torah teaches man two things. First, obedience to the will of God through the observance of the *mitzvot;* by these, man learns to fear God. Second, man is taught the knowledge of God as revealed in the Torah; this leads man to love Him. The knowledge of God and the fulfillment of the will of God are therefore indivisible elements in the Torah. Needless to say, according to Maimonides, love of God motivated by a greater knowledge of Him is by itself of little value unless man observes His will by the performance of the *mitzvot.* Observance of *mitzvot* alone, without real knowledge of God, leads one to the virtue of fearing Him out of a dread of the punishment He can visit on those who violate the commandments. But knowledge of God leads to love of God, and subsequently acceptance of the will of God out of love for Him.

In still another source Maimonides declares that love of God is attained through the study of the Torah and the observance of the *mitzvot,* but only when this is done out of love and not in hope of a reward or out of fear of punishment:

Whoever serves God out of love, engages himself in the study of the Torah and the fulfillment of the Commandments, and walks in the paths of wisdom, impelled by no other thing in the world, motivated neither by fear of misfortunes, nor that he may inherit benefactions, but practices the truth, because it is the truth, ultimately benefactions will come to him as a result of his conduct. This virtue is a very high one and not every sage is privileged to attain it. This was the high standard of our Patriarch Abraham whom God called His friend, because he served Him only out of pure love. ~his is the standard which the Holy One blessed be He instructs us through Moses our Master to achieve, as it is said, "And thou shalt love the Lord thy God with all thy heart and all thy soul and all thy might."[106] When one loves God with the proper love he will straight-away fulfill all the Commandments out of love.[107]

Judging by the above citations, culled from rabbinical literature, Philo and Maimonides, it appears that the highest standard of "serving God out of pure love" can be attained in the following ways: by totally committing one's being and possessions to the service of God; by accepting in the spirit of trust and thankfulness the judgment of God under all conditions; by serving God without being motivated by the expectation of reward, though such reward for one's good deeds will certainly come; by acquiring knowledge of God and of his unity, as revealed in the Torah and in His creation.

### LOVE OF MAN: THE GREAT RULE OF THE TORAH

The duty of loving one's fellow man is clearly stated in Leviticus 19:18, "Thou shalt love thy neighbor as thyself." Our Sages chose to use the negative rather than the affirmative in their explanation of the duty to love one's fellow. Thus, in the classical example, when a foreigner asked Hillel to teach him the whole Torah while standing on one foot, Hillel taught him, "Whatever is hateful to you, do not do to your fellow."[108] This implies that all that the Torah requires of man to fulfill the obligation of loving his fellow man is that he do nothing harmful to others.

It is often suggested that this substitution of the negative for the positive expresses a lesser concept in human relations. The positive, it is argued, conveys a more forceful approach to human intercourse. This assumption, however, is a mistaken one. Our Sages did not regard the mere performance of positive commandments to be a virtue, nor, in their view, does the failure to perform them mean that one has not attained certain desirable virtues in his intellectual and moral development. They ruled that the non-performance of a positive command required by the Torah is a transgression of a positive precept; a subversion of the will of God. Thus, the positive command, "Thou shalt love thy neighbor as thyself," carries the implication that he who does not love his neighbor violates this positive precept. The opposite of love is hatred; therefore our Sages taught that any hateful act or any contemplative act which may either imply hatred or finally lead to hatred is truly a transgression of the positive precept, "Thou shalt love thy neighbor as thyself."

As an illustration we may recall the law pertaining to prohibitive vows.[109] A man has the legal right, by means of a vow, to prohibit upon another person the derivation of any benefit from him or his property. Rabbi Meir, however, said that the court may find an opening to release an individual from such a vow by saying to him: "Didst thou know that thou wouldest transgress the commandment, 'Thou shalt not take vengeance,' or 'Thou shalt not bear any grudge,' or 'Thou shalt not hate thy brother in thy heart,' or 'Thou shalt love thy neighbor as thyself?...' If he said: 'Had I known this I would not have made my vow,' then he may be released from his vow."[110] Hence an anti-social action, though legal and binding, since it is motivated by a form of hatred is a violation of the positive precept of "love thy neighbor."

Similarly, Rabbi Meir said that if a man marries a woman who is not suitable for him, and the union can ultimately lead him to dislike or hate her, he transgresses the command of "love thy neighbor."[111] So, too, is it forbidden for a man to marry a woman without meeting her lest he later discover in her something unseemly,[112] for if she should become repulsive in his eyes and he grow to hate her, he will transgress the commandment of "love thy neighbor."

In this spirit our Sages admonish the court to choose a pleasant, that is, a less painful death for one who is to be executed, for the Torah said "Thou shalt love thy neighbor as thyself."[113] In other words, not only hatred but also lack of consideration for the pain and emotions of another, even though the latter may be a man condemned to death, is in every sense a transgression of the command to love one's neighbor.

The *Sifre* also voices this view: If he transgresses the command of "Thou shalt love thy neighbor as thyself," he will later transgress the command of "Thou shalt not hate," and "Thou shalt not take vengeance," and "Thou shalt not bear any grudge" and the positive command of "That thy brother may live with thee" and finally he will come to the shedding of blood.[114] According to this *Sifre*, one does not necessarily have to feel a deep hatred against his neighbor in order to transgress the command of "Thou shalt love thy neighbor as thyself." Much less than hatred—even a slight annoyance which may possibly lead to hatred—is therefore considered a transgression of this positive command.

On how a man fulfills his obligation to love his fellow man, our Sages are silent. Maimonides, it is true, reformulated the precept of "Thou shalt love thy neighbor as thyself" into a positive "All the things that you wish others to do to you, do you to your brothers."[115] But when he had to define the exact acts by which one can fulfill this command, he merely asserted that under the precept of "Thou shalt love thy neighbor as thyself" are included many good deeds which are not specifically commanded in the Torah, such as visiting the sick, comforting the mourners, burying the dead, and participating in the rejoicing of bride and groom. Our Sages had already listed these acts among those through which a man imitates the ways of God: "As He visits the sick, do thou also visit the sick. As He comforts the mourners, do thou also comfort the mourners. As He buries the dead, do thou also bury the dead."[116] Similarly Rabbi Judah ben Ilai said that to attend upon a bride is an act of *Imitatio Dei*, for God Himself engaged in attending to the needs of Eve and served as best man for Adam and Eve, as noted, "And He brought her unto the man."[117] It appears that our Sages looked upon the positive precept of "Thou shalt love thy neighbor as thyself" as an all-embracing principle which underlies the moral structure of the Torah. Unlike other precepts, it is not a commandment which is fulfilled merely by the performance of one act. This rule has to serve as the motive for all the positive duties which the Torah requires of man to perform for the betterment of society. Indeed, all the duties man owes his fellow man have as their primary object and ultimate goal nurturing a genuine affection among all men. It is this attitude which made it possible for Rabbi Akiba to say that this commandment is the "great principle of the Torah."[118]

This great general rule has as its particulars and corollaries all the positive and negative precepts of the Torah pertaining to the relationship of man to his fellow man. Thus, the duty to love one's fellow as one loves himself is defined by all the *mitzvot* pertaining to one's relationship to his fellows. At times one should be concerned with another's welfare as much as he is concerned with his own. At times, it is man's duty to be even more concerned with another's welfare than with his own. A neighbor may be wicked and animosity toward him may even be sanctioned by law, yet nevertheless, a person must be as concerned with the welfare of his enemy as with his own welfare. Thus it is clear that the duty to love one's neighbor is a general, all-inclusive principle whose fulfillment rests on the fulfillment of all the precepts of the Torah.

As further illustration of the compass of this rule, we can examine the precept in Exodus 23:5, "If thou see the ass of him that hateth thee lying under its burden, thou shalt forbear to pass by him, thou shalt surely release it with him."[119] The accepted halakah is that the law applies here not only to unloading a burden but also to helping load the burden, whether it be for an enemy or a friend.[120] An old man, however, or a distinguished scholar, is exempt from fulfilling this *mitzvah* since such work is beneath his dignity or beyond his strength.[121] The Tosefta lays down the norm: "The rule is that whoever does such work for himself should also do it for others, and whoever does not do it for himself is not bound to do it for others."[122] The Talmud also sets down the principle, "Whoever loads and unloads for himself is bound to load and unload for others,"[123] a direct application of the affirmative "do unto others as you would do for yourself." However, if one desires to meet the higher moral standards of the Torah, it is his duty to help another with loading and unloading even if he would not do such things for himself.[124] Maimonides succinctly sums up this general rule,

"If the animal were his own, he would load and unload, then in every case he must load and unload another's too. But if one is a man of piety (*hasid*) and conducts himself beyond the line of the law, even if he is the Patriarch of the highest rank (*hanasi hagadol*), it is his duty to load and unload."[125]

The rabbinic approach to this particular precept illustrates their point that the general rule of "Thou shalt love thy neighbor as thyself," applies to all commandments and means that one should be as concerned with the welfare of others as with his own. A man of piety must practice supererogation and be more concerned with another's welfare than with his own. Moreover, this law applies to helping any man, even one who "hateth thee." In this connection, it is striking that some of our Sages interpreted the phrase "who hateth thee" to refer not to a personal enemy but to a "religious enemy,"[126] a non-repentent transgressor. Maimonides, following this view, declares: "Even if he has not yet repented and one finds him under difficulties with his burden, it is one's duty to help load or unload, and not leave him in danger of death.... Indeed the Torah is very solicitous for the lives of Israelites, whether of the wicked or the righteous."[127]

Others of our Sages went on to say that the words "who hateth thee" apply to a heathen who hates a Jew.[128] Judging by these sources, it appears clear that the Rabbis saw in this particular precept a divine instruction: one must be concerned with another's welfare, at times even more than with his own, even with the welfare of one whom he cannot love for one reason or another.

Rabbi Akiba, in his disagreement with Ben Paturi, it will be recalled,[129] interpreted the verse in Leviticus 25:36, "And thy brother shall live with thee," to mean that the preservation of one's own life takes precedence over the life of another. How, one may well ask, can this be reconciled with the positive precept of loving thy neighbor as thyself and giving him prior consideration in accordance with the higher law? The answer is simply that every case must be weighed in its own context. Every action must be measured against the requirements of the higher principle. In other words, the full significance of the great and general rule of "Thou shalt love thy neighbor as thyself" is always measured by the particular definitions of every positive and negative precept in the Torah, all of which have as their ultimate aim the love of every human being. Only through continuous training in the moral duties as stipulated in the Torah and defined by the oral tradition, and only by continued concern with the welfare of others, as outlined in the Torah, can man attain the great virtue bound up in the command "Thou shalt love thy neighbor as thyself."

It is in this spirit that Ben Azzai, the younger contemporary of Rabbi Akiba, declared that the central pillar in the moral structure of the Torah is to be found in Genesis 5:1, "These are the generations of man in the day that God created man; in the likeness of God made He him."[130] He announced that the general and great rule of the Torah which directs Jewish morality is based upon the concept of the sacredness of the human personality. Every man is sacred because the human personality is created in the likeness and image of God. The Midrash further defines Ben Azzai's statement: "Do not say: Inasmuch as I have been put to shame, my fellow man also shall be put to shame with me. Rabbi Tanhuma said: If thou dost so, reflect upon whom thou dost put to shame, for, 'in the image of God He made him.'"[131]

It must be recognized that even our love for man ultimately is dependent upon our love of God. Any wrongs done to a fellow man reflect our own disregard for the Almighty Who graced man with His own likeness. Clearly, the sacredness of the human personality and the infinite worth of the individual are deeply imbedded, irremovable and irreplaceable cornerstones in the moral and religious structure of Judaism.

# NOTES

## INTRODUCTION

1. Cf., J. Guttmann, *The Philosophy of Judaism* (Hebrew), 225.
2. See H. A. Wolfson, *Philo*, I, 146–47.
3. Josephus, *Contra Apionem*, II, 165 (all references are to the edition of the *Loeb Classical Library*, 1951).
4. *Ibid.*
5. Berakot 2, 2.
6. Gittin 4, 3.
7. *Spec. Leg.* IV, 237 (all references are to the F. H. Colson translation in the *Loeb Classical Library*, 1950).
8. See E. R. Goodenough, *The Politics of Philo Judaeus*, 86–90; and F. H. Colson, *Philo*, VIII, Appendix, 437–38.
9. *De Conf. Ling.* 108.
10. H. A. Wolfson, *Philo*, II, 427–28. Prof. Wolfson's analysis, in this passage, of Philo's unique use of the term "democracy" in relation to the "constitution of the Torah" is very interesting and illuminating.

## CHAPTER I

1. *Genesis Rabbah* 1, 2.
1a. *Sifra* on Lev. 19:18; Yer. Nedarim 41 c.
2. Gen. 1:27; 5:1; 9:6.
3. *Leviticus Rabbah* 34, 3.
4. Num. 15:30–1.
5. *Sifre* Num. 112.
6. *De Virt.* 167–72.
7. Berakot 35 a-b.
8. *De Cherubim* 83–119.
9. *Sifra* on Lev. 25:23.
10. Lev. 25:3–4.
11. Sanhedrin 39 a.
12. *Spec. Leg.* II, 113.
13. Abot 3, 7.
14. *Midrash Mishle* 31, on *Eshet Hayil*.
15. Cf., *Abot de R. Nathan* c. 14.
16. *De Cherubim* 83.
17. *Quaes. in Gen.* 23:2–3, Book IV, No. 73.
18. Rosh Hashanah 31 a (the Hebrew word used to denote "acquired possession of" is *shekanah*).
19. Menahot 99 b.
20. Hilkot Me'ilah 8, 7.
21. *Spec. Leg.* II, 180.
22. *Tanhuma*, Re'eh, 16 (on Deut. 14:22).
23. Deut. 14:22.
24. *Pesikta Rab.*, 26:2 (*aser t'aser*).
25. Gen. 15:9.
26. Ex. 25:2.
27. *Quis Rer. Divin. Heres*, 103–123.
28. Sotah 14 a.
29. *Mekilta* on Ex. 20:5.
30. *Midrash Tehillim*, 24:3.
30a. Cf., Akiba's view in Abot 3, 14.
31. Ex. 15:17.
32. *De Plant.* 54–55.
33. Abot 6, 10 (baraita, *Kinyan Torah*).
34. Maimonides, beginning of *Mishneh Torah*.
35. Ex. 20:2.
36. *Mekilta*, Ex. 20:3 (*al panai*). See also Rashi, *ad. loc.*

CHAPTER II

1. Berakot 7 b.

2. *Sifre* Deut. 313.

3. See, e.g., the prayers recited on Mondays and Thursdays before returning Torah to Ark; cf., G. F. Moore, *Judaism*, II, 204.

4. Deut. 14:1.

5. *Sifre*, Deut. 96.

6. There is an isolated statement in the Midrash which seems to indicate that, when the Temple was still in existence, a sinner who brought a sin offering confessed his sins to the priest. It reads: "Why did the Holy One blessed be He ordain that the bullock of the sin offering which the High Priest brought shall be burned publicly outside the camp?... to teach... that the sinner should not be embarrassed to confess his sin to the priest.... The sinner may now say: The High Priest was not embarrassed [to confess his sin] in my presence. I shall not be embarrassed because of his presence." But, as we shall see, this midrashic statement in no way contradicts the fact that the priest was not an intermediary for atonement. (See A. F. Epstein *Kadmoniot*, Midrash Tadshe, Sec. 18, XXXV; See also A. Büchler, *Sin and Atonement*, p. 418, and S. Belkin, "Midrash Tadshe," *Horeb*, Vol. 11, No. 21–22, pp. 47–48.)

7. Lev. 4:29.

8. Yer. Yebamot, 9 c.

9. *Spec. Leg.* 1, 238–241.

10. Sotah 32 b.

11. Psalms 32:1.

12. Prov. 28:13.

13. Yoma 86 b.

14. Hilkot Teshubah 1, 1. Not all rabbinic scholars, particularly Nachmanides, agreed with Maimonides that *teshubah* and *vidui*, repentance and confession, are synonymous. In fact, the Talmud states that if a thoroughly wicked man marries a woman on the express stipulation that he is righteous *(zadik)*, the marriage is valid, for he may have thought to repent (Kiddushin 49 b). According to this *baraita* it would seem that repentance does not require a formal pronouncement of confession; mere meditation of repentance is sufficient to make one a righteous man. This *baraita*, however, does not seem to have been accepted as *halakah* (Kiddushin 40 a). It seems that the real purpose of our Sages in this law was to declare that it is impossible to talk of a "thoroughly wicked" or "thoroughly righteous" man, for no one can tell what goes on in another's mind. It was for this reason that they ruled that any such stipulation is void.

15. Hilkot Teshubah 2, 5.

16. *Yalkut Shimoni* 532, on Hosea 14:2 (Horeb ed., p. 853.)

17. Philo, as indicated, agreed with the Palestinian Tannaim that at the bringing of the sin offering, the sinner is permitted to confess in such a manner as to protect him from humiliation and that therefore the sin offering brought for offenses committed against God in error did not require a public confession. But he, too, speaks about "open confession" *(De Praem. 163)*. It is most likely, however, that he refers to sins committed against one's fellow man, and that he would agree that for unintentional sins committed against God, a silent confession made in general terms would

suffice. (See Belkin, *Philo and the Oral Law*, 155–156n; H. A. Wolfson, *op cit.*, II, 256–57.)

18. Sanhedrin 6, 2.
19. Kiddushin 65 b.
20. Ketubot 18 b; Sanhedrin 9 b.
21. Hilkot Sanhedrin 18, 6.
21a. *Ibid.*
22. Hilkot Sanhedrin 19, 1–4.
23. Sanhedrin 6, 2.
24. Hilkot Teshubah, 1, 1.
25. Yoma 87 a.
26. Yoma 8, 9.
27. Baba Kamma 84 a.
28. Deut. 25:2–3.
29. *Sifre* Deut. 285.
30. Deut. 25:2.
31. Ketubot 37 a.
32. Makkot 1, 2.
33. *Ibid.*
34. Ketubot 32 b.
35. Baba Kamma 8, 7.
36. Leviticus 5:23.
37. Tosefta Baba Kamma 10, 5; Gittin 55 a.
38. *Ibid.*
39. *Ibid.* (see Maimonides, Hilkot Gezelah, 1, 5).
40. Gittin 5, 5.
41. Baba Kamma 103 b. The rule that restitution must be made directly to the person robbed, applies also to a robber who did not swear falsely (according to the opinion of R. Akiba). See Tosafot *ad. loc.*
42. Baba Kamma 9, 5.
43. Baba Kamma 103 b.
44. Baba Kamma 66 a.
45. *Mekilta* on Ex. 22:24.
46. Tosefta Baba Metziah 6, 17. See also Baba Metziah 71 a.
47. *Sifra* on Lev. 25:37 (see also A. Büchler, *Sin and Atonement*, 92).

48. Cf., Berakot 28 b; (Rabban Johanan b. Zakkai's said: "Fear God as much as you fear man").
49. Ex. 22:6.
50. Baba Kamma 76 a.
51. See *Encyclopedia of Religion and Ethics*, IV, p. 217.
52. Hullin 139 a.
53. *Spec. Leg.* III, 83–84.
54. Cf., *Harper's Dictionary of Classical Literature s. v. crimen*, and Josephus, *Antiquities*, IV, 280; *Encyclopedia of Social Sciences*, Vol. 9, 228.
55. Hilkot Rozeah 1, 4.
56. *Mekilta* on Ex. 20:13.
57. Abot 3, 14.
58. Tosefta Yebamot 8, 4.
59. *Sifra* on Lev. 19:18.
60. See Mommsen, *Roman Strafrecht*, 661 ff (see also above Note 54).
61. *Spec. Leg.* IV, 2.
62. *Ibid.*, IV, 23 (Büchler, *Sin and Atonement*, 390–91, mistakenly took Philo's use of non-Jewish terminology for ignorance of Jewish law).
63. Josephus, *Contra Apionem*, II, 216 (see S. Belkin, "The Alexandrian Halakah in Apologetic Literature of the First Century B.C.E.," 17 ff).
64. According to the Torah, only if the thief killed or sold the stolen animal.
65. Josephus, *Antiquities*, XVI, 1, 1.
66. *Mekilta* on Ex. 22:6 (see also Tosefta Baba Kamma 7, 2).
67. Lev. 5:21.
68. *Sifra* on Lev. 5:21.
69. *Spec. Leg.* IV, 30–32.
70. Yer. Rosh Hashanah 59 c.
71. Tosefta Kiddushin 1, 14–15.
72. Berakot 29 a.
73. See Kiddushin 40 b; Hilkot Teshubah 3, 5.
74. Hilkot Teshubah 2, 2.

75. See H. A. Wolfson, *op cit*, II, 253.
76. *De Praem.* 163.
77. Yoma 8, 8.
78. *Spec. Leg.* I, 236.
79. *De Virt.* 177.
80. *Spec. Leg.* I, 187.
81. *De Virt.* 176; *De Abr.* 26; *De Somm.* I, 91.
82. Berakot 34 b. (See also Wolfson, *Philo*, II, 258.)
83. See *De Abr.* 17.
84. *De Praem.* 17–20.
85. Hilkot Teshubah 2, 4.
86. *Quod Deus Immut.* 162.

87. *Spec. Leg.* IV, 102.
88. Hilkot Deot. 1, 4.
89. Hilkot Deot. 1, 5.
90. *Moreh Nebukim* III, 46 (Friedlander translation, 237).
91. *Testament of Reuben* 1, 9.
92. *Testament of Simeon* 3, 4.
93. *Testament of Judah* 15, 4 (see G. F. Moore, *Judaism*, II, 257–58).
94. *Quod Deterius Potiori* VII, 19 ff.
95. *Spec. Leg.* II, 20.
96. *Ibid.*, 21.
97. *Probus* 75 ff.
98. *Ibid.*, 72.

## CHAPTER III

1. Lev. 21:10–12.
2. Sanhedrin 2, 1.
3. Yoma 3, 8.
3a. *Ibid.*
4. Yoma 1, 1 and 4, 2.
4a. Cf., S. Zeitlin, *Perushim v'ha-Zadukim* (Hebrew), Horeb, 1936.
5. Mishnah Yadaim 4, 7. Based upon the Pharisaic perspective, the Mishnah records that if a Canaanite slave injures someone, the injured party can collect indemnity only in the unpredictable future, i.e., when the slave, at the good will of his master, may be set free. The reason is that during the period of his enslavement, though the slave may be legally responsible for his own actions, he does not possess any property with which to pay his legal indebtedness. Thus, the ultimate loser is the injured party.
6. See Ex. 20:10.
7. *Ozar ha-Gaonim*, Yebamot, Vol. 7, 119–20. (A contrary view is held by Maimonides, Hilkot Shabbat 20, 14.)
8. Ex. 21:20.
9. *Mekilta, ad. loc.*

10. Yer. Baba Kamma 5 d (see also I. Herzog, *The Main Institutions of Jewish Law*, II, 5).
10a. See Abot 2, 4; Berakot 29 a, which stress that "one should not be sure of himself till the day of death" and apply the statement to Johanan the High priest. See above p. 54.
11. Kiddushin 66 a.
12. Josephus, *Antiquities*, 13, 10, 5–6.
13. *Ibid.*
14. Cf., G. F. Moore, *Judaism*, I, 59.
15. Deut. 22:13–19.
16. *Sifre* Deut. 238.
17. Lev. 19:16.
18. Ketubot 46 a.
19. Deut. 22:18.
20. See Maimonides, Hilkot Deot. 7, 2; Hilkot Sanhedrin 18, 1 and 19, 4: Negative command punishable by stripes, No. 133.
21. Yer. Sanhedrin 19 d.
22. Tosefta Sanhedrin 4, 1.
23. I Samuel 24:6.
24. I Samuel 26:9.
25. Tosefta Sanhedrin 3, 4.
26. *Spec. Leg.* IV, 157; cf., *Sifre* Deut. 137.

27. Deut. 33:5.
28. *Midrash Tannaim, ad. loc.*
29. Ex. 4:29–31.
30. *Mekilta*, Beshallah 6 (on Ex. 14:31).
31. *De Praem.* 54.
32. See H. A. Wolfson, *Philo*, II, 326–31.
33. Sanhedrin 2, 3–5.
34. Ketubot 17 a.
35. Kiddushin 32 a, according to R. Joseph's opinion.
36. Sanhedrin 49 a.
37. Shabbat 56 a.
38. See I Samuel 8:11–18.
39. Tosefta Sanhedrin 4, 5.
40. Sanhedrin 2, 4.
41. See E. R. Goodenough, *The Politics of Philo Judaeus*, 44, 86 ff.
42. *Legat. ad Gaium* 76.
43. *Ibid.*, 119.
44. E. R. Goodenough, *The Politics of Philo Judaeus*, 112–13.
45. Gen. 17:17.
46. *De Mutatione Nominum* XXXIV, 181–85.
47. *Ibid.*
48. Tosefta Kiddushin 1, 13–14; Kiddushin, 40 b. See Rosh Hashanah 16 b, and Maimonides, Hilkot Teshubah 3, 1.
49. Josephus, *Antiquities*, IV 223.
50. *Ibid.*, XV, 9 ff.
51. Tosefta Sanhedrin 4, 8.
52. I Chronicles 23:4; 26:29; II Chronicles 19:4–11; Sanhedrin 19 a.
53. *Spec. Leg.* IV, 190.
54. *Ibid.* (See Loeb Classical Library

ed., VIII, Appendix, 436, Note 188.)
55. Deut. 17:8–9.
56. *Sifre* Deut. 152.
57. On the term "synedrioi" in Philo, see H. A. Wolfson, *Philo*, II, 350–52; S. B. Hoenig, *The Great Sanhedrin*, 6 and 228.
58. *Spec. Leg.* IV, 192.
59. Josephus, *Antiquities*, IV, 218; cf., S. B. Hoenig, *op. cit.*, 165 ff.
59a. Cf., however, Tos. Sanhedrin 4, 6, speaking of regal punishments in contrast to those of the Beth Din.
60. *Spec. Leg.* IV, 170.
61. *Ibid.*, 170–71.
62. Tosefta Sanhedrin 4, 2: *Sifre* Deut. 161.
63. Ex. 22:27.
64. *Mekilta of R. Ishmael, ad. loc.*
65. See Sanhedrin 49 a; Maimonides, Hilkot Melakim 3, 9 (cf., J. Ginzberg *Mishpatim L'yisrael* 9 a).
66. Pirke Abot 6, 6.
67. Abot 3, 5.
67a. Yoma 71 b.
68. Horayot 13 a.
69. See *Quaest. in Gen.* IV, 76.
70. See Gittin 62 a.
71. *De Plant.* 68.
72. Sanhedrin 2, 2; cf., S. B. Hoenig, *op. cit.*, 186.
73. Deut. 19:17.
74. Sanhedrin, 19 a–b.
75. Josephus, *Antiquities*, XIV, 9, 4.

## CHAPTER IV

1. Sanhedrin 1, 6 (see S. B. Hoenig, *The Great Sanhedrin*, 86 ff.)
2. Sanhedrin 1, 1.
3. Abot 4, 8.
4. Sanhedrin 5 a, and Tosafot *ad. loc.*
s.v. *mumhe le' rabim.*
5. Sanhedrin 3 a.
6. Hilkot Sanhedrin 5, 18.
7. Sanhedrin 8 a.
8. Sanhedrin 1, 6.

9. On the requirement of a majority of two, see Hilkot Sanhedrin 9, 2.

10. Rosh Hashanah 16 b.

11. See Kiddushin 40 b.

12. Yoma 86 b; Hilkot Teshubah 3, 5. See RaBaD *ad. loc.*

13. I Kings 14:13.

14. Eccl. 9, 18.

15. Hilkot Teshubah 3, 2.

16. Tosefta Sanhedrin 3, 8.

17. *Mekilta de R. Simeon* on Ex. 23:2 (see also Rabbi M. M. Kasher, *Torah Shelemah*, Vol. 18, 159, Note 32).

18. Hilkot Sanhedrin 10, 1; *Sefer ha-Hinuk*, Mitzvah, 77.

19. Eduyot 1, 1–4.

20. Eduyot 1, 6; I. H. Weiss, *Dor Dor v' Dorshav*, IV, 300. Cf., Ch. Tscherno-witz, *Toldot ha-posekim*, I, 271 ff. See also *Encyclopedia Talmudit*, IX (Jeru-salem, 1959) s.v. *halakah*, 261 ff.

20a. See RaBaD, *Hasagot on Maimonides*, at end of Introduction to *Mishneh Torah* and Hilkot Killaim 6, 2.

21. Eduyot 1, 5.

22. Tosefta Eduyot 1, 4.

23. Eduyot 1, 4.

24. *Sifre* Deut. 188.

25. Ketubot 2, 8.

26. Gittin 2 b (see Rabbi Joseph Rosen [Ragotshover Gaon], *Tsafnat Paneah*, "Hilkot Issure Biah," I, Chap. 20, 74).

27. *Spec. Leg.* IV, 53–54.

28. *Sefer ha-Hinuk*, Mitzvah 526.

29. Makkot 1, 7; Makkot 5 b; Maimon-ides, Hilkot Edut. 5, 3.

30. Deut. 17:6.

31. Makkot 1, 7.

32. Lev. 19:15.

33. *Sifra* on Lev. 19:15.

34. *Ibid.*

35. Ex. 23:6.

36. *Mekilta, ad. loc.*

37. Shebuot 30 b.

38. Deut. 17:6.

39. Deut. 19:15.

40. Sanhedrin 37 b.

41. Ketubot 18 b; Sanhedrin 44 b.

42. Abot 1, 9.

43. See *Rashi*, Sanhedrin 44 b; Yer. Sanhedrin 23 a.

44. Sanhedrin 5, 1.

45. Sanhedrin 26 b–27 a.

46. Sanhedrin 3, 3.

46a. Sanhedrin 27 a.

47. Sanhedrin 24 b.

48. The answer offered by the Talmud to this question is that the consent of the loser of the money is merely an *asmakta.* This term is part of one of the most com-plicated legal principles in the Talmud, and in this particular case may apply on-ly in its most elementary sense—that a person who obligates himself to pay in the event he loses a gamble, does so pri-marily in the hope that he will win, otherwise he would not gamble. Since it is on this hope that he leans *(samak),* his obligation is not valid and therefore whatever the gambler acquires is consid-ered a form of robbery *(gezel).*

49. Sanhedrin 24 b.

50. Kiddushin 1, 10.

51. Kiddushin 40 b.

52. Hilkot Edut, II, 1–3.

53. *Ibid.*

54. Ketubot 1, 8–9.

55. Ketubot 13 a–b.

56. Baba Metziah 3 b; Baba Kamma 73 b; Makkot 5 a.

57. Ex. 23:1.

58. Sanhedrin 27 a.

59. Shebuot 47 b; Baba Bathra 31 b.

60. Maimonides, who accepts this prin-ciple in his *Yad Hahazakah,* (Hilkot Edut 22) apparently concurs with Rashi's

thinking (Ketubot 22 a, *cit*: "Trei vetrei Ninhu") that while the two sets of witnesses retain their *hezkat kashrut*, the trustworthiness of the person against whom the conflicting testimony was given, remains in doubt.

The logic behind the position of Rashi and Maimonides seems to be that as soon as the first set of witnesses gives evidence that the man is a *rashah* he immediately loses his *hezkat kashruth*. Even though the evidence of the first witnesses is contradicted by later testimony, the man does not automatically regain his presumption of trustworthiness, for once voided this *hazakah* can be regained only by unqualified proof of innocence. At best, he can only be classified as a *safek*, as a doubtful case. Since this is a *safek deoraitha*, he is no longer eligible to give evidence in court.

Rabbenu Hananel, the outstanding North African scholar of the eleventh century, and the Tosafists of the French school, however, do not agree with Rashi and Maimonides. They are of the opinion that when the evidence of the first set of witnesses is contradicted, the doubt concerning the principal's trustworthiness falls away and he regains his *hezkat kashruth* (Tosafot, Ketubot 22 a, s.v. "Trei vetrei ninhu").

61. Sotah 3 a.

62. Makkot 3, 15.

63. Hilkot Edut 12, 4.

CHAPTER V

1. Sanhedrin 4, 5.

2. Terumot 8, 12.

3. Tosefta Terumot 7, 20.

4. Cf., *Maimonides*, (Hilkot Deot. 5, 5) who also understood this to be the intent of the Tosefta.

5. Lev. 25:36.

6. *Sifra, ad. loc.* A variant of this statement in Baba Metziah, 62 a, omits Ben Paturi's reference to Leviticus 25:36 (which only Rabbi Akiba uses as text-proof) and records the full declaration of Ben Paturi, "let them both die and let not either of them witness the death of the other."

7. Cf., Yitzhak Baer, *Yisrael b'amim* (Mosad Bialik, Jerusalem, 1956), 102.

8. Lev. 19:16.

9. *Sifra, ad loc.*

10. Sanhedrin, 73 a. (See also Maimonides, *Sefer ha-Mitzvot* by Ch. Heller, 175. The duty to risk one's life applies not only to the prevention of criminal acts but also to exacting justice. A judge must pronounce his verdict even at the risk of losing his life. On the verse in Deut. 1:17, "Ye shall hear the small and the great alike, ye shall not be afraid of the face of any man," the *Sifre* states: "Perhaps you may be afraid to pronounce the judgment because you might say, 'this man will kill my son, or set fire to my house, or cut off my plants;' therefore it is said, "ye shall not be afraid of the face of any man." Cf., *Maimonides, Minyan Hamizvot*, 415, and the *Sefer-ha-Hinuk*).

11. Niddah 5, 3; Niddah, 44 b.

12. Ohalot 7, 6 (see Jacob Ginzberg *Mishpatim L'yisrael* 224, 239 ff).

13. On the question as to what extent a foetus is considered a human being in rabbinic law, see *Hiddushe Rabbenu Chaim Halevi* (by Rav Chaim Soloveit-

chik) on *Mishneh Torah*, Hilkot Rozeah
1, 9, 95–6.

14. *Spec. Leg.* III, 117–18.

15. Gittin 23 b.

16. When, however, Philo writes *(Spec. Leg.* III, 108–09) that according to the Torah, killing a fully developed foetus is an act of murder punishable by death, he bases himself upon a mistranslation of the LXX which renders the verse in Exodus 22:22 as if it referred to the death of the foetus instead of the death of the mother. It is ironic that the non-Jewish sources Philo quotes support the Halakah, while his interpretation of a verse goes contrary to the Halakah.

17. Pesahim 25 b.

18. Horayot 3, 7–8.

19. Sanhedrin 74 a; Abodah Zarah 27 b.

20. Leviticus 18:5.

21. Abodah Zarah 27 b, 54 a.

22. Hilkot Yesodei ha-Torah, 5, 4.

23. Gen. 9:5.

24. *Gen. Rabbah*, 34, 19; Hilkot Rozeah 2, 3.

25. Josephus, *Bellum Judaicum* III, 375 ff.

26. Josephus, *Antiquities*, IV, 202.

27. *De Cherubim* 114–19.

28. *Abot de Rabbi Nathan* Chap. 14; the end of *Midrash Mishlei*, 31.

29. See above, Chap. I, p. 25.

30. *Leg. All.*, I, 103; III, 69.

31. *Conf. Lin.* 176; *Fuga.* 68–70; see also H. A. Wolfson, *Philo*, I, 269.

32. See *Tanhuma* (ed. Buber), Lev. 12; Sanhedrin 91 a–b; cf., G. F. Moore, *Judaism*, I, 486–89.

33. See Taanit 11 a.

34. Nedarim 10 a.

35. Yer. Nedarim 9, 1 (41 b).

36. Hilkot Deot 3, 1.

37. *Sifre* Deut. 318.

38. Deut. 16:20.

39. *De Pot.* 19–20; see also *De Cher* 5.

40. Baba Kamma 8, 1.

41. Where, however, no permanent injury is inflicted, but a man becomes bedridden, in the opinion of many rabbinic scholars, the victim is to be paid for his enforced idleness in accordance with his actual loss of income. See *Maimonides,* Hilkot Hobel U-Mazik 2, 11; Alfasi and Tosafot on Baba Kamma 85 b.

42. Tosefta Baba Kamma 9, 12.

43. Baba Kamma 86 b.

44. Baba Kamma 8, 3.

45. Baba Metziah 58 b.

46. Abot 3, 11.

47. Baba Kamma 86 a.

48. Baba Kamma 8, 6.

49. Lev. 24:12.

50. Sanhedrin 78 b and *Rashi* s. v. "*l'daas ha-hahamim*"; cf., J. Ginzberg, *Mishpatim L'yisrael*, 31 ff.

51. Ex. 21:19.

52. *Mekilta, ad. loc.* (see also M. M. Kasher, *Torah Shelemah*, Vol. 17, 102, Note 360).

53. Sanhedrin 9, 5.

54. Sanhedrin 81 b.

55. *Ibid.* (see also *Rashi, ad loc*).

56. Prov. 28:17.

57. I Kings 21:25.

58. Num. 16:22.

59. I Kings 22:21.

60. I Kings 22:22.

61. Hilkot Rozeah 4, 9.

62. Fragments of the XII Tables, III, 1 (see *Library of Original Sources*, III, 10).

63. The term *shibud haguf*, personal obligation, which was coined by Rabbi Jacob Tam, the Tosafist, (Baba Bathra 175 b) has not even the remotest relation to the ancient Roman concept of personal *obligatio*, which actually meant that the creditor acquired ownership, in the

literal sense of the word, over the person or personality of the debtor. *Shibud haguf* merely means that the debtor has a *personal obligation* to pay his debt, not that his person becomes the property of the creditor (see Baba Bathra 174 b). In rabbinic law, the property of a person is his surety, and the law of surety is that the primary responsibility falls on the debtor, that is, that the creditor must approach the debtor first before he can sue a guarantor for payment. On the same principle, the creditor cannot seize the estate of the debtor unless the debtor either cannot or does not want to pay his debt (see I. H. Herzog, *Main Institutions of Jewish Law*, II, 7). Furthermore, this term implies that even if the property, either because of sale or gift, is no longer subject to the creditor, as in the case of a *milveh al peh*, the debtor still has an obligation to repay his debt.

64. Ex. 22:1.

65. Cf., Malbim, *Hatorah v'hamitzvah* 144, on Ex. 22:2, and *Sefer Ha-mikneh* on Kiddushin 18a.

66. Arakin 29 a.

67. Baba Metziah 6, 2.

68. Baba Metziah 77 a.

69. Lev. 19:15.

70. *Ibid.*, 25:55.

71. Baba Metziah 10 a.

72. Baba Metziah 77 a.

73. *Ibid.*, Rashi, *ad. loc.*

74. The rabbinic concept, that any obligation which involves one's own person is in effect a form of slavery and is therefore not binding, is applied in a decision handed down by the late Judge Sulzberger of Philadelphia. The Pennsylvania legislature adopted a statute permitting a laborer to pledge his future wages for indebtedness previously incurred.

Judge Sulzberger opposed this statute for the following reason: "The first action of the Bill of Rights is still a living force in this Commonwealth. One of the inherent and indefeasible rights thereby granted, is the enjoyment and defense of liberty. It is a declaration against slavery in any form however modified or disguised. The distinction between a man's acquired estate (that is, his freedom) is carefully preserved and sedulously guarded. A man may pledge his property but not his person. However great may be the volume of police power entrusted to legislature, it cannot extend to the impairment of the mere right of a man, even though he be a debtor, to earn a living by labor and to apply his earnings to the support of himself and his family.... And after mature consideration, we cannot resist the conclusion that there is no power of contract in the individual," (See Louis E. Levinthal, *Mayer Sulzberger*, Philadelphia, 1927, 100–01).

75. Hilkot Mekhirah 5, 14.

76. Hilkot Shelukhim U-Shutafin 4, 2. According to Rabbi Abraham Ben David, however, a partnership in which two people obligate themselves to share their future earnings is valid (RaBaD *ad. loc.*). Disagreeing with Maimonides, he argues that since the institution of Israelite slavery did exist in ancient times, it becomes self-evident that one can bind oneself to another, through a proper *kinyan*, for his future earnings and that the law does not require a property obligation. Maimonides believed either that, with the abolition of the institution of the Israelite slave during the Second Commonwealth, the entire concept of *personal obligation* became extinct, or

that the binding of one's personality was
limited only to the particular instrumentality of *abdut*; one could not bind
himself to another person through any
other means.

77. Ex. 21:6.

78. Kiddushin 22 b.

## CHAPTER VI

1. Sanhedrin 10, 5.

2. Sanhedrin 15 b (see also Rosh Hashanah 17 b).

3. Sanhedrin 112 a.

4. Tosefta Sanhedrin 14, 4.

5. Sanhedrin 111 a.

6. Abot 1, 7.

7. Hilkot Deot 6, 1.

8. See *Sifre* Deut. 144 *(Shofetim)*.

9. Megillah 26 a.

10. Baba Bathra 8 b.

11. Nedarim 5, 4–5.

12. The concept of state, in our judgment, would be included under the institution of kingship, which is not the
core of our problem.

13. See Sanhedrin 5 a, 8 a.

14. Ex. 22:8.

15. Cf., Onkelos, *ad loc.*; Baba Kamma
75 a.

16. See Ex. 21:37 and 22:3.

17. See Gittin 53 a. Cf. *Encyclopedia
Talmudit*, VIII, 703 ff.

18. Baba Kamma 5 a.

19. *Ibid.* 98 a (see also Tosafot *ad. loc.*, s.
v. *achurin u-tzelulin*).

20. Gittin 5, 4 (see Bartenoro, *ad loc*).

21. Tosefta Gittin 4, 6; Gittin 54 b.

22. Josephus, *Antiquities*, IV, 278.

23. *Spec. Leg.* III, 108.

24. See E. R. Goodenough, *The Jewish
Courts in Egypt*, 113 ff., and F. H. Col-
son's note in the Appendix to *Spec. Leg.*
III, 108, p. 637.

25. *Mekilta* on Ex. 21:22.

26. In one place (Shabbat 139 a), the
Talmud vaguely refers to *hilkot zibur*,
"community laws," interpreting a verse
in Isaiah (14:5), as an admonition to
scholars not to teach "Community
Laws" to ignorant judges. In my opinion, however, this has no bearing on the
concept of a community as we are
discussing it. It is fairly clear that in
Talmudic times individuals not of the
highest caliber were, on occasion, appointed to oversee specific municipal
institutions. On the other hand,
institutions and functions which can be
characterized as "religious"—schools,
synagogues, supervision of charity
funds, and so on—were entrusted only
to men of great scholarship. The Talmud (Kiddushin 76 b) records that in
one Babylonian community two scholars of unequal stature were engaged in a
dispute over which one should be placed
in charge of the community. When the
dispute was brought before Rabbi
Joseph, he ruled that to the one who was
more distinguished in learning should be
assigned the "affairs relating to heaven,"
and to the one less distinguished in
scholarship and lineage be assigned the
"affairs of the city." It is, therefore, a
fair assumption that when the Rabbis
spoke out against the appointment of
ignorant people as judges of the *hilkot
zibur*, they had in mind the supervision
of the "affairs of the city" (*cf.* S. W.
Baron, *The Jewish Community*, I, 134).

27. Baba Bathra 1, 5.

28. Tosefta Baba Metziah 11, 23.
29. Baba Bathra 22 a.
30. *Ibid.*
31. *Ibid.*, 8 a.
32. Ketubot 49 b; Baba Bathra 8 b.
33. Hilkot Matnot Aniyim 7, 10.
34. Baba Bathra 8 a.
35. Rabbi Jacob Tam, Tosafist of the French school, among others, claimed that the court could only "force with words," that is, by using its influence, but could not actually and legally compel one to give charity (see Tosafot, Ketubot 49b). Most rabbinic authorities, however, accept the view of Maimonides that the giving of charity is enforceable in court.
36. Ex. 22:25.
37. *Mekilta, ad. loc.*
38. Baba Metziah 108 b.
39. *Ibid.*
40. *Ibid.*
41. Hilkot Shekhanim 12, 5.
42. Deut. 6:18.
43. Baba Bathra 2 b.
44. Baba Bathra 6 b.
45. Baba Bathra 2, 3.
46. Baba Bathra 21 a.
47. Baba Bathra 2, 4, and discussion in Gemara thereon.
48. *Ibid.*, 2, 9.
49. *Ibid.*, 2, 8. This law is particularly interesting because legally a man cannot be held responsible for injuries caused by chaff blown by the wind (Baba Bathra 26 a). Morally, however, this was considered a serious offense, of which Maimonides wrote: "all of these cases are similar to doing damage with one's arrow" (Hilkot Shekhenim 11, 1).
50. Lev. 19:18.
51. Deut. 20, 19.
52. Hilkot Melakim 6, 10.
53. See Baba Kamma 91 b; Kiddushin 32 a; Makkot 22 a.
54. Deut. 4:9.
55. Baba Kamma 91 b.
56. Terumot 8, 4; Tosefta Abodah Zarah 6, 6; Abodah Zarah 12 b.
57. Hilkot Rozeah 11, 5.
58. Lev. 19:2.
59. *Sifra* (Kedoshim) on Lev. 19:2.
60. Lev. 22:32.
61. Pesahim 49 a.
62. Yoma 86 a.
63. Berakot 6 a.
64. Sanhedrin 1, 6.
65. Megillah 4, 3.
66. Megillah 23 b.
67. Berakot 21 b.
68. See above, p. 102.
69. Sanhedrin 74 a–b.
70. Abodah Zarah 27 b.

## CHAPTER VII

1. Taanit 3, 8.
2. See below, p. 140.
3. Abot 2, 4.
4. Taanit 11 a.
5. Rosh Hashanah 17 a.
6. *Rashi, ibid.*, quoting *Seder Olam* (see *Dikduke Soferim* on Rosh Hashanah 17a, Notes).
7. Hilkot Teshubah 3, 11.
8. *Ibid.*, 4, 2.
9. Maimonides employs a different phraseology when he enumerates the people for whom relatives should not mourn (Hilkot Abel. 2, 8). Included in that list are those in the class of *haporshim midarkei zibur*, whom Maimonides, bas-

ing himself on a rabbinic source (Sema-
kot 2, 10), defines as those who cast off
the yoke of the Torah and observe none
of its commandments, making no mention of failure to participate in public
fasts or refusal to share in the distress of
the community. It is therefore apparent
that Maimonides distinguishes between
two kinds of *porshim*. A man who does
not join the community, even if in private he is observant and fulfills his religious duties, is considered a person who
has no share in the Jewish community
and is therefore denied a share in the
world to come. But a man who con-
sciously rebels against God and refuses
to observe any of the laws and identify
himself with his coreligionists is no longer considered even a member of his immediate family. The laws of mourning
therefore, do not apply to him.

10. Tosefta Kiddushin 1, 14; Kiddushin
40 b; cf., same passage in name of *Dorshei
Reshumoth, Kohelleth Rabbah* 10, 1.

11. Prov. 10:25.

12. Yoma 38 b.

13. *Ibid.* 86 b.

14. Sanhedrin 103 b.

15. Hagigah 12 b.

16. Sukkah 45 b; Hullin 92 a.

17. Hullin 92 a.

18. *De Sacr. Ab.* 121-26.

19. Gen. 12:3.

20. *Mig. Ab.* 120-25.

21. Gen. 20:17.

22. Berakot 12 b.

23. Baba Kamma 92 a.

24. Cf., G. F. Moore, *Judaism*, II, 208.

25. Berakot 29 b.

26. Taanit 3, 8; Taanit 23 a.

27. Sanhedrin 27 b; Shebuot 39 a.

28. Shabbat 54 b.

29. Ex. 19:6.

30. *Mekilta de Rabbi Simon* on Ex. 19:6.

31. *Mekilta de Rabbi Ishmael* on Ex. 20:2.

32. Cf., S. Schechter, *Some Aspects of
Rabbinic Theology*, 194-95.

33. Tosefta Taanit 1, 8.

34. See above, p. 37, for a discussion of
public confession.

35. Lev. 19:16.

36. See Shabbat 56 b; Pesahim 87 b,
118 a: Yer. Peah 16 a.

37. Hilkot Deot. 7, 2.

38. Arakin 15 b.

39. Shebuot 39 a; Sanhedrin 27 b.

40. Arakin 16 b.

41. Yoma 86 b.

42. Baba Bathra 8 b.

43. Shabbat 118 b; *Rashi, ad. loc.*

44. See Salo W. Baron, *The Jewish
Community*, I. 118-56 and Notes.

45. Abot 2, 2.

46. Rosh Hashanah 17 a.

47. Hilkot Teshubah 3, 13.

48. Hagigah 5 b.

49. Sanhedrin 7 b.

50. Hilkot Sanhedrin 25, 2-3.

51. See above, p. 68.

52. Berakot 55 a.

52a. Cf., S. B. Hoenig, *The Great Sanhedrin*, 90, ff.

53. Sanhedrin 46 a.

54. Abodah Zarah 36 a.

55. Gittin 36 b.

56. See Hilkot Mamrim 2, 2; Tosafot,
Gittin 36 b.

57. Yer. Shabbat 3 d.

58. *Ibid.*, Peah 20 c.

59. *Sh'elot U'teshubot Ha-Rosh*, Kelal
55:10 (page 105 in 1954 reprint).

60. Soferim, 14:18.

61. Yer. Baba Metziah 11 b (see *ad.
loc.* [Krotoshin ed.]

62. I. H. Herzog, *The Institutions of
Jewish Law*, I, 21-22.

63. Baba Metziah 7, 1.
64. Cf., the different view expressed by Dr. Chaim Tchernowitz, *Toledot ha-Halakah* I, 146 ff.
65. Erubin 62 b.
66. *Ibid.* 72 a.
67. Taanit 26 b.
68. This seems also to have been Rashi's interpretation (see *Rashi, ad. loc.*).
69. Cf., G. F. Moore, *Judaism*, II, 244–45.
70. *Pirke Abot*, Chap. 6.
71. *Ex.Rabbah* 6, 2.
72. Yer. Pes. 30 b. The talmudic texts (see next note) use the word *talmud*. A parallel text in Abot 1, 17 reads: "not learning (*midrash*) but deed is the essential." Apparently both words were used for "study," but *midrash* was used in its original sense, which meant research as well as study.
73. *Sifre*, Deut. 41 (Ekab); Kiddushin 40 b; Yer. Hagigah 76 c.
74. See Josephus, *Antiquities* XVIII, 6, 3.
75. E. R. Goodenough, "Philo and Public Life," *Journal of Egyptian Archeology*, 1926, XII 77–79; *The Politics of Philo Judaeus*, New Haven, 1938, 16 ff.
76. *Spec. Leg.* III, 1–7.
77. Num. 4:3.
78. *Fuga* 37.
79. *Ibid.*, 26.
80. *Ibid.*, 35–39.
81. Prov. 29:4.
82. *Ex. Rabbah* 30, 10.
83. *Tanhuma*, Mishpatim 2.
84. Yer. Berakot 8 d.
85. Deut. 4:5.
86. Nedarim 37 a; Bechorot 29 a.
87. Bechorot 4, 6.
88. *Ibid.*
89. Baba Metziah 2, 9.
90. Baba Metziah 31 b.

91. Rashi understood the Talmud to mean that if a man is engaged in fulfilling a religious duty and thereby sustains a loss of money, he is compensated in accordance with the following standard: If his normal occupation is heavy work, he is paid the wage any laborer would be willing to accept for giving up his heavy work and doing light work instead, obviously a lesser amount. This is also how Rashi explained the mishnah which notes that if by fulfilling the duty of returning a lost article a man loses the value of a *sela*, "he may not say to the owner, 'Give me a *sela*'; the owner need pay him only his hire as a *poel batel*." (See Baba Metziah 2, 9; *Rashi*, Baba Metziah 31 b, *cit.*, *Kepoel batel*). Maimonides, however, interprets *poel batel* to mean that he is paid the amount a laborer would accept in order to be rid of the particular work in which he is engaged. In other words, he should be paid the sum he would accept to refrain from work altogether and take a rest. If, for instance, he would be satisfied with half the amount he would have earned had he worked, that would be his payment for time spent while fulfilling a *mitzvah* in behalf of his fellow man.

Maimonides' legal and religious philosophy is very interesting. When a man performs a religious duty, regardless of how difficult the performance may be for him, he should never consider it work. He should look upon himself as taking a rest, and therefore he cannot ask to be paid as much as if he had labored at his particular type of work (see Hilkot Gezelah VeAbaidah 12, 4).
92. Ketubot 105 a.
93. *Ibid.* See J. Brüll, *Mebo Hamishnah*, 53.
94. The exact nature of this court is still

obscure, but it is interesting that the Mishnah (Ketubot 13, 1) states that the sons of the High Priests disagreed with its decisions.

95. Baba Metziah 2, 9.
96. Hilkot Sanhedrin 23, 5.
97. Nedarim 37 a.
98. See *Pesikta* (Buber ed.) 178 a–b.
99. Yer. Hagigah 76 c.
100. *Ex. Rabbah* 27, 8.
101. Deut. 27:26.
102. Yer. Sotah 21 d. The duty of community leaders to protest the transgressions of individuals, and their responsibility for the wicked actions committed in the community, was apparently derived by our Sages from the same text (see commentary on Deut. 27:26).

103. Arakin 16 b.
104. *Sifra* (Kedoshim IV, 9) on Lev. 19:17.
105. See above, p. 140 ff.
106. Sanhedrin 27 b.
107. Arakin 16 b; *Sifra* (Kedoshim IV, 8) on Lev. 19:17.
108. Onkelos *(ad. loc.)* interpreted "thou shalt not bear sin because of him" to mean, "thou shalt not share in the guilt because of him" which Nachmanides *(ad. loc.)* suggests implies that one shares a sinner's guilt if he does not reprove him.
109. Mitzvah 205.
110. Hilkot Deot 6, 5 ff.
111. *Seder Eliahu Rabbah*, Chap. 19 (Friedman's ed.), 109.

## CHAPTER VIII

1. *Spec. Leg.*, II, 233.
2. *Ibid.*
3. Niddah 45 b.
4. Deut. 22:16.
5. *Sifre*, Deut. 235.
6. Ex. 21:7.
7. Num. 30:6.
8. See *Mekilta* (Mishpatim) on Ex. 21:7.
9. *Sifre* Num. 153.
10. Ex. 21:8–9.
11. Kiddushin 19 b.
12. Ex. 21:2.
13. *Mekilta, ad. loc.*
14. Kiddushin 20 a.
15. Arakin 29 b.
16. Ex. 21:17; *Maimonides*, Hilkot Abadim 4, 2.
17. Kiddushin 41 a.
18. Tosafot, Kiddushin 41 a; s.v. *assur l'adam sh'yekadesh et bito.*
19. Kiddushin 12 a.

20. Yebamoth 13, 1–2 (see also Yebamoth 107 b).
21. Baba Kamma 87 a–b.
22. Baba Bathra 125 b.
23. Deut. 24:16.
24. *Sifre*, Deut. 280.
25. See Pesahim 118 a and particularly *Midrash Tadshe*, Chap. 16.
26. Shabbat 32 b.
27. Hilkot Teshubah 6, 1.
28. Deut. 11:19–21.
29. *Sifre*, Deut. 46.
30. Ketubot 50 a.
31. Kiddushin 4, 14.
32. Berakot 47 b.
33. Shabbat 54 b.
34. See Deut. 13:7 ff.
35. Hilkot Teshubah 4, 1.
36. Deut. 21:18–21.
37. Sanhedrin 8, 1.
38. See Sanhedrin 69 a.

39. Sanhedrin 8, 5.

40. *Ibid.*, 8, 4.

41. Sanhedrin 71 a.

42. *De Ebrietate* 93.

43. *De Mut. Nom.* 206.

44. Ex. 20:5.

45. Deut. 24:16.

46. Berakot 7 a: Sanhedrin 27 b.

47. Gen. 9:25.

48. *De Sobrietate*, 31–48.

49. *De Virt.* 226–27. It is quite probable that when Philo criticized those who entertain the doctrine that pious men of ignoble birth can never attain real moral nobility, he addressed himself to a group of Alexandrian Jews who looked with antipathy upon heathens who became proselytes. He regarded them not only as enemies of the Jewish people but as enemies of the world, for they "kindled the fuel of enmity into flame," and rebuked them most vehemently: ". . . you stand accused, you who spring from great houses, which boast in the splendor of their race. For though you have good models on your side... you have never been minded to reproduce any of their excellence" *(Ibid,* 197).

50. *Ibid,* XXXVII, 198 ff.

51. Deut. 32:39.

52. *Sifre* on Deut. 32:39 (329).

53. *De Virt.* 194.

54. *Num. Rabbah,* Chap. 19, 20 (see also S. Schechter, *Some Aspects of Jewish Theology,* 185 ff.)

55. Shabbat 55 a; *Lev. Rabbah* 36, 6 (see also G. F. Moore, *Judaism* I, 543 ff).

56. *Spec. Leg.* IV, 179–80.

57. *De Praemtis* 165–66.

58. Cf., *Mekilta* (Mishpatim) on Ex. 21:10 for a similar exposition of the three "intercessors" who plead for the Jewish people.

59. *Mekilta* on Ex. 21:11.

60. Ketubot 5, 6.

61. *Ibid,* 5, 7; Ketubot 63 a–b.

62. Ketubot 7, 6.

63. *Ibid.,* 7, 10.

64. See Baba Bathra 108 a; Ketubot 89 b.

65. Hilkot Ishut 12, 3; Hilkot Nahalot 1, 8.

66. *Hasagot ha-Rabad, ad. loc.*

67. Ketubot 62 a.

68. *Ibid.*

69. See Gittin 12 a; *Maimonides,* Hilkot Ishut 12, 4.

70. Tosafot, Ketubot 63 a, *s. v.* "*Rab Huna Amar.*"

71. See commentary of *Ran* on Ketubot 64 b.

72. Ketubot 5, 5.

73. Ketubot 59 b.

74. Ketubot 6, 1.

75. Baba Metziah 12 b.

76. Yebamot 7, 1; Ketubot 4, 4; (Tur) Eben ha-Ezer 85.

77. Hilkot Ishut, 12, 3.

## CHAPTER IX

1. On the difference between these two terms see Michael Higger, *Intention in Jewish Law,* 19 ff.

2. Berakot 2, 1.

3. See Erubin 95 b; Pesahim 114 b; Berakot 13 a.

4. Hilkot Tefilah 4, 15–16.

5. *Quod Deus Immut.,* 100.

6. H. A. Wolfson, *Philo,* II, 224.

7. Pesahim 8 a; Baba Bathra 10 b; Rosh Hashanah 4 a.

8. See R. Rabbinowicz, *Dikduke Soferim*

on Baba Bathra 10 b, notes.

9. Abot 1, 3.

10. Shabbat 30 b.

11. *Ibid.*; Pesahim 117 a.

12. *Lev. Rabbah* 34, 9.

13. *Seder Eliahu Rabbah* Chap. 16, p. 82.

14. Kiddushin 40 a.

15. *Ibid.*

16. See Num. 30:9.

17. Nazir 23 a.

18. Num. 30:8.

19. See *Sifra* on Lev. 5:17; Nazir 23 a; Kiddushin 81 b.

20. Kiddushin 49 b (see also Nedarim 28 a).

21. Deut. 23:24.

22. Ex. 35:5.

23. Shebuot 26 b (for application of this principle in relation to charity, see below pp. 195–6.

24. Kiddushin 1, 6.

25. Makkot 23 b.

26. *Ibid.*, 24 a.

27. Psalms 15:2.

28. Makkot 24 a.

29. *Ibid.*, Rashi, *cit.* "R. Safra." This incident, in full detail, is recorded in *Sheiltot de R. Ahai Gaon*, Sheiltah 36 (Parshat Vayehi).

30. Psalms 15:3.

31. Makkot 24 a.

32. Psalms 15:5.

33. Makkot 24 a.

34. Psalms 15:5.

35. Makkot 24 a; Ketubot 105 b.

36. Ex. 20:17.

37. Deut. 5:18.

38. *Mekilta de Rabbi Simeon ben Yohai* on Ex. 20:14.

39. See *Midrash Hatannaim* and *Midrash Hagodol* on Deut. 5:18.

40. Hilkot Gezelah 1, 9–11 (see also M. Kasher, *Torah Shelemah* Vol. 16, p. 118

[on Ex. 20:15] Note 394).

41. *De Decalog* 142.

42. H. A. Wolfson *(Philo,* II, 226–30) has shown conclusively that Philo did not take the tenth commandment to be a prohibition against desire in general.

43. *Spec. Leg.* IV, 84–87.

44. Baba Metziah 49 a.

45. *Ibid.*

46. Kiddushin 59 a.

47. Baba Metziah 4, 2.

48. Baba Metziah 48 b.

49. Baba Bathra 133 b; Kiddushin 28 b.

50. Baba Kamma 36 b.

51. Alfasi, *ad. loc.,* Maimonides, Hilkot Matnot Aniyim 8, 1 ff.

52. Nedarim 7 a; Rosh Hashana 6 a.

53. Hilkot Mekhirah 22, 17.

54. Yoreh Deah, 259, 6.

55. I. H. Herzog, *The Main Institutions of Jewish Law,* I, 287 ff.

56. *Ibid.*

57. Peah 6, 1; Eduyot 4, 3. Cf., S. Zeitlin, "Hefker v'yeush," *Louis Ginzberg Jubilee Vol.* (1945), Heb. Sec., 365 ff.

58. Hilkot Nedarim 2, 14.

59. Num. 30:3.

60. See I. H. Herzog, *The Main Institutions of Jewish Law,* 21–33 (see also Kiddushin 9 b: "These are the things in which a word of mouth is binding." Cf., Maimonides, Hilkot Zekiah Umatanah 6, 17).

61. See below, p. 234.

62. Baba Kamma 55 b.

63. Baba Kamma 6, 4.

64. Baba Kamma 60 a, Baba Bathra 22 b, Tosafot *ad. loc.* For a listing of sources and distinctions between these two terms, see the novellae of Nachmanides on Garmi.

65. See Baba Kamma 56 a; Sanhedrin

77 a; Kiddushin 43 a.

66. Hilkot Rozeah 2, 2.

67. Deut. 19:19.

68. Makkot 1, 4.

69. See above, p. 94, for discussion of laws of *hazamah* and *hakhashah*). Cf., A. Weiss, *Seder Hadiyun*, pp. 110 ff.

70. Makkot, 1, 6.

71. Josephus, *Antiquities*, XX, 19, 1.

72. Makkot 4 b.

73. Hilkot Sanhedrin 18, 2.

74. Arakin 15 a–b.

75. Deut. 30:12 ff.

76. Cf., Bahya's interpretation of this verse—its similarities and differences with Philo's interpretation are striking.

77. *De Mut. Nom.* 236–44.

78. It is not quite clear whether Philo meant that oral transgressions are punishable in court but only in a more lenient manner, or whether his terms *apologon* and *euthunas* imply merely that one must defend himself when he is accused of such transgressions and correct his former wrongdoings. The latter interpretation would accord more with rabbinic thinking. However, regardless of how we interpret Philo's words, the entire passage reveals a thinking very similar to that of the Palestinian Rabbis in the distinction they make between man's intentions, his articulation, and his action.

79. Ketubot 2, 3.

80. Ketubot 18 b.

81. Ex. 20:13.

82. See RaN on Sukkah, Chap. 3, *vide* "*l'hidur mitzvah*" (Perek Lulab Hagazul) in name of RaBad; also Joel Sirkes (Bach) on *Tur Orach Haim*, 656.

83. Baba Kamma 117 a.

84. Lev. 19:13.

85. Hilkot Hobel Umazik 8, 1–2.

86. In talmudic terminology a distinction is made between vows and oaths: A vow forbids upon a person the *use* of a certain thing *(issur heftza)*; an oath forbids the swearer *to do* a certain thing *(issur gabra)*.

87. Nedarim 28 a.

88. The Mishnah (Nedarim 3, 4) rules that "Persons may vow to murderers, robbers, and publicans that their produce is *terumah*, though it is not *terumah*; or that they belong to the king's household, though they do not belong to the king's household." The School of Shammai and the School of Hillel disagree over the form of the vows, over whether this applies to vows and oaths or only to vows, and over whether the victim can volunteer the vow or must wait until he is compelled to do so, as well as over what produce is covered by such vows.

The words "murderers and robbers" imply men who either threaten to rob him or to take his life. "Publicans" refers to unauthorized tax-collectors. Though criminals, they would nevertheless not take *terumah* or that which belongs to the royal household. According to the School of Hillel, vows and affirmative oaths taken under duress to save produce are not binding. According to the School of Shammai *oaths* (signifying the *person*) taken under duress to save money are binding. Moreover, even *vows* (signifying the *article*) taken under duress are binding, but these must be forced upon the person, not initiated by him.

89. This is indicated by the report of Rabbi Ilai recorded in the Talmud, (Ketubot 50 a; Arakin 28 a) that at a conference held at Usha the rule was laid

down that one should not spend more than a fifth of his possession for the fulfillment of a positive command. It was asked (Yer. Peah 15 b): "In such cases would he not dissipate his property in a period of five years?" The answer given is that during the first year he may spend a fifth of his capital, but during the four succeeding years a fifth of his income only. Hence, if a man should be told: "Give me more than a fifth of your income or I will prevent you from performing a positive command," his non-action would be permissible, because he was under duress.

90. Hilkot Yesodai Hatorah 5, 4.

91. Nachmanides, *Milhamot*, Sanhedrin, at the very end of Chapter 8 (Ben Sorer).

92. Tosafot Abodah Zarah 27 b, *vide* "*yachol*."

93. Yer. Shebiit 35 a.

94. Sanhedrin 74 a (see above, pp. 102, 132).

95. Hilkot Yesodai Hatorah 5, 4.

96. *Ibid.*

97. RaN on Sanhedrin, end of Chap. 8, commentary on Alfasi.

98. Baba Kamma 2, 6.

99. Baba Kamma 26 b.

100. *Ibid.*, 27 a. See above, p. 105 ff.

101. *Sifre* Deut. 286.

102. Ketubot 32 b. If, however, the amount of damage the injury causes is more than a *perutah* and makes the striker liable for money indemnity, then the rule is: "He is liable for money indemnity and is exempt from corporal punishment" *(Ibid).*

103. Hilkot Nezikin 4, 10.

104. Hilkot Hobel Umazik 5, 9.

105. See Tosafot, Baba Kamma, 27 b, *vide "amai patur"; Mahane Ephraim* by Rabbi Ephraim Nabon, on Hilkot Nizkei Mamon, 4, 10.

## CHAPTER X

1. Joshua 1:8 (see elaborations in Yoma 35 b, Baba Metzia 84 a–b).

2. Hilkot Talmud Torah 1, 9.

3. Peah 1, 1.

4. Pesahim 50 b.

5. Joshua 1:8.

6. Josephus, *Contra Apionem* II, 177–78.

7. Ex. 18:20.

8. *Mekilta, ad loc.* See above p. 190.

9. Baba Metziah 30 b.

10. Gen. 2:4.

11. *Gen. Rabbah* 12, 15.

12. See Berakot 5, 3; Berakot 33 b; Megillah 4, 9; Yer Megillah 75 c.

13. Ex. 22:27.

14. *Mekilta, ad. loc.*

15. Ketubot 9, 2.

16. Lev. 19:15.

17. *Sifra* on Lev. 19:15. See above, p. 87.

18. Baba Kamma 87 a.

19. Tosefta Abodah Zarah 8, 4.

20. Baba Kamma 38 a.

21. Hilkot Talmud Torah 1, 13. The Talmud (Baba Kamma 87 a) also relates that R. Joseph, who was blind and fulfilled the *mitzvot* of the Torah, once said: "Whoever would tell me that the *halakah* is in accordance with Rabbi Judah that a blind man is exempt from fulfilling the precepts of the Torah, I would set a day of festivities for the Sages. It is not obligatory upon me to fulfill the *mitzvot*, yet I do them." Later, however, R. Joseph changed his mind because he learned that the reward for

fulfilling the *mitzvot* which the Torah imposes upon one is greater than that gained by fulfilling the same *mitzvot* if one is exempted from performing them.

22. Lev. 24:22.

23. For a full discussion of this concept see above, p. 20.

24. See Tosefta Baba Kamma 6, 16; Maimonides, Hilkot Hobel Umazik 2, 7.

25. Baba Kamma 56 a.

26. Tosefta Shebuot 3, 2–4.

27. Tosefta Baba Kamma 6, 16.

28. See Baba Metziah 37 a.

29. Baba Metziah 3, 3.

30. Prov. 2:20.

31. Baba Metziah 83 a.

32. Baba Metziah 2, 11.

33. Baba Metziah 33 a.

34. *Ibid.*

35. Hilkot Abadim 9, 8.

36. Berakot 5, 1.

37. Yer. Terumot 46 b.

38. See above, p. 97.

39. *Exodus Rabbah*, 31, 17.

40. Sanhedrin 6 b; Yebamot 92 a.

41. Abot 1, 18.

42. *Ibid.* 1, 12.

43. Yer. Sotah 16 d; Gittin 52 a.

44. *Sifre* Deut. 199.

45. See *Lev. Rabbah* 9, 9.

46. Eduyot 8, 7.

47. Ukzin 3, 12.

48. Sanhedrin 6 b.

49. *Ibid.* 6a.

50. Psalms 99: 4.

51. Ex. 23: 5.

52. *Tanhuma* Mishpatim 1 (see also *Midrash Agadah, loc. cit.*).

53. *De Virt.* 116–18.

54. Yebamot 87 b.

55. Hilkot Melakim 10, 12.

56. Baba Metzia 10 a.

57. Gittin 5, 8–9.

58. Eduyot 1, 13; Gittin 4, 5.

59. Asheri on Gittin 40 a.

60. Gen. 4:10.

61. Sanhedrin 4, 5.

62. *De Decalog.* 36–43. The similarity between Philo's statement and talmudic sources is not confined to the idea alone; verbal similarities also exist. Thus, just as Philo drew upon the image of a banquet arranged by God in honor of the first man, to express the concept of the sacredness of each human being, so did our Sages compare the original creation of a single man to a full banquet prepared by God for the benefit of one individual. (See Sanhedrin 38 a).

63. Sanhedrin 37 b.

64. *Ibid.*, 40 b.

65. Makkot 1, 10.

66. Makkot 16 a; Shebuot 21 a.

67. Sanhedrin 46 a.

68. Yer. Haggigah 78 a; Yebamot 90 b.

69. Ketubot, 86 b. See *Or Sameah*, Hilkot Mamrim, 4, 3.

70. See above, p. 111.

71. Sanhedrin 9, 5 and 81 a. The penalty of life imprisonment was apparently restricted to cases of homicide. In other capital offenses, if the court could not put the offender to death in accordance with the strict penal code of the Torah, he was set free (see Hilkot Rozeah 4, 9).

72. Hilkot Sanhedrin 24, 4.

73. Baba Kamma 6, 4.

74. Kiddushin 43 a.

75. *De Decalog.* 111–112.

76. Num. 15:30.

77. *De Virt.* 172.

78. *Ibid.*, 171–74.

79. *De Praemiis* 69.

80. Ex. 21:13.

81. *Spec. Leg.* III, 122.

82. Makkot 10 b.

83. Berakot 9, 5.

84. Job 13:15.

85. Job 1:1.

86. Sotah 5, 5.

87. Deut. 10:20.

88. Abot 1, 3.

89. Maimonides in his commentary on this Mishnah, however, adds that even if a man serves God out of pure love, he must at the same time fear him.

90. Deut. 11:13.

91. *Sifre, ad loc.*

92. *Quod Deus Immut.* 62–69.

93. *De Abr.* 127 ff.

94. *Spec. Leg.* I, 229.

95. H. A. Wolfson *(Philo,* II, 295–96) has very perceptively pointed out that "The phrase 'virtue for its own sake' is of course Stoic. Whereas among the Stoics, and in Greek philosophy in general, we have seen it means an admission that the practice of virtue may not be rewarded, in Philo, as in Judaism, it means that the worship of God out of love will bring the highest reward."

96. *Spec. Leg.* II, 257–62; cf., Nachmanides on Ex. 20:12, who follows Philo's line of thinking but reaches different conclusions.

97. *De Decalog.* 106–07.

98. Deut. 5:16, not found in Ex. 20:12.

99. Hullin 142 a; Kiddushin 39 b.

100. See Kiddushin 40 a.

101. Deut. 11:22.

102. Sifre, *ad loc.*

103. Hilkot Yesodai Hatorah 2, 2.

104. Deut. 28:58.

105. *Moreh Nebukim* III. Chap. LII (Friedlander translation, 392).

106. Deut. 6:5.

107. Hilkot Teshubah 10, 1–5.

108. Shabbat 31 a.

109. See above, p. 208.

110. Nedarim 9, 4.

111. Tosefta Sotah 5, 11.

112. Kiddushin 41 a.

113. Sanhedrin 45 a.

114. *Sifre* Deut. 187 on Deut. 19:11.

115. Hilkot Abel 14, 1.

116. See above, p. 29.

117. *Abot de R. Nathan* (ed. S. Schechter), 10 a. Maimonides believed that all such acts of *Imitatio Dei* are enjoined by the command "Thou shalt love thy neighbor as thyself." Nachmanides (on Deut. 6:18), however, felt that they are intended in the verse "And thou shalt do that which is right and good in the sight of the Lord."

118. *Sifra* on Lev. 19:18.

119. See above, p. 227, where this was discussed.

120. See *Mekilta* on Ex. 23:5; Baba Metziah 2, 10.

121. Cf., *Mekilta de R. Simeon ben Yohai* on Ex. 23:5; Baba Metziah 32 b.

122. Tosefta Baba Metziah 2, 24.

123. Baba Metziah 30 b.

124. *Ibid.*

125. Hilkot Rozeah 13, 4.

126. Pesahim 113 b (see also Rabbi M. M. Kasher, *Torah Shelemah,* Vol. 18, 202).

127. Hilkot Rozeah 13, 14.

128. *Mekilta* on Ex. 23; 4.

129. See above, p. 98.

130. *Sifra,* Lev. 19:18.

131. *Gen. Rabbah* 24, 8.